Edward Miller

The History and Doctrines of Irvingism

Or of the So-called Catholic and Apostolic Church

Edward Miller

The History and Doctrines of Irvingism
Or of the So-called Catholic and Apostolic Church

ISBN/EAN: 9783337002961

Printed in Europe, USA, Canada, Australia, Japan

Cover: Foto ©ninafisch / pixelio.de

More available books at **www.hansebooks.com**

IRVINGISM,

VOL. II.

THE
HISTORY AND DOCTRINES

OF

IRVINGISM,

OR OF THE

SO-CALLED CATHOLIC AND APOSTOLIC CHURCH.

BY

EDWARD MILLER, M.A.,

VICAR OF BUTLER'S MARSTON,

AND FORMERLY FELLOW AND TUTOR OF NEW COLLEGE, OXFORD.

IN TWO VOLS.—VOL. II.

LONDON:
C. KEGAN PAUL & CO., 1, PATERNOSTER SQUARE.
1878.

Bungay
CLAY AND TAYLOR, PRINTERS.

CONTENTS OF VOL. II.

DOCTRINES.

CHAPTER I.

DOCTRINES.

Introduction—§ 1. Immediate expectation of the Second Advent—§ 2. Doctrine of the Incarnation—§ 3. Bible Symbolism—§ 4. The Church—§ 5. The Fourfold Ministry—§ 6. The Restored Apostolate—§ 7. Prophets—§ 8. Evangelists—§ 9. Pastors—§ 10. Hierarchy—§ 11. Church Services—§ 12. Other Doctrines—§ 13. Finance .. .. 1—75

CHAPTER II.

GENERAL EXAMINATION.

I. Irvingism now an anachronism—II. Its failure—comparison with the Early Church—futile objection—III. Deadness and dulness—IV. Destructive internal forces—opposition between Apostles and Prophets—iron rule—unwieldy Hierarchy—dreamy mysticism .. 76—95

CHAPTER III.

EVIDENCE AND CATHOLICITY.

Objection considered—right use of human intellect—sanctified intellect—judging by the fruits—objection—literature and enquiry—constructive objection—not a bare question between Heaven and Hell—good points admitted—good life in the Members does not prove the system true—three standards of appeal—English and Roman Catholicity—Irvingism not Catholic—Doctrine—continuity of life .. .. 96—118

CHAPTER IV.
APOSTLES.

Fourfold Ministry—types and symbols no proofs—the two passages inconsistent—Catholic interpretation—other passages condemnatory—no real foundation—credentials of the Twelve—rest mainly upon our Lord—their association with Him—St. Paul—call and direct appointment from our Lord—St. Matthias—St. Barnabas—four credentials—Irvingite Apostles can only claim one—futility of this claim—self-condemned—by seventeen centuries of Church history—Irvingite plea   119—153

CHAPTER V.
BISHOPS THE SUCCESSORS OF THE APOSTLES.

Difference between Apostles and Bishops—when equals appoint equals—local and general jurisdiction—nature of the Bible testimony—threefold Ministry—in the Jewish Church—in our Lord's time—after His Ascension—early indistinctness of terms—Bishops appointed by the Apostles—Clement of Rome—Ignatius—Hegesippus—Irenæus—Tertullian—Council of Carthage—Cyprian—Firmilian—Eusebius—Augustine—Jerome—Ambrose—Optatus—universal Doctrine—Cardale's position—utterly unsound—why people fancied Apostles would come   154—187

CHAPTER VI.
PROPHETICAL GIFTS.

Gifts in Apostolic times—after the Apostles' deaths—Montanism—about the era of the Reformation—Quakers—Camisards—Wesleyans—Swedenborg—Joanna Southcote—Shakers—Mormons—Plymouth Brethren—Agapemonites—Mrs. Girling—credentials of Prophets—Moses—schools of the Prophets—Samuel—Elijah—Elisha—Amos—Isaiah—Ezekiel—Daniel—Jonah—Jeremiah—John the Baptist—our Lord—later Prophets—coincidence with Truth before revealed—miracles—verified predictions   ..   ..   ..   188—222

CHAPTER VII.
ARE THESE MEN PROPHETS?

Duty of reverential enquiry—Irvingites receive a great part of Catholic Truth—but in characteristic points contravene it—surrender the proof from miracles—their "miracles" not wrought publicly—can be explained naturally—illustrations—no verified predictions—vapidity of these "prophecies"—treatment of their Prophets—travesty of the Pentecostal events—misunderstanding of the passage in 1 Cor. xiv.—disuse of the tongues—cessation of extraordinary gifts—unconscious simulation of Divine gifts—concentrated attention—constructive objectivity—weakness of will—imagination—reflex power of prayer—infection—expression of covert sentiment—hysteria—ecstasy—Satanic influence—Theology and Physiology—ordinary supernatural agency .. .. 223—258

CHAPTER VIII.
EXPECTATION OF THE GREAT ADVENT.

Change of argument—strength of this motive—this not the great motive—ecclesiasticism—frequent study of this subject—I. Futurists—II. Præterists—III. Continuous Historic Scheme—IV. Spiritual Exegesis—millenarianism rejected—spiritual is literal—periodical expectation—true attitude .. .. 259—281

CHAPTER IX.
THE DOCTRINE OF THE INCARNATION.

Calvinism—Moralism—straining of the Doctrine—combination with Deism—neglect of Church Festivals—Present rendering of the Doctrine—Hypostatic Union—Unfallen Nature—sanctification of St. Mary—four possible theories—her Immaculate Conception rejected—would trench upon His—unscriptural—opposed to Patristic opinion—our Lord's true but unfallen human nature—danger of forming our own notions .. .. 282—305

CHAPTER X.
TYPES AND SYMBOLISM.

Sanctioned in the Incarnation—neglected—strong feelings about—how taught in the Body—good features—necessitated by human nature—taught in the Mosaic Law—erroneous teaching—Catholic Rule .. .. 306—315

CHAPTER XI.
EFFECT OF THE EXAMINATION.

Fairness—the demand made upon all Christians—good characteristics enumerated—condemned by the Catholic Church—by Holy Scripture

—at variance with Catholic Doctrine—no continuity of life—not real Apostles—cannot answer to the four credentials—numerous prophetical claims—three canons—these Prophets condemned—and accounted for—other considerations—Irvingite reply—candid and reverent enquiry both permissible and demanded—materials for it exist—recent advance in the Church of England—prejudice—misconception of change—the chimera of Romanism—the English as a Branch of the Catholic Church—national acceptations of Christianity—resort to the Undivided Church—Ecclesiastical Legislation in England now abnormal—the reform of it before us—contemporaneous infidelity—its weakness—the causes of it—a new Christian Philosophy—a new School of Theology—the strength of the Faith .. .. 316—354

CONCLUSION.

General lessons—expostulation—return to our Mother-Church—Catholic Unity .. .. 355—360

APPENDIX II. The two Smaller Testimonies .. .. 361—380
APPENDIX III. The Mystery of the Candlestick .. .. 381—382
APPENDIX IV. List of Offices in the Liturgy or Prayer-book 383—386
APPENDIX V. Selections from the Catechism .. .. 387—390
APPENDIX VI. Passages from Manual .. .. .. 391—394
APPENDIX VII. Account of the Catholic Apostolic Church in the Census of 1851 .. .. 395—397
APPENDIX VIII. The Tabernacle .. .. .. 398—403
APPENDIX IX. The Regulations for Distribution of Tithe 404—413
INDEX .. .. 415—420

DOCTRINES OF IRVINGISM.

CHAPTER I.

DOCTRINES.

THE history of this sect of religionists, which has been gradually unfolded in the first volume of this work, shows them to be a remarkable Body of Christians. Their system of doctrine and discipline has been worked out with the utmost labour and ingenuity. For the short period of its existence, it is really a marvel of intricacy and of careful adjustment of force and counterforce. Yet an examination reveals defects which are plainly fatal to the entire conception. It is only suited for those who have education enough to enable them to enter into its intricate details, if we pass by those who are ready to accept a new system with unquestioning credulity. But it fails to arrest such as have been previously well instructed and brought up in the wider doctrines of the Catholic Church.

Irvingism is emphatically the child of the nineteenth

century. It has arisen out of the throes and seething thought of the earlier part of this eventful period. And if logic wins its way in the realms of religious belief, if long habit does not remove from the disciples of these doctrines the power of candid judgment, and usages and interests do not become too deeply rooted to yield when their *raison d'être* is no more, it must die, when, if the providence of God so orders, the present age is swallowed up in the next.

But I must not anticipate the criticism, which I hope to make with all the candour at my command, after my readers are put in possession of the chief facts of the history of this Community, and of the doctrines which they profess.

§ 1. *Immediate expectation of the Second Advent.*

The mainspring of their system is their belief in the near approach of our Lord's second Coming. This belief, as is well known, they share with a large number of Christians who do not participate in the peculiar views of these people. But the members of this Community have carried it, if not in their authorized documents which they keep wholly to themselves, yet in the wide-spread tenets of their members, to applications peculiar to themselves.

This belief arose, as has been narrated, out of the extraordinary events which accompanied the entrance of the present century. The wonderful career of the first Napoleon, painted in the terrified imaginations of those who anticipated coming evil as much more wonderful than it really was, led people to fancy that still greater commotions and changes were at hand. "The French Revolution of 1793 was but the partial outbreak of that universal convulsion which is now preparing, the first shock of that earthquake which will throw down every civil and ecclesiastical fabric."[1] These striking occurrences, added to the fact that a great change in society generally was then setting in, caused many good and earnest people to attribute to passing events an importance which concerned all history and all time. The disturbances in France and in other countries in 1830, the revolutions almost throughout Europe in 1848, the various wars in Europe or in India, the war in America which has been waged since that era, the internal struggles between contending parties in the united kingdoms, have thus been regarded, each in its own time, as ominous of the approaching end. These were supposed to be the foretold "wars and rumours of wars," and plenty of signs were discovered of "the love of many waxing cold." The grievous state of the Catholic Church, with yawning abysses between the several Branches of it which appeared to defy all attempts to fill up or abolish them by bringing their banks together, the prevalence of wickedness and crime, the increase of ungodliness, as it was judged to be, seemed to betoken that period of falling away which was to precede the Advent of the Lord.

Accordingly, to many troubled spirits which have been cast down at present sinfulness and at the advance

[1] *Testimony to the patriarchs, archbishops, bishops,* &c., p. 71. See Appendix I.

and development of evil principles, and which have yearned for a vast improvement, the idea of the nearness of the Lord's second Coming has been inexpressibly grateful. The longings of the Christian heart have found rest in this contemplation of futurity. Whether it be justified by facts and by revelation is another question. Many, as is well known, in this and the last generation have felt it a sacred duty to quell all doubts in their own minds about the grounds of this expectation, and to expect the Lord's Advent in their own days as an acknowledged prospect. "He must be manifested speedily; for amid the increasing tumults and confusion of all people in every country of Europe, in this distress of nations with perplexity, the time foretold in God's Word rapidly approaches, when the Son of Man shall come in the clouds of heaven to judge the nations, and to set up that kingdom which shall never be destroyed."[1]

Before our Lord's coming, Antichrist is expected. "Lawlessness shall pervade and prevail, tossing men to and fro as the waves of the sea, until it shall put forth its concentrated energy in that 'wicked,' that lawless one who shall be revealed, 'the man of sin,' 'who opposeth and exalteth himself above all that is called God, or that is worshipped; whose coming is after the working of Satan, with all 'power, and signs, and lying wonders.'"[2] This belief, too, is shared by many others, as is well known. Indeed, various treatises have issued from the press, proving, as the authors imagined, that different public men of note, such as the late Emperor Napoleon,

---

[1] *Testimony*, p. 72; *Appendix* I.   [2] Ibid. p. 72.

were severally, as each author made out, Antichrist, or the Beast of the Revelation. This is a subject of great mystery, demanding anxious but cautious attention on the part of Christians. The special point which these people insist on is, not that Antichrist shall be revealed, whoever or whatever he is to be, which every believer in the Bible must hold, but that some personage is coming at some time in these our days. And they promulgate this as a dogma of faith.

In preparation for these events, and as harbinger of our Lord's coming, they believe that He has sent what they call "an Elias-ministry." For as Elias came to prepare for our Lord's first coming, and is said by the prophet Malachi to be coming before "the great and dreadful day of the Lord," and came formerly only "in spirit and power," they suppose that he has now appeared, though not as a single individual, in the new ministry of apostles, prophets, evangelists, and pastors, who are thus the messengers preparing the way before the Lord.

The Coming of the Lord is expected by these people to take place before the great outburst of Antichrist. The *Testimony* states "when He cometh, that lawless one stands already revealed; for it is written that 'the Lord shall consume him with the spirit of His mouth, and destroy him with the brightness of His coming.'"[1] But this more rudimentary teaching was carried out into further detail in later times. After the Church is first warned we are told[2] that those who sleep in Christ

---

[1] *Testimony*, p. 72; 2 Thess. ii. 3; *Appendix* I.
[2] *Creation and Redemption*, p. 263.

shall be raised. Then those who are alive at the time of His coming, together with the dead who have risen, will be caught up to meet Him in the air, before His descent upon the earth. By this time the fourth empire has[1] assumed its complete form, as having ten horns. The man of sin, or Antichrist, who is the eighth and last head of the beast, has now[1] appeared, accompanied by the false prophet. There will now be a war in heaven, and Satan will no longer be allowed to appear before God, or to act as the "accuser of our brethren," or to hinder the Lord in His spiritual operations in the Church.[2] But he is cast down to the earth, and, finding that to be his only place, will seek to do as much injury as he can to the Church. Yet the Lord will not leave Himself without witnesses against Satan. Accordingly, He will raise up "the two witnesses," who after fighting for the truth will be slain by the Beast, but only to his own destruction.

Then the Beast with his ten kings is to destroy Babylon. The seven vials are to be successively poured out, and the other events recorded in the early part of the Revelation which have not yet been fulfilled are to be accomplished. Then is to ensue the great battle of Armageddon, between the Lord and His saints on the one side, and Antichrist and the false prophet with all their hosts on the other, followed by vast results. The Beast and the false prophet are to be cast alive into the

---

[1] The exact time of these, however, whether antecedent or consequent upon the good being caught up into the air, appears not to be settled.
[2] *Creation and Redemption*, p. 290.

lake of fire, and their followers slain. Satan is to be bound in the bottomless pit. The Jews and the tribes of Israel are to be settled again in Palestine. But the restoration of the Jews is to take place in successive stages. Some of them will repair to the holy city before His second Coming, after the first-fruits are "caught up," and before the Lord descends. Then Antichrist and his hosts will besiege Jerusalem.

At this moment the Lord appears, delivers His city and people, and destroys Antichrist and his hosts, as has been just related. Then all the Jews and the ten tribes will be restored to their own land by the mighty hand of God.[1] These events usher in the millennium, or the reign of our Lord with His saints on earth for a thousand years. This is the "intermediate stage between" the present dispensation and the one in which the new heaven and the new earth, the eternal kingdom of God, shall be established.[2] At the end of it they say will be "the last rebellion of the nations;" for Satan will be loosed, and another terrible conflict will follow, but the end of it will be that Satan will meet his final doom. He will be cast for ever into the lake of fire, where the beast and the false prophet are. And now comes the end.

Almighty God is revealed, seen on the great white Throne. All those will rise at this, the second resurrection, who were not thought worthy to attain to the first resurrection. "The last enemy, Death," will be destroyed. The great day of judgment will have arrived, and the

---

[1] *Creation and Redemption*, p. 318.   [2] Ibid. p. 306.

awful scene of the judgment of all nations and people will be transacted. The heavens and the earth will pass away. New heavens and a new earth will be created. And the Lord will deliver up His kingdom to the Father for ever and ever.[1]

It will be observed that the chief periods in this consummation are the following:—First, the great tribulation, reaching from the appearance of the Lord in the heavens till His descent upon the earth for victory, and for the establishment of the millennium. During this time the first-fruits have been caught up to Him in the air, and continue with Him, having been sealed till the day of redemption.[2] Secondly, the millennial reign of the Lord on earth. Thirdly, the last rebellion of the nations. And lastly, the eternal kingdom over new heavens and the new earth. There are three gatherings:—First, of the first-fruits of the harvest, the wise virgins who follow the Lamb whithersoever He goeth; next, the abundant harvest gathered afterwards by God; and lastly, the assembling of the wicked for punishment.

I do not mean to say that all the details of this teaching, and the many more details into which it is pursued, are regarded as *De Fide*, the necessary belief of every member of the Catholic Apostolic Church who would be saved. But this sketch which is taken from one of their accredited works, ascribed to a deceased apostle, gives an idea of the manner in which Irvingites have worked out into a definite order of events the mysterious pictures in the Revelation and hints from

---

[1] *Creation and Redemption*, Part IV.   [2] Ibid. p. 262.

other parts of Holy Scripture. This is their moving doctrine, the mainspring of their religious life. They teach their people, as has been said, to pray to God at night that the Lord may come before morning.[1] Many keep their affairs wound up and in perfect order, as a matter of religious duty, that they may be ready at any time to be caught up to meet the Lord. Frequently at their various periods they expect the Advent in the next month, or the next week. It is easy to see what tremendous moral power such a persuasion, if it is embraced with all the heart and soul, must perforce exercise over the whole life—thoughts, words, and actions. The belief that without all doubt the Lord Himself is coming immediately, and that He has already in the special arrangements of His Church vouchsafed for the very purpose, made preparations for His Advent, and that titles of precedence in His kingdom are within reach of the faithful and may now be had, must constitute a most powerful engine of influence—perhaps the most powerful in the world for those few who can accept the slender force of argument by which it is built up.

It has been already stated that in spite of difficulties, and, in later times, of previous errors, there has been a strong tendency in the Body to fix upon definite dates for the coming of the Lord. Such was July 14, 1835, when the apostles were separated. Such were also the tenth, twentieth, thirtieth, and fortieth anniversaries of that day. Such again was Christmas Day, 1838, the

[1] *Consecration of the Catholic Apostolic Church, Constitution Road, Dundee*, p. 10.

1260th day after the day of the separation. The multiples of seven were also brought into requisition. But more than all, perhaps, the year 1866 was looked upon as fulfilling the numbers of the Apocalypse, because 1260 years from the decree of Phocas in A. D. 606 would end at that time. In fact, ingenious calculations of almost all sorts have found their place in the imagination of one or other of these people, the fundamental article in whose creed is that the Advent is to occur in our own days.

Upon this foundation, therefore, not only historically as matter of fact, but by a development of thought, the building of Irvingite doctrine is reared. The near approach of the Lord necessitates preparations for His reception. Hence came the idea and the phrase of "the Elias-ministry," though the expression is, I believe, less commonly used now than it was during earlier stages of their career. The phrase speaks for itself, showing how the passages in the Bible which relate to the great Forerunner of the Lord are applied to a special ministry supposed to be sent "as couriers before Him" at the end of the present dispensation. "There was an Elias-work to the Jews; . . . . . there must be an Elias-work in the Christian Church previous to the final restoration and establishment in the kingdom. In everything the type and the antitype go double."[1]

[1] *Creation and Redemption*, p. 310.

§ 2. *Doctrine of the Incarnation.*

The other grand Feature in the peculiar Tenets of these people is their mode of holding the Doctrine of the Incarnation. This great Doctrine, as has been already pointed out, was placed very much in the background in the Theology of the eighteenth century. The beautiful system of observances in the Catholic Church had lost its vigour and had become pale; and the earliest revival in England under the Evangelicals[1] and Wesley had only fixed itself with a narrow and indeed an exclusive grasp upon the wondrous Scene enacted on Calvary. The recovery of the grand truth of the Incarnation with its marvellous detail and amazing features is perhaps the great characteristic of the onward movement made in Theology during the present century. It is the glory of Irving and his friends—not so much his followers—Messrs. Campbell, Story, Scott, and others, that they were the pioneers of the advancing march. But the chief of the labour and success was wrought in the Oxford movement. Excesses have been found in the cases of Irving himself and of his followers in the "Catholic Apostolic Church," and practically as I believe, if not theoretically, in the Roman Catholic adorations to Parts of our Lord's Human Nature, and—owing to a too exclusive contemplation of the Humanity apart from the Divinity—in the celebrated Treatise *Ecce Homo.*

Amongst the Religious Body of which we are now

---

[1] That the Evangelical movement in the Church was independent of the Wesleyan, and had an origin of its own, was proved by Venn. See *Dean Hook's Sermons on the Catholic Church.*

concerned, the tendency to outstep the proper bounds circumscribing this grand Doctrine has arisen from their anxiety to bring out with full relief the powers of exaltation communicated to human nature through the Incarnation, and the Grace which has flowed through that wondrous channel. Hence Irving insisted so strongly upon the taking of man's nature and the close relationship effected between the SON of GOD and ourselves, that he asserted that the nature that He took was not our nature purified through His Heavenly Birth, and planted again in a fresh growth,—but our fallen nature, corrupt since Adam through sin, though cleansed by its attachment in Him to the Divine Nature, and so preserved without sin.[1] He lowered too much the Human Nature of our Lord, in order to bring the closer to Him sinful and erring, though penitent people.

This special tenet, viz., that our Lord took our fallen nature at His Birth, not purified and renewed human nature, is to some extent in words repudiated in the "Catholic Apostolic Church." But there is nevertheless a tinge derived from it which has coloured the entire System professed by these Religionists. And it has coloured this both in the Doctrine held, and in the nature and working of their entire constitution.

First, there is amongst them an imperfect appreciation of the Doctrine. Such an appreciation really

---

[1] See Vol. i. p. 85. "Sin inhered in the Human Nature of our Lord; as He was made under the law, He must have been inclined to all those things which the law interdicted."—*The Orthodox and Catholic Doctrine of our Lord's Human Nature*, by the Rev. Edward Irving, M.A., London, p. 127. Bellett's *Dialogue on Irvingism*, p. 14.

requires, it should be said, professional study. No one should attempt without such study to speak or teach upon this mysterious subject, any more than an amateur should discourse upon the anatomy of the human body. Now such a professional study has not fallen to the lot of most of the Ministers in this Community. It is not surprising therefore to find such teaching as the following: "Being God, He is infinite in all Divine attributes. Being Man, He is in His human nature perfectly, that is to say entirely, a creature." This expression can only imply, that our Lord has human personality, which is of course only in His Divine Nature, because otherwise He would have two Persons. Else what can be the meaning of our Lord "*being perfectly*, that is to say *entirely*, a creature?" And when the same writer, speaking dogmatically, goes on to say that "the Human Nature of our Lord is, as we have said, our common human nature," and with the knowledge of Irving's error, adds no guard, or limitation, or explanation of the phrase to exclude that error, we are plainly upon unsafe ground. That this is actually the case, the Author of *Apostolic Lordship*, who has recorded the teaching given, positively shows.[1] When it was maintained that our Lord offered sacrifice *for His own sins*, and the thesis was supported by others in high office besides the original promulgator, it is clear that sin was being brought perilously near to His spotless Nature.

Again, the following teaching expresses the objectionable doctrine without any concealment:—"so that,

[1] *Apostolic Lordship*, pp. 36—42.

despite it was *fallen flesh*[1] He had assumed, He was, through the Eternal Spirit, born into the world the *Holy Thing;* and ever continued, through the same Eternal Spirit, by the perfect faith which He had also begotten, and so sustained, to present our fallen flesh, rescued out of Satan's hand, and without spot, unto the Father — approving Himself to be indeed the Word made flesh, the Truth, God's Holy One."[2] At the same time, it appears that such a heresy has been condemned by others amongst them, and would probably, if presented in an undisguised form, be opposed by most of the influential people in the Body.

The undue stress laid upon the Human Nature of our Lord as apart from His Divine, both in teaching and in their general system, constitutes also a chief result of Irving's error. This is found generally. They come insensibly to look upon the "Son of Man" more than upon the Son of God. But this feature in their teaching is exemplified more than all in the rigid, intensely human character of their general Doctrine and their Ministry. They teach that after the pattern of the Incarnation, everything is done in the Church by living agency. They insist strongly that Almighty God sends His Salvation and His Blessings by the hands of men.

---

[1] These Italics are mine.

[2] *God: Christ: The Church,* a Discourse, 1863 ("delivered to the Ministers—printed for circulation among us"). So "this act of the Son . . . coming into the very lowest position of our flesh to work out literally and truly our restoration."—*The Word made Flesh,* a sermon, &c., by the Rev. G. Freer, A.M., &c., London: Bosworth, 1865, p. 11. Our Lord came into a low position in the world, but not into "the lowest position of *our flesh.*"

Hence comes their strict and hard ecclesiastical system, reduced to an elaborate machinery, burnished, stiffened, hardened to the last degree of imperative necessity.

The nature of this elaboration will be explained afterwards. The idea of it came from making the human arrangements of the Church, which our Lord set up on earth through His Incarnation, as perfect as possible. True that the Catholic Church has ever had perfect arrangements also. But the recollection of the Divinity has ever been present with Her maintenance of the Human system bequeathed by our Lord, and has tempered and moderated all Her machinery of outward rites. For she has ever taught, that necessary as outward order and ceremonies are to all who are constituted with human bodies, and essential as they are for conveying and ensuring Blessings which are promised in no other way, yet there is a Divine Power also above which is superior to all finite agencies, which will overreach their weakness, and supply their unavoidable absence. The importance of this outward machinery has been, and is being, gradually taught in this our day; but not with the heedless impetuosity of Irving, not by newly-invented methods, but upon the old lines which have been proved and accepted throughout the Church's existence.

§ 3. *Bible Symbolism.*

Various instances of the manner in which the Symbolism of the Bible is employed and extended has been recorded in the course of this work. A good exemplification may be found in the "Mystery of the Candlestick,"[1] and in the application of the various parts of the Jewish Tabernacle to the Ministries in this Body. This is one of the most remarkable characteristics of their System.

Symbolism presents great charms for minds which are of a poetical or dreamy cast; and in some provinces of the religious movement in the earlier part of the present century was pursued with eagerness and ingenuity. Indeed as long as symbolism is kept within bounds, and is merely the interpretation or the legitimate application or even the expansion of doctrines otherwise ascertained, it is not open to objection. And if the tyranny of matter-of-fact minds, prone sometimes to condemn and scout all that they cannot themselves realize, prevailed so far as to ostracize all symbolism, not only the poetry of Christians would suffer inestimably, but a cold preciseness would repel many warmer hearts, and the free flow of the numerous springs of reverential and loving thought in the Catholic Church would be dangerously impeded.

But symbolism merely of this moderate and guarded kind is not pursued amongst these people. They employ types and symbols not merely as the application or the corollaries of doctrines otherwise established, but as the grounds upon which those doctrines are adopted and recommended for adoption. Such for example is the reference to the four streams of Paradise, the four colours in which the cherubim were embroidered on the

[1] *Appendix* III.

Tabernacle, the four ingredients of Incense, and the four living creatures in the Apocalypse, for typifying the Four Ministries.[1] Similar to these were the interpretations of the bullock offered for a sin-offering as symbolizing the priesthood, and the goat as showing forth the whole Church;[2] of the two lights at the Altar as standing for Apostles and Prophets;[3] and of the "ministry" of the Angel every morning, addressed principally to the Elders, and the "united Ministry of Adoration" every evening by the Seven Elders, as being foreshadowed by the trimming of the seven-branched candlestick in the morning by Aaron, and the lighting of it before the Lord every evening by the priests.

Nearly all the observances of the Catholic Apostolic Church are built upon types or symbols, some of which are sound and good, but others and perhaps the great majority are far-fetched or fanciful. A large number of these are derived from the observances of the Jewish Law. The same idealistic method of interpretation which has led to the application of passages in the Apocalypse to current or past events, has prompted this symbolical system. Such for example is the employment of gold-colour for the Apostles' and Elders' stoles, of blue for the Prophets', scarlet for the Evangelists', white for those of the Pastors. For gold is held to be the symbol of Faith, of which the Apostles and Elders are

---

[1] Drummond's *Discourses*, p. 98.
[2] *Three Discourses on Certain Symbols used in Worship*, &c., 2nd Edition. London: Thomas Bosworth, 1874, p. 19.
[3] Ibid. p. 7.

supposed to be the guardians; blue marks the heavens into which the Prophet soars like the eagle; scarlet is taken to designate the Evangelists' message, peace through the blood of the Lamb; and white, as the emblem of righteousness, indicates the Pastor. Besides these, purple, as the symbol of rule, may be worn by the Angel, except at the Holy Eucharist, or in the presence of the Apostle, when he wears white; and also by an Elder or by any priest when preaching or presiding.[1]

§ 4. *The Church.*

After considering the great motive which is presented to all the members of the "Catholic Apostolic Church," so called, and the general principles of their mode of interpreting the Incarnation, and of their fondness of pressing out of almost everything that can be found in the Bible, references to the system constructed, we now come to the various features which that system presents to our consideration. I do not find in their conception of the Church anything different from the ordinary Catholic doctrine, unless it be that there is an exaggerated stress laid upon the undoubted need of human ordinances and human agencies, with the exception that they include all the baptized, without let or distinction, within the fold of the Catholic Church.

They maintain the doctrine of regeneration and incorporation with Christ, and accept lay baptism with the necessary restrictions, and the Theological distinctions of "form" and "matter." But they carry their

[1] *On Symbols*, pp. 36, 37.

idea of the indelible character of baptism so far as to deny in consequence the possibility of apostatizing. "Every baptized man is a Catholic, and as he cannot be unbaptized, so he cannot cease to be a Catholic. Where the room for heresy and schism, and excision from the Church, is to be found under such conditions, or how St. John could speak of certain whilom disciples as 'going out from us, because they were not of us,' are questions we have often asked, but to which we have never elicited a reply."[1]

In consequence of this fundamental tenet, we arrive at the attitude in which they stand towards other Christians. In their eyes the Roman, Greek, and Anglican Communions, Alt-Katholiks, members of the Swedish, Norwegian, Danish, and Dutch Churches, Presbyterians, Lutherans, Calvinists, the various Nonconformist Bodies in England, America, and elsewhere, Armenians, Jacobites, Copts and other Monophysites, Nestorians, and all who have been once baptized, however much they may have abjured the Catholic faith, or violated their baptismal nature by deadly sin, are within the pale of the Universal Church. Upon this broad way of viewing other Christians, and taking account of their various stages in the direction of what they deem to be the highest type of Christian, and upon their really tolerant manner of treating all who differ from them, unless they are of their own communion,[2] they rest in great measure the claim which they make strongly and

---

[1] *Union Review*, No. 81, p. 42.
[2] The perusal of *Apostolic Lordship* compels me to add this limitation. See also McNeile's *Letters*, p. 125.

emphatically, of being pre-eminently Catholics. Their largeness of mind in dealing with other Christians has been pointed out in the last Volume, and several exemplifications of it have been given.

The position which they maintain is mainly this:— they assert that the Church Catholic has by degrees sunk deeply from the condition in which it was left by our Lord, when the Holy Spirit, according to His pre-arrangement and promise, came upon it on the Day of Pentecost. At that time He descended not upon the Church generally, but upon the Apostles alone.[1] The Apostles therefore were "the link between Him in the Heavens, and His body on the earth." At this time the intention of the Lord was, according to His words on the Mount of Olives foretelling the destruction of Jerusalem and the end of the world, to come to His Church during the first ages of its existence. Accordingly preparations were begun for the consummation of all things. A Gentile Apostleship must be added to the Jewish College of Twelve. St. Paul and Barnabas were therefore called and separated. But then, notwithstanding the various words of the Apostles, speaking of the return of the Lord as drawing nigh, the faith of the Church waxed feeble. People began to give up waiting for the Lord. Therefore His purpose was changed. No more Apostles were appointed. The early sproutings of the Gentile Apostleship were nipped. And in course of time the Jewish Apostles died, one by one. Then the Church was

[1] *Apostolic Lordship*, p. 63.

maimed of its most important ministry, for the Apostles were not only the link between Heaven and the Church on earth, but they were also the channel through which grace flowed down from the former into the latter.

When therefore the original Apostles were removed, the link "being snapped by the loss of Apostles," the Church "fell as a dead thing to the ground."[1] The ministry of Apostles to the Church being interrupted, she drifted from Christ.[2] Hence, inasmuch as less grace now was bestowed from Heaven, there ensued various defects and evils. The Bishops, who alone now remained to guide and rule the people of God, not being successors of the Apostles, but only holders of an inferior office, as these people assert, and having only local duties over their own Dioceses, not universal prerogatives or responsibilities reaching throughout the Church, that part of the original constitution which was meant for keeping God's people in one, was now wanting. What wonder therefore, they ask, if the Church fell asunder? If sad schisms followed, and the love of many waxed cold? But then, when centuries of this maimed and mutilated state had elapsed, how could the diseases of the Church be healed, or the schisms closed, except by the restoration of the long-lost ministry? Since the Lord is now, as they imagine, evidently coming, He has called and separated His Gentile-Apostles so that they may prepare His Church for His approach, and so present it to Him when He arrives.

[1] "A Ministry," quoted in *Apostolic Lordship*, p. 63.
[2] *Truths for our Days*, No. vi. *The Apostleship*. *Apostolic Lordship*, p. 74.

This sketch will show the relation in which the members of this Body believe that they stand towards the several Branches of the Catholic Church. They look upon themselves as alone possessing plenary grace. They think that others have grace increasing in abundance according as they approach nearest to the perfect constitution which they themselves display. Bishops have the succession from the first Twelve, and can therefore bestow valid ordination. Therefore Priests and Bishops ordained or consecrated by them are real Priests and Bishops. But they do not possess the same amount of grace which they would have if an Apostle's hands were laid upon them. Therefore these people have an office for Confirmation by the Apostle of the Orders bestowed by a Bishop.[1] It is under this belief in the essential, though inferior, position of other Bodies in the Universal Church, that they are often unwilling to remove Clergymen from the work which they are doing outside of their Community into offices directly under Apostolic guidance.

But if the standard of action is thus marked by tolerance and liberal consideration towards those who are

[1] I regret that in a letter to the *Guardian* newspaper written in the Autumn of 1875, I stated through some inadvertence that Irvingites re-ordain those who have been ordained elsewhere. This is entirely a misstatement, the truth being as explained in the text. But the other part of my sentence is true, "they suffer themselves to be re-ordained." That is to say, Priests or Angels, holding "Catholic Apostolic" orders, accept, when wishing to get employment in the Church of England, ordination from a Bishop. What can be more un-Catholic than re-ordination? Especially when, as in this case, ordination by a supposed "inferior" is accepted by one who has been according to his own belief validly ordained by a minister of the superior order.

outside their pale, there is no lack of strict discipline within the Body itself. Upon the question of obedience to authority, these people have ever been the highest of high Tories. They are among the strongest in animadverting upon lawlessness (ἀνομία) as a glaring fault in our times. They will permit nothing such themselves. If their chief Rulers are appointed directly by the voice of prophecy, if Apostles are "not of man nor by man, but by Jesus Christ,"[1] then their official commands have indeed a high sanction and imperative force. The strong rule of the Apostles has been exercised over many opponents of their imperious sway, and has led several thoughtful men to secede from communion with them.

§ 5. *The Fourfold Ministry.*

The evidence of the Fourfold Ministry is based first upon certain passages and types in Holy Scripture and upon other considerations, and secondly upon the fact, as these Religionists deem it, that Apostles, Prophets, Evangelists, and Pastors have been duly appointed with Divine promptings and sanction. "When He ascended up on high, He received gifts (δόματα) for men; and He gave some *men* (τοὺς μὲν, not τὰ—*men*, not *gifts*), apostles; and some *men*, prophets; and some *men*, evangelists; and some *men*, pastors and teachers."[2] This is the rendering of the *Testimony*. The passage too in the First Epistle to the Corinthians mentions apostles, prophets, and teachers, which latter designation may, it is contended, reasonably include evangelists as the teachers

[1] Gal. i. 1.   [2] Eph. iv. 11.

of the world without, and pastors as the teachers and trainers of the members within the Church.

Then there are the types, viz., the Four Cherubim mentioned by Ezekiel,[1] and the Four Beasts in the Revelation.[2] "The Prophet in the visions of God beheld figured forth under the form of the Cherubim, each with four faces, the fourfold ministry of the Lord in His Church, by which ministry the Glory of God is revealed. The vision is a vision of the appearance of the glory of the Lord, the Incarnate Word.

"The whirlwind out of the north is the emblem of spiritual power manifested in the cold death of nature; the great cloud, God hiding Himself; the fire infolding itself, and the brightness about it, the purity and holiness of God reflected in His instruments, which like a fire at once consumes and purifies. The colour of amber is the savour of truth, as St. Paul says, 'by manifestation of the truth commending ourselves to every man's conscience in the sight of God.'

"The likeness of four living creatures coming forth out of the midst of this vision is the fourfold ministry of the Lord in men, for they had the likeness of a man: the four faces and four wings represent the character of the ministries, and the endowment by which they are borne up above the earth into the spiritual region, into the heavenlies.

"Their feet being straight feet, and their motions straightforward, represent the uprightness of their walk, and their progress towards the fulfilment of the purpose of God, without any turning aside.

[1] Ezek. i. 10.   [2] Rev. iv. 6—8.

"The sole of the foot like a calf's foot, the patience and pastoral care of their ministry; the burnished brass, the spiritual understanding wherein they minister.

"The hands of a man under their wings, the power of taking hold of men and lifting them up into the spiritual region wherein they move; the joining of the wings one to another, the unity of purpose wherein they work harmoniously together, always pressing straight forward.

"The faces represent the characteristics of that fourfold dignity and office of the Great Shepherd which are exercised by them.

"The lion, the symbol of the Ruler, full of majesty and dignity, calm and quiet in his motions, who walketh in his dwelling and none maketh him afraid, represents the authority, dignity, and supremacy of the Lord, the Lion of the Tribe of Judah (the royal tribe, to whom the sceptre belongs); and such ought to be the demeanour and character of those by whom this His office of rule and authority is to be manifested and exercised—His Apostles.

"The eagle, soaring up into the heavens, dwelling on high, living solitary, keen-sighted to see the things afar off, represents the Lord as the Prophet, the foreteller of things to come; and this His office He exercises through the Prophets.

"The man, having sympathies and affections in common with suffering humanity, represents the character of the Lord as the Evangelist, the herald of mercy, peace, and reconciliation; and this His office He exercises through the Evangelists.

"The ox or calf, patient, strong to labour, bearing the yoke, treading out the corn, represents the character of the Lord as Pastor and Teacher; and this His office He exercises through the Pastors.

"The appearance of the burning coals of fire and of lamps, indicate their ministry as being a ministry for cleansing and for enlightening.

"Their running and returning as a flash of lightning represents the suddenness of the fulfilment of the different steps or stages in the purpose of God, and the want of any sign or appearance which is left behind, so that as God's purpose shall go forward towards its fulfilment, it shall appear, even to the spiritual, but as a flash of lightning, which passes and leaves no trace behind; and thus shall the coming of the Son of Man be,—as lightning in the heavens, seen for a moment by the dwellers upon the earth, causing a temporary fear, and straightway forgotten (Luke xvii. 24—30).

"The wheels upon the earth beside the living creatures, having the form of a wheel within a wheel, being of the colour of beryl, with their rings full of eyes, so high that they were dreadful,—this, which the Prophet saw while contemplating the living creatures, represents the workings of the Providence of God in the affairs of the world, whereby He orders all things according to His purpose in the Church. The wheel within a wheel represents the complicated movements of the Providence of God; the dreadful rings represent the shadow of the eternal purpose of God, of which every specific act of His Providence, whether to human eye having the appearance of accident or design, is a small but certain portion; and the dreadfulness of the rings full of eyes expresses the indescribable awe and reverence which results from the workings of the Providence of God, in all that occurs, and are the visible results of the incomprehensible, unseen purpose of Him who seeth all things, and whose eyes are everywhere beholding the evil and the good. The spirit of the living creatures in the wheels, shows the affairs of the world following the purpose of God in His Church. The beryl is the colour of the sea, and signifies the workings of God's Providence, having the appearance of being the result of the workings of man, according to that expression, *Vox populi, Vox Dei;* man thinking he is working when God is working by him.

"The likeness of the firmament over their heads, like unto crystal, is the eternal condition of the heavenly things,—that state of purity, whereof the saints who shall have part in the first Resurrection shall be made partakers, and whereunto they aspire (Rev. xv. 2; iv. 6).

"The noise of their wings is the spiritual utterances and manifestations accompanying the going forth of the Fourfold Ministry.

"The throne of the colour of sapphire, the colour of Heaven, the body of Heaven in his clearness (Exodus xxiv. 10), is the depth and intensity of that heavenly-mindedness, whereby it is seen that the Heavens do rule, and that all things on earth are ordered by Him who sitteth upon the Throne, as exemplified in the vision of Stephen at his martyrdom; the appearance of a man on the Throne is the continual seeing by the spiritual of the Man Jesus at the Right Hand of God, who as our forerunner is entered into the Heavens for us.

"The appearance as of the bow in the clouds in the day of rain, the sign of the covenant of God with us, is the continual remembrance of His promise, and the hope of its fulfilment; for by hope we are saved.

"This vision is not discerned by man's eye, it is a vision of God; it is the form wherein the pure in heart see God in his waking, and it belongs to this dispensation, and to those only who see His glory" (John xvii. 24).[1]

This passage, which I have quoted from the *Narrative*, shows us in the words of a leader in this Body what is the nature of the evidence for a Fourfold Ministry which is derived from the visions of Ezekiel and St. John. And it is a good instance of the ingenious symbolism which has extracted the application and discovered, as is supposed, recondite features of adaptation. Besides this, we learn that other types are believed to set forth the same doctrine.

"The four ministries of Apostles, Prophets, Evangelists, and Pastors," says Drummond,[2] "are obviously typified by the four streams which watered the garden of Eden; by the four colours in which the cherubim were embroidered on the curtains of the tabernacle; by the four ministries (the bestower of the Comforter, the

---

[1] *Narrative of Events*, pp. 71—73.
[2] *Drummond's Discourses*, &c., Bosworth and Harrison: London, 1858, p. 98.

Voice crying in the wilderness, the teller of good tidings, and the feeder of the flock) by which Isaiah (xl.) calls on the Church in the latter days to arise and shine; by the four living creatures in the Apocalypse. These bind into unity the different Churches presided over by their respective independent bishops, and carry on the whole Church, as one, to perfection. These are typified by the Cherubim."

To these types we may add "the cherubim, placed at the gate of the garden of Eden;" "the four standards of Israel's host which came in triumph out of Egypt, with the ark of God in the midst of them;"[1] "the same four-foldness of things subsidiary, the bowls, the dishes, the covers, the spoons;"[2] "and the four carpenters," and "the spirits of the earth," mentioned by Zechariah.[3]

Such are the Scriptural types, which are supposed to represent the Fourfold Ministry. But besides this kind of evidence, these people believe that they find arguments to support their conclusion from man's own nature, and from the provinces of work which they say naturally divide into four distinct groups.

They urge that our mental and moral being may be divided into the Will, the Imagination, the Understanding, and the Affections. Of these the Will is placed by them as "the highest faculty in man, the great parent of his active and distinctive character;"[4] according to its strength or weakness the decider whether a man is

---

[1] Groser's *Four Ministries*, p. 7.   [2] *Groser*, p. 8.
[3] Zech. i. 20; vi. 5. *Groser*, p. 9.   [4] *Groser*, p. 9.

resolute and influential, or vacillating and inauthoritative. The Will of the Church is therefore embodied in the Apostolic Ministry. The Apostles are "heads under Christ, and supreme rulers of the Catholic Church; the fountains and teachers of the doctrine of the Church; and lastly, the bestowers of the Holy Ghost by the laying on of their hands, whether for sealing all who believe, or for ordaining ministers of the House of God."[1]

Next to the Will comes the Imagination, which "ranges and expatiates over the fields of knowledge and of fancy—soars into the heaven of sublimest thought and feeling—is the parent of invention, of eloquence, and poetry; and this is the portion of our nature which the Prophet addresses."[2] He gives utterance to the "living word." And such is the power of this living word, that "it touches a cloud, and behold! a rainbow. It strikes upon a stone, and turns up heaps of gold and jewellery. It opens mines of wealth and wonder, such as Oriental fancy never pictured, and that where drossy scurf and barrenness alone had hitherto appeared. It is not a matter of theory; we speak of what we have seen and heard, and experienced."[3] The Prophet is therefore "the channel whereby the secret mind of God is brought into the Church by revelation;" for the purpose of conveying the light of God, and for opening hidden mysteries.[4]

[1] *A Manual or Summary of the Special Objects of Faith and Hope in the Present Times.* For the use of the Catholic Churches in England. London: Printed by Moyes and Barclay, 1843, p. 22. (Testimony.)
[2] *Groser*, p. 11.   [3] Ibid.
[4] *Manual* (Testimony), p. 30. *Appendix* I.

Thirdly, we have the Understanding, the intellectual faculty, "by which we lay hold of principles, both of truth and action;" which draws logical inferences, and deduces general conclusions from particular cases; which "in the schools originates scientific analysis; in the ordinary intercourse of life is called common sense."[1] This faculty is supposed to find exercise pre-eminently in the ministry of the Evangelist, whose business it is with keen and brightened weapons to fight the battles of the Lord, and with all the resources of reason and illustration to convince the minds of men. The field of the Evangelist lies without the fold. He is to preach the Gospel, to convert, to prepare for admission into the true flock, and to receive by baptism. When admission is effected, his office is fulfilled, and that of the Pastor succeeds.

Lastly come the Affections, as a constituent of our mental and moral nature. "Sorrow and joy, love and hatred, fear and hope, desire and aversion, all that is kept in such continual commotion and unrest by the various changes and chances of this mortal life—all this is the region of Pastoral care."[2] The Pastor's scene of operation lies inside of the fold. His duty is "to descend into the interior of Christian experience—to comfort the mourner—to admonish the guilty—to soothe the penitent—to receive the confession of sin, and sprinkle the conscience with atoning blood—to unloose the heavy burdens and bid the oppressed go free—to exercise the care of the Good Shepherd over His flock—to

[1] *Groser*, p. 12.   [2] Ibid., p. 13.

see that they do not stray—to watch that they be never over-driven; "for if they be over-driven one day," said Jacob, "they will die"—to gather the lambs in his arm, and carry them in his bosom; if need be, to lay down his life for the sheep;—all this pertains to the Pastor's work."[1]

We see here the grounds upon which the doctrine of a Fourfold Ministry is reared. I have thought best to represent them mainly in the words of the maintainers of this doctrine, in order that they may not suffer from inadequate explanation. We can now pass on to the consideration of each Ministry separately.

§ 6. *The Restored Apostolate.*

In the fourth chapter of the Revelation, twenty-four seats are represented as encircling the Throne of the Lamb, and upon the seats twenty-four elders were seen in the vision to be sitting. These twenty-four, who are thus admitted into honoured proximity to the Lord, are supposed to consist of the Jewish and Gentile Colleges of Apostles. St. Paul and St. Barnabas, being the only products of an attempt to form a Gentile College in the lifetime of the first Apostles, which proved unsuccessful through the want of faith enough in the Church for the Lord to close this dispensation at that time according to His pre-existing desire, are excluded from the favoured Twenty-four.[2] The first College marks the

---

[1] *Groser*, p. 13. See also *Readings upon the Liturgy*, Vol. I. Part I. pp. 148—152, p. 263, *note.*

[2] At Albury there are twenty-four carved stalls round the Sacrarium which are said to be set in preparation for the Lord's Coming, though I cannot vouch for this. See *Union Review*, No. lxxi. p. 41, *note.*

commencement of the life of the Christian Church; the last College, or more correctly, the second division in the main Apostolic College, is sent in order to present the Church to the Lord on His return. Hence arose the belief, only shattered by the stern arrival of inexorable death, that the twelve Apostles would be preserved by supernatural power all together in their entire number, or when that was impossible, in the person of at least one representative, till His long-desired appearance.

"Men ought to demand a proof," writes Drummond, "of the mission of Apostles, because, whilst all other ministers exercise their office in virtue of the authority conferred upon them, they exercise their office by immediate appointment from Christ.' The proofs then rest upon two grounds: first, the method of their original sending forth; and secondly and above all, that to which the Apostle Paul, the first Apostle of the Gentiles, appealed when he wrote to the Churches which he had planted:—'Ye are my Epistle,' *i. e.* my testimonials, my letters of orders, 'seen and read of all men.' If they have not planted and established Churches, fulfilling all the conditions which the New Testament declares to be characteristic of Christ's Church:—if there is not found combined in these Churches all the truths which are found separately in all the different sects, then truly there are no Apostles; and we should pray to God continually to raise up Apostles to guide us, in the full confidence that He will hear and answer us, because we can never be guided truly in His ways, never can be prepared to be caught up to meet the Lord in the air, never can be baptized with the Holy Ghost, never can be sealed from the great destruction that is coming, never can be filled with all the truth of God, but by Apostles, as the spiritual instruments of God, and the means by which He will give us these blessings."[1]

Of these two grounds of Apostolic credentials, the first which concerns their appointment, claimed to be Divine, is clear from the course of this history. As St. Peter, St. James, St. John, and their companions received on the Day of Pentecost a descent of the Holy Spirit, which was attested by tongues and by other supernatural signs, so these Apostles were appointed through Prophets who had spoken with tongues, and had exhibited strange signs of an unearthly character. And as St. Paul was confident that he had received his appointment directly from the Lord Himself, so each of these Apostles had his own settled conviction that he was sent forth by the same Lord. Again, as SS. Paul and Barnabas, though Apostles "not of man, nor by man, but by Jesus Christ," were yet formally "separated" for the active duties of their office by the Church at Antioch, guided thereto directly by the Holy Ghost; so under the orders of the Lord through His Prophets, the Church of the faithful "separated," with due circumstances of formality, the Gentile Twelve. When the Lord speaks, who can gainsay it?

Materials too for estimating Mr. Drummond's second reason for concluding that these men were really Apostles, have been supplied in the course of this history. Their adherents point to their wisdom in managing the

[1] Drummond's *Discourses*, p. 117.

Body, the largeness of their Catholicity, the compact and well-considered system of doctrine which they have consolidated and completed, the ingenious and perfect machinery of the different Ministries which in detail at least has grown up under their superintending care, their Liturgy and elaborate Ritual, and the high character which their Members have borne, and the zeal universal among them, which must be a proof of the soundness of their Faith, and of the presence of the Divine Blessing. So high is the appreciation of these services, which is general throughout the Body, that if people who have never heard even the names of these Twelve men remark that if Apostles indeed, they have effected marvellously little, the surprised answer is that they have achieved marvellously much. The original appointment of them is referred to as if it was without doubt the Lord's doing; and the success which is supposed to have attended them is quoted as the proof from actual experience that this was no mere human agency.

If indeed they are not duly appointed, but have usurped so high an office, they must, as the Members assert, have been actuated by Satan. What could be more presumptuous and wicked than to have professed to bestow the Holy Spirit as they have done without being duly authorized? Such awful profanity could not co-exist with such a manifest production of the fruits of the Spirit as have been seen in this Body. And as this supposition appears to be preposterous, we are perforce led —so they allege—to conclude that these men are really Apostles.

Their great characteristic is taken to be that they are the channels of the influx of the Holy Spirit into the Church. This involves all their functions.[1] They are next to Heaven. The gift of the Holy Ghost is imparted to them to divide to every man severally. Accordingly, they ordain all the other Ministers, and they "seal" the faithful. The effect of imposition of hands in the former case is to confer ordinary ordination, only that Apostles do so with plenary grace. The latter has acquired a higher sense, in not being merely Apostolic Confirmation, but being supposed to be the conveyance of a talisman of security against the great tribulation, and of a title of membership in the immediate suite of our Lord on His Approach. Their "functions none other can fulfil, as far as is revealed in Scripture, save Apostles, and those only who are immediately and personally delegated by them."[2]

Then the Apostles are also "the fountains and teachers of the Doctrine of the Church." They are the ultimate court of appeal in cases of dispute about Doctrine. In Drummond's time, proceedings were conducted as follows: "In the ultimate court of appeal, the Twelve Apostles are assisted by the Twelve Prophets. The Senior Apostle presides to preserve the order of the Council; six sit as judges, and five open the proceedings by laying down the principles on which the matter is bound to be decided. The elders and deacons give their opinions; the angels and bishops collect the light which

---

[1] *Testimony in Manual*, p. 22.
[2] Ibid., p. 23.

has come up from all; if the Holy Spirit please to speak, He does so through the Prophets; and after all is concluded, the Twelve Apostles apart consider the judgment which is ultimately to be delivered to the Churches."[1] This description, which of course could only be true throughout during the survival of all the Twelve, and indeed during the short period of their unbroken unity, shows the relation in which practically the Apostles stood to the other Ministers upon questions concerning doctrine and the faith.[2]

And indeed in practical matters also. They are the heads under Christ, and supreme Rulers of the Catholic Church. This position has never been abandoned; and time and prescription have rather heightened relatively the eminence on which they stand, than brought them more upon a level with their followers.

Indeed, as the difference claimed between the Apostleship and the other Ministries amounts to a difference of kind rather than degree,—for all the others are by them, and they alone by the Lord Himself,—it is clear that every occasion of collision must leave them only the more securely established. For the strength of the title of the one—supposing it to be acknowledged—and the comparative weakness of the titles of the others, which draw all their virtue and force from the first, must be made gradually more conspicuous. Apostles move upon a higher platform, and claim to do so, however much they and their immediate friends may disguise the fact.

---

[1] Drummond's *Discourses*, p. 107.   [2] See *Appendix* IV.

That Apostles ought to have this pre-eminence, they consider to be proved, not only from the nature of their office, but also from the manner in which our Lord treated the original Twelve. He retained them near to Himself, for instruction, not only private, but public. He cleansed them by His blood, and went in to and out from them between His Resurrection and His Ascension. "Apostles, and Apostles alone, are in Scripture declared to be the centre of authority, of doctrine, of unity, in all things, to the visible Church of Christ on earth, until His second and glorious appearing to those who look for Him without sin unto salvation."[1] In the Acts of the Apostles, we hear of "continuing in the Apostles' Doctrine and Fellowship," of "laying things at the Apostles' feet," of the Twelve appointing the Deacons, of the Apostles, when persecution drove away the rest, abiding at Jerusalem. Apostles are foundations of the Church, which receives from them the title "Apostolic."

§ 7. *Prophets.*

The position of Prophets in the Church is defended upon the grounds that Prophets existed in the days of the First Apostles and for some time after their decease, and that in fact they were so well known, and so essential a part of the Church's life, that St. Paul gave in a long and important passage directions about the exercise of the prophetical gift.

The position of Prophets in the Jewish dispensation cannot be doubted. They were the means during a

---

[1] *Testimony in Manual*, p. 24. *Appendix* I.

lengthened period of the conveyance of the revelations of the Holy Spirit about Divine Truth, and of guidance in various cases of practical business. If these prophetical gifts were the evidences and the means of the continued action of the Holy Spirit in the inferior state which was to minister to the introduction of a better order of things, why should they not be conspicuous when confessedly the Holy Spirit came to dwell in the Church in the higher dispensation?

And such was actually the case. On the Day of Pentecost the descent of the Holy Ghost was evidenced by the use of tongues, and by a vast development of the small germ of the Church which had met during the week before in the upper Chamber. The inspired account says that this was in fulfilment of ancient prophecy, which said :—" It shall come to pass in the last days, I will pour out My Spirit upon all flesh: and your sons and your daughters shall prophesy, and your young men shall see visions, and your old men shall dream dreams: and on My servants and on My handmaidens I will pour out in those days of My Spirit; and they shall prophesy."[1]

And so they did prophesy. "God hath set some in the Church, first Apostles, secondly Prophets."[2] The Church "is built upon the foundation of the Apostles and Prophets, Jesus Christ Himself being the Head Corner-stone."[3] There were Prophets at Jerusalem in the first days; for the passing account

---

[1] Acts ii. 17, 18 ; Joel ii. 28, 29.
[2] 1 Cor. xii. 28 ; Eph. iv. 11.   [3] Eph. ii. 20.

states that they went "from Jerusalem to Antioch."[1] There were Prophets in the Church at Antioch; for through them the Holy Ghost ordered that St. Paul and St. Barnabas should be sent out on their celebrated journeys.[2] The twelve disciples of St. John the Baptist, upon the imposition of St. Paul's hands, "prophesied."[3] We know the names of some of the prophets, such as Judas, Silas,[4] Agabus,[5] besides those who were mentioned at Antioch as "prophets and teachers." Accordingly St. Paul warns the Thessalonians: "Despise not prophesyings."[6] And to the Romans he says: "Having then gifts differing according to the grace that is given to us, whether prophecy, let us prophesy according to the proportion of faith."[7] St. Peter uses very much the same language, though the actual term "prophesy" is not employed by him. "As every man hath received the gift, even so minister the same one to another, as good stewards of the manifold grace of God. If any man speak, let him speak as the oracles of God."[8] St. John speaks of "false prophets"[9] which presumably would not exist, unless there were also true prophets: "Beloved, believe not every spirit, but try the spirits whether they are of God: because many false prophets are gone out into the world." And St. Paul tells the Ephesians that "the mystery of Christ" "is now being revealed to His holy apostles and prophets by the Spirit."[10]

[1] Acts xi. 27. [2] xiii. 1, 2. [3] xix. 6.
[4] xv. 32. [5] xi. 28. [6] 1 Thess. v. 20.
[7] Rom. xii. 6. [8] 1 Pet. iv. 10, 11.
[9] 1 John iv. 1. [10] Eph. ii. 4.

So too the early records of the Church show that the spirit of prophecy was continued for some time, even after the first Apostles died. But when their quickening power was removed, this spirit gradually waned, and at last ceased from the Church. It is clear, so they assert, from the writings of Justin Martyr, Irenæus, Tertullian, Origen, and Eusebius, that spiritual gifts remained in the Church for about a century and a half following the departure of the Apostles, and that then they gradually disappeared.[1]

But the most important passage by far is that which is found in the First Epistle to the Corinthians. St. Paul comes gradually into this subject in the course of his long and weighty letter. In the eleventh chapter he speaks of both men and women " praying or prophesying," as if the latter were almost as common an occurrence as the former. In the twelfth chapter he first really grapples with the subject. He says, "Concerning spiritual gifts (περὶ τῶν πνευματικῶν), brethren, I would not have you ignorant." Afterwards, "But the manifestation of the Spirit is given to every man to profit withal.

---

[1] *Justin Martyr*, Apolog., i., p. 45. Dial. cum Tryph., pp. 308, 315, 316. Ad Orth., Q and R, v., &c.
Irenæus, Hæres., ii. 57; iii. 11; and v. 6.
Tertullian, Apolog., xxiii.; Ad Scapul., iv.; De Anima, ix.; Præscript., ix., &c.; De Charism. in Apostol. Constit., xiii. 1, published in the work attributed to Hippolytus.
Origen, Contra Celsum, lib. ii. and iii.
Eusebius, lib. iii. c. 37; iv. 15; v. 1, 7, 24; vi. 40; and vii. 7, 9.
See also Dodwell's *Dissert. in Irenæum*, ii., and Biscoe's *Boyle Lecture*.
These references are taken from a Pamphlet *On Miracles and Miraculous Powers*. Three discourses delivered in the Catholic and Apostolic Church, Gordon Square, London. Bosworth and Harrison, 1856, p. 40, note.

For to one is given by the Spirit the word of wisdom; to another the word of knowledge by the same Spirit; . . . to another prophecy." And after showing how all these gifts are to be exercised, not by the individual for himself, or at his own will, but by each for the good of the Body, and in subordination to authority in the Body, he ends after the passage relating to "first apostles, secondarily prophets," by asking "Are all apostles? are all prophets? are all teachers? are all workers of miracles?" Then, after first exhorting all Christians to " covet earnestly the best gifts," he passes off into the beautiful digression about Charity, before pursuing the subject of prophecy into more practical detail.

On his return to this subject, he urges us to " desire spiritual gifts (τὰ πνευματικὰ), but rather," he says, " that ye may prophesy." A distinction is thus drawn between the two, spiritual gifts and prophesying. Spiritual gifts are shown in the next verses to be chiefly exemplified in the use of tongues, which are also declared to be not for the intelligence of man, but to be primarily addressed to God. "He that speaketh in an unknown tongue (γλώσσῃ) speaketh not unto man but unto God: for no man understandeth him; howbeit in the Spirit he speaketh mysteries." What can be clearer? Prophesying, on the other hand, which is here not taken in the popular acceptation of foretelling future events, which latter is indeed only a striking application of the general power of prophetic insight, is open in meaning and communicative. It is addressed to man, not to God. "He that prophesieth speaketh unto men to edification, and exhortation, and comfort. He that speaketh in an unknown tongue edifieth himself; but he that prophesieth edifieth the Church. I would that ye all spake with tongues, but rather that ye prophesied: for greater is he that prophesieth than he that speaketh with tongues, except he interpret, that the Church may receive edifying."

This character of tongues (γλῶσσαι,—the word "unknown" in our English version having no Greek equivalent) in being primarily addressed to Almighty God, and having only a secondary purpose as being for signs to men to attract them to a supernatural manifestation, is further shown repeatedly by St. Paul. He speaks of the probability of words being uttered in the tongue which are hard to be understood (μὴ εὔσημον λόγον). He ends an amplification upon this subject by the conclusion, "Wherefore let him that speaketh in an unknown tongue pray that he may interpret. For if I pray in an unknown tongue," he adds, "my spirit prayeth, but my understanding is unfruitful." And after further discussion and explanation, he says: "Wherefore tongues are for a sign, not to them that believe, but to them that believe not: but prophesying serveth not for them that believe not, but for them that believe." He then in contrast to this gives a striking description of all prophesying, and of an unbeliever or an ignorant man coming into the assembly, and being convinced by the disclosure of the secrets of his heart, and falling down prostrate before God in conversion and repentance.

After this, St. Paul, still taking for granted that

tongues and prophesying would exist in Churches, gives rules for the employment of these spiritual gifts. Not too many are to speak in a tongue; and some one is to interpret. If there be no interpreter, no speaking publicly in a tongue is to be permitted. Prophets also are to speak in limited numbers, and are to be subject to judgment. For "the spirits of the prophets are subject to the prophets." He winds up the subject by saying to the Prophets, that any one who thinks himself a prophet, or spiritual, should admit that the Apostles' directions are the commandments of the Lord. And to Churchmen generally, that they should "covet to prophesy, and forbid not to speak with tongues." And generally, that order and decency should govern all proceedings.

This long and weighty passage is thus supposed by the Members of this Body to enjoin and regulate prophesying in all ages of the Church. For it cannot be doubted that prophesying formed a very real and important part of the religious proceedings in the Corinthian Church at the time when St. Paul wrote. There is also no expression which might lead people to infer that he was speaking of ephemeral gifts. Accordingly, prophesyings have been attempted to be exercised and regulated after the rules and principles which the Apostle here unfolds.

If it be asked why, although Prophets, as they assert, belong to the essential constitution of the Church, they have failed to be present from the third century of the Christian era till the outburst of the spirit of prophecy in Scotland in 1830, the answer is, as they maintain, clear.

"The second of the two ministries, the Prophetic ministry, has necessarily ceased with the first. Prophecy is a gift of the Holy Ghost. The Holy Ghost, for the fulfilment of ministry, is conferred by the imposition of hands of Apostles. The suppression of the Apostleship carried with it necessarily the suppression of prophecy."[1] Prophecy was restored, when the Lord, seeing the rising faith of some amongst His people, began through His faithful to make preparations for His second coming.

Prophets are "men of high spiritual characteristic, whose intellectual energy naturally moves in a *spiritual* region of the thing in hand; whose ministry is of a quality by which it is adapted to go straight to the spirit, and from thence embrace the reason and affections and will; whose natural gift it is to invest authoritative dogma with the attractions of heavenly benignity and supernatural majesty; to steep the intellectual form of the truth in heavenly unction, and in the depths of men's own spiritual consciousness, so that they shall possess in the spirit that which they know in the mind."[2]

"The gift of prophecy may be exercised in the Church by any of its members."[3] But to be a Prophet is different from mere prophesying. Prophesying must be

---

[1] *Appeal to all who believe on the Lord Jesus Christ* (mostly translated from the French), p. 6. London: Bosworth and Harrison, 1859.

[2] *The Present Sorrows of the Lord Jesus and the power of the English Church to meet them.* London. The Author of this tract has since writing this tract returned from the Body to the English Church.

[3] *A Short Discourse on Prophesying*, &c., printed for the use of the Churches in England, p. 6. This tract is known to possess as much authority as anything not issuing from the united Apostolic College can enjoy.

exercised in subordination to the authorities existing in the Church: to the Angel in each Church, and to the Apostle of the Tribe over him; but prophesying does not make a Prophet. A Prophet is one who has been duly ordained to the office of Prophet. And a Prophet in a particular Church is under the Angel, and must be careful to act in submission to him, and not to transgress the "border" of his ministry. "Prophets set in the particular Church receive from the Angel the things revealed; they feed upon them in their hearts, and bring them forth in such form as to give light thereon to the Angels and ministers, and to all the people."[1]

The gift of prophecy may be easily abused. In the first place, false prophets may arise, who ought to be detected and silenced by the Angel in each Church. Secondly, the people "may hear words of prophecy intimating new and strange things, conveying new matters of faith and views of doctrine, new revelations, new facts, hitherto unknown to the Church, and of which the proper evidence is the senses."[2] To prevent the acceptance of these false prophecies, no prophecy is received as binding or valid till it has received the impress of legitimate authority, recognizing and stamping it as part of the lawful and true coinage. That is to say, all prophecies must be submitted to the Apostle of the Tribe before they are acknowledged as valid and authoritative.

The functions of the Prophets embrace three provinces. First, they have to convey the light of God to enable Apostles and others to "direct their course in exercising

[1] *Short Discourse*, p. 8.   [2] Ibid., p. 11.

rule in the Church of Christ." Secondly, they open "the hidden mysteries contained in the law and in the prophets of the Old Testament, in order that Apostles may minister them forth in holy doctrine to the Church." Lastly, they "declare the mind of God concerning His servants whom He would call in the ministry, which predicted mind the Apostles may effectuate by ordination."[1] That is to say, as St. Timothy received the gift of his Ministry "by prophecy, with the laying on of the hands of the presbytery," so the Prophets previously call those who are afterwards ordained.

This is effected as follows:—Certain persons present themselves for ordination. On an appointed day, *The Office for Presentation and Dedication for the Holy Ministry* is used. During that service, after prayer that the Lord may make known His Will, some are chosen or not by the Voice of Prophecy, *i. e.* through the Prophet or Prophets, out of the Candidates for the Ministry who have solemnly presented themselves. This choice is generally made in prophetic language, *e. g.* to a future prophet: "The Lord hath numbered thee among His Prophets: thou shalt offer His word." When the call has been confirmed by the Apostle, he proceeds to the ordination. A Prophet is attached to each Church, and takes part in the Service, as has been and will be further explained.

§ 8. *Evangelists.*

The term Evangelist is not taken in the restricted meaning with which it is applied to St. Matthew, St.

---

[1] *Testimony in Manual,* pp. 30, 31.

Mark, St. Luke, and St. John, but in the wider sense, which includes all the official bearers of the glad tidings of salvation through the Lord. Under this acceptation the name is applied to Philip the Evangelist; and St. Paul tells St. Timothy[1] to "do the work of an Evangelist," and "make full proof of his ministry." So, it is maintained, the word is employed by St. Paul in his mention of the four ministries.[2]

The office of Evangelist was also called into action when our Lord sent out His first Twelve to preach the Gospel. And again, when the Seventy went through Samaria and Galilee, towards the end of His Ministry. From the passages in the Gospels relating to these two events are derived the chief instructions about the work of Evangelists. Thus the Evangelist is one kind of "Teacher."[3] But his province is chiefly outside, not inside the Church. His teaching is especially addressed to the understanding and common sense of his hearers, whom he tries to convince, rather than persuade.[4] He is the preacher of the Gospel. He carries "forth both the light of the truth and the power of the life;" he bears "the tidings of the coming kingdom, and so of the coming judgment, and the news of the ordained refuge, the Church of Christ, wherein alone is salvation."[5] According to the *Testimony*, he was to "heal the sick, cast out devils, raise the dead," as he went. When he has converted people, and taught, and baptized them, then his work ceases, and

---

[1] 1 Tim. iv. 5.   [2] Eph. iv. 11.   [3] 1 Cor. xii. 28, 29.
[4] *Manual,* p. 33. Note K.   [5] *Testimony,* § 39.

they come under the Pastor. Evangelists are thus either members of a company who are constantly engaged in doing the work of preaching the Gospel generally in the Tribe, or else they are attached to each Church. Each Tribe should have sixty Evangelists, who are divided into five bands, each of which is headed by an Angel-Evangelist, answering to the sixty Pillars encompassing the Court of the Tabernacle, and the five Pillars at the entrance.[1] Each Church too has an Evangelist, who takes an appointed part in the Service, and finds his duty in seeking for converts, and preparing catechumens within the sphere of that Church's operations.

There is thus a province, defined by its own "border," for Evangelists. And it is urged that the work of the Church must suffer if there be not a duly-ordained Ministry to attend to this province.

§ 9. *Pastors.*

The oversight of the Church was provided for from the earliest times. Men were appointed as "Bishops" or "overseers," who should "watch for souls, as they that must give account." The Lord Jesus Christ included this duty especially in the commission which He gave to His Apostles. And they in turn delegated it to others. That there is thus a definite office and province for the Pastors to fulfil and occupy cannot be disputed.

Following then their acceptation of the Fourfold Ministry, and assigning special duties to Pastors as well

---

[1] *Readings upon the Liturgy*, Vol. I. Part I. p. 260. See *Appendix VIII.*

as to Apostles, Prophets, and Evangelists, the Members of the so-called Catholic Apostolic Church consider them to possess the supervision and care of the Church and of the baptized, and to be the guardians of the souls of the latter. They are thus placed in every Church by the Apostles, and consist of two grades. The lowest of these includes those Priests who are Pastors. Such a Pastor in each Church "has the especial supervision and care of the children of God; he is the immediate and intimate guardian of their souls." All the direct pastoral care of the flock is in his hands. The second or highest grade consists of the Angels or Bishops of Churches. Each Church has its Angel, who has (1) the higher supervision and care of all the flock, (2) the supervision and care of the Priests under him, and (3) the care of the Church itself. The Pastor of the Church works in the pastoral office under the Angel. Accordingly, he is the channel for the conveyance of rule, and of instruction, and of ministrations of the Spirit from the Apostles to those who are placed under him.[1]

§ 10. *Hierarchy.*

Such are the four kinds of Ministers. They have their several places in the complete Hierarchy of the Church.

First, the old Orders of BISHOPS, PRIESTS, and DEACONS are preserved in the Irvingite Body, only that Bishops are designated by the Scriptural name, which is not applied in the Bible to Priests, viz., ANGELS.[2]

---

[1] *Testimony*, § 40.   *Manual*, § 41. M.   [2] Rev. ii., iii.

Of these, Angels have the power of imposition of hands in the ordination of Deacons, and if specially deputed by the Apostle, in the ordination of Priests. Angels celebrate the Holy Eucharist, absolve, and bless. Priests celebrate the Holy Eucharist in the absence of the Angel, and absolve, and bless. Deacons are excluded from the Choirs in Churches, sitting at the head of the laity, and are chiefly engaged in distributing alms, searching out members of the Congregation, providing and taking care of the externals of worship, and generally acting under the direction of the Angel and Elders.

It must be understood that the Fourfold Ministry has no special reference to these Orders. The two are "cross divisions." Apostles, Angels, Priests, and Deacons constitute a Fourfold Order of degree, each step being higher than the previous step. But Apostles, Prophets, Evangelists, and Pastors constitute a Fourfold Ministry of kind, each kind being different from the others. The relation of the three subordinate Orders or Ministries may be illustrated from the Army. We may suppose for a moment, though with not too close a resemblance, the Cavalry, Infantry, and Artillery to correspond to the three Ministries of Prophets, Evangelists, and Pastors. It will be readily seen how the three latter may have their Angels, Priests, and Deacons, just as in the three branches of the Military Service respectively we find Colonels, Captains, and Subalterns. Only as the sphere of labour for Prophets and Pastors is usually the same, we do not find that their Orders have any distinctive title, beyond the title of their jurisdiction or mission. But the names Angel-Evangelist, Priest-Evangelist, and Deacon-Evangelist, which tell their own story, are very common.

It should be noticed next that Apostles are distinct from all the rest. They with their staff may be considered as the general officers of the Church Militant. But they have also a most remarkable distinguishing feature. All other Ministers, of whatever kind or grade, receive their Ministry or Orders from the Apostles. The Apostles are supposed to receive their Apostleship immediately from the Lord Himself. Thus the Apostle consecrates Angels, and ordains Priests; and Deacons are ordained by Angels in their authority derived from Apostles. But Apostles are "not of man, nor by man, but by Jesus Christ." They therefore stand at the head of all, and upon a platform exclusively their own. This point is brought out strongly and repeatedly in the *Testimonies*, and has been asserted and maintained over over and over again in practice in the face of all opposition. The supreme rule is in the hands of the Apostles.

The staff of each Apostle consists of a Prophet, Evangelist, and Pastor. Each of these is the head under the Apostle of the Ministry to which he belongs in the Tribe. All appeals pass to and fro through him. Suppose for example that any complaint or difficult question is referred to the Apostle of the Tribe from any Prophet. The paper of particulars is sent to the "Prophet with the Apostle,"—such is the official phrase,—who lays it before the Apostle, and afterwards forwards the decision. There is no direct communication between the Apostle

Hierarchy. 53

and Members of the Church except through the authorized channels, which in some instances may involve some six or seven stages.

The number of Clergy in a Church, where there is a full complement, is what would be considered very large. The ideal complement is as follows, but it presupposes a congregation of 3000 communicants:—

I. Angel, who has an Angel's Help . . 2
II. Six Elders, each with an Elder's Help . 12
III. Six Prophets, each with a Prophet's Help . 12
IV. Six Evangelists, each with an Evangelist's Help 12
V. Six Pastors, each with a Pastor's Help . 12
VI. Seven Deacons, each with a Deacon's Help 14

64

Besides these, there might be more Deacons, if desired.

But this ideal has never been realized. At Gordon Square, which ever since the days of Irving has been by far their largest Congregation, only one of the six columns of Elders, so to speak, exists. That is to say, instead of there being six Elders to correspond to the six lateral lamps of the Candlestick, there is only one. But he has his colleagues of the Prophetical, Evangelist, and Pastoral Ministries respectively, he with them representing in their order the Fourfold Ministry. In this state of the development of the Hierarchy of a Church, the four Priests, viz., Elder, Prophet, Evangelist, and Pastor, are rather considered as holding four of the six places designated for the Priests officially assisting the Angel.

There is a provision also for affiliated Churches or Chapels. Such an offshoot of a parental Church is called "the Horn." It may be presided over by an Angel with four Priests, one of each Ministry, under him, in which case it is considered to have a full complement; or an Angel with an assistant Elder, or even an Elder alone without an Angel, may preside over and conduct the Services held there. The Services in the Horn are dependent upon the size of the Staff of Clergy.

A Horn is supposed to have a quasi-independent existence. When a Congregation assembles entirely under the Mother Church, or even under the Horn, it may be committed to a single Priest, either alone, or with Assistant-Priests, and is then called a "Helpship." A "Helpship" may be under the general charge of some Elder of the Mother Church, with only a Deacon upon the spot.

But the Ministry of the Body does not end here. There should be seven Deacons for each Church, and more may be added according to the needs of the Congregation as decided by the Angel. The members of the Congregation elect Deacons into the seven places. Additional Deacons are appointed by the Angel.

HELPS (ἀντιλήψεις[1]), a general name for Assistants, one of which may be provided for each official Minister, have been already explained. These "Helps" are chosen by the Minister whose coadjutor each respectively is to be, but only with the sanction afterwards given of

[1] 1 Cor. xii. 28.

Hierarchy. 55

the Angel of the Church. Upon a similar principle, the Angel's Help is chosen by the Angel, but his choice must be confirmed by the Apostle.

The above include the Hierarchy of the Church, and are included amongst the Clergy. There are also several Offices for the devoted amongst the laity.

DEACONESSES assist the Priest and the Deacon in their several ministrations towards the women of the flock. A Deaconess is considered to possess "no original or independent jurisdiction." Her office is not to be taken as constituting any distinct order in the Church, nor does she cease to be one of the laity, and consequently ranks after all the Ministers of the Church. She must carefully attend to the directions of the Priest or Deacon under whom she is serving. But—and this is remarkable as showing the strictness which prevails in the regular transmission of orders, or messages, or questions, or appeals, step by step, without any leap from any one even to the next but one—the Priest is specially allowed to direct the Deaconess without the intervention of the Deacon. Deaconesses are chosen with reference to fitness of age, and opportunities of service. They are nominated, and subsequently elected by the "Angel in Council." After which due notice is given in the Congregation for objections, if any, to be stated. They are admitted with the use of a special Service provided in the Liturgy. They do not require re-admission on removing to another Church.

UNDER-DEACONS are nominated and subsequently elected by the Angel of the Church in Council. As in the case of Deaconesses, notice is given in the Congregation after the Communion at least two Sundays, or as these people say, "Lord's-days," before proceeding to the election, in order that objections, if there be any, may be stated. Only communicants are entitled to advance objections, and these are made through the Deacons of the Church. Under-Deacons are either employed under the seven Deacons of the Church, or not. In the former, case, they ought to be heads of families, and are chosen by preference from the candidates for the Ministry. The Under-Deacon's duty is to assist the Deacon in keeping order in the Lord's House; to take oversight of the walk and conversation of those who are within the Deacon's charge; and to visit according to the Deacon's instructions. Under-Deacons not wholly under the seven Deacons of the Church are to be chosen exclusively from the "Candidates for Ministry." They are all admitted with a special Service, and do not require re-admission upon moving to another Church.

LAY-ASSISTANTS are such lay-people as voluntarily undertake works of charity and piety under the Ministers of the Church, and are regularly organized, the men under the Deacons, and the women under the Deaconesses. At least once in every year the Angel of the Church invites members of his Congregation to devote their spare time to charitable and pious purposes. They are searched out by the Deacons, and their names with the particulars of the services which they can render are entered in a book kept in the vestry for the purpose. As long as their names remain there, they are held to be bound to render the services specified. But their names can be removed, or their services altered, whenever they choose to make application. They are presented to the Angel for special Benediction by him, at some time to be appointed by him for the purpose, which should be by preference Christmas, Easter, Pentecost, or All Saints' Day.

If either Deacons, or Deaconesses, or Under-Deacons, or Lay-Assistants are going to work under the Angel-Evangelist, they are presented to him, instead of to the Angel of the Church.

None of the Clergy of this Body take any title or address in ordinary life from the office which they bear. If a Clergyman joins them, and becomes Elder or Angel, he is still addressed under the conventional title of Reverend. But even an Apostle, if regarded as a Layman outside of the Sect, notwithstanding his presumed promotion to a post above all Patriarchs and Archbishops, repudiates everything beyond the ordinary Esquire or his legal title. Whether this neglect of outward distinction, which extends also to their dress, be wholly due to the modesty which has undoubtedly marked all their public action, or in part also to a secret want of that confidence in the truth and reality of their mission which, in a case of such enormous and universal importance as is involved in their claims, would perforce bear them, even if unconsciously, to a high degree of inalienable magnifying of their office, may well afford matter for consideration.

§ 11. *Church Services.*

The regular hours of Divine Service are six o'clock

A.M. and five o'clock P.M. daily. Besides these, Services are held at ten o'clock A.M. and at two o'clock P.M. These hours are regulated strictly by the central authority. Also, the Holy Eucharist is to be celebrated by the Angel immediately after the ten o'clock Service on every Lord's Day, and the Communion is to be administered immediately after the two o'clock Service. This is the order to be observed in Cathedral Churches, which have a sufficient staff of priests. In these, if the number of priests and deacons admits, there is to be daily Service also at nine and three, and at such other hours as the Angel, with the sanction of the Apostle, may appoint.

But in smaller Congregations, this number of Services may be lessened, according to the strength of the staff of Clergy. If there are not enough for more, there may be Services only at ten o'clock and in the afternoon on Sundays,—the latter at what hour is most convenient,—with no week-day Services. In that case the Holy Eucharist is to be celebrated in the morning, but there is to be no afternoon Administration. If there is only a Deacon in charge, there must be no Celebration, and the Service in that case should be later than ten o'clock, lest the members of the Congregation on their return meet other people going to their own places of worship.

Two forms are given in the Liturgy for the Office of the Celebration of the Holy Eucharist. The longer of these is to be used only in Cathedral Churches, or Angels' seats, and on the Lord's Day. And even then it is to be used only by the Angel, or by some one duly qualified and authorized to act for him, assisted by two Ministers. It will be remembered that Deacons are not technically "Ministers." The Shorter Form is to be used in smaller Churches, and when there is not any one duly authorized to take the Angel's place, or two assistant Ministers are not present.

On the Lord's Day a sufficient quantity of both Elements are consecrated at the Holy Eucharist, and reserved during the week for three purposes, viz., (1) "proposition," before the Lord at Morning and Evening Prayer, which act is supposed to bring all the Worship of the Church nearer to the One great Sacrifice for Sins, by means of the weekly Celebration; (2) for Communion on Sunday afternoons, and after Morning Prayer; (3) for the communion of the sick. The Sacrament thus reserved is kept in a "Tabernacle," and a lamp is kept burning before it, as in Roman Catholic Churches. Whatever remains of it is to be taken into the Vestry on the succeeding Sunday after the Celebration at the Forenoon Service, and is then to be consumed upon the return of the Priests. But when there is no Angel to make the daily Intercession, only so much is consecrated as is sufficient for communicating the sick during the ensuing week. In this case, no "proposition" is made, nor is there any Communion apart from the Celebration. The Afternoon Communion is intended for those who cannot attend at the Forenoon Service. It should be conducted by at least one Priest,—if the Angel be not present, —assisted in the administration by another Priest, or in the absence of such, a Deacon. The Priest must have himself received the Holy Sacrament before in the day.

"The Shorter Office for the Celebration of the Holy Eucharist" ought, when it is used on the Lord's Day, or on any Feast or special occasion, to be performed by not less than three Ministers, the Celebrant and two Assistants. But on ordinary occasions, on week-days, there should be only one Assistant. The Office is of a simpler character than the longer one.

In the Morning Prayer on each day, the Angel delivers what is technically called his "Ministry." This Ministry, which is specially addressed to the Elders of the Church, should relate to "the Faith of the Church, or the works and goodness of God therein. He should seek to set forth matter rather suggestive of meditation, than calculated to draw forth from the Elders systematic reasonings, teachings of doctrine, or exhortations to duties." The Elders on hearing this Ministry are supposed to feed in thought upon it during the day, and in the evening at the Service they deliver "Ministries" grounded upon it. These Ministries ought to be in the form of meditations, "uttered as before God, and not addressed directly to the people, though delivered in their hearing, that they may participate therein."

The various arrangements of all these Services are regulated with great care and minuteness. Each Minister has his copy of "General Rubrics," answering to the Roman "Directorium," which is replete with authoritative directions about all Services and most ministerial purposes, and extends beyond 150 pages.

Provision is thus made for all the occasions that may occur when either at the " Horn " or a " Helpship " fewer Clergy are present than are required for conducting the service.

There are four chief Feasts in the year, Christmas, Easter, Pentecost,—" Whitsuntide " and its cognate terms are seldom used,—and All Saints' Day. Besides these, the " days of Observance " in this Body include Christmas Eve, the Circumcision, the Presentation in the Temple, the last four days in Holy Week,—which, after the fashion that prevailed in the earlier part of the present century, and still remains in many quarters, they call Passion-Week,—Ascension-Day, and All Angels. They also commemorate Advent. Lent is marked by them as Quadragesima, as in the case of the First Sunday in Quadragesima, the Second Sunday in Quadragesima, &c., but only the last quarter of it is observed. Indeed, the only fast-day in the year is Good Friday. Ember-days, Fridays, and the other ordinary fast-days, receive no recognition, except that the Litany is to be used on Fridays. The Epiphany is not found in their calendar, and the Sundays up to Septuagesima are reckoned in order after the Circumcision. There is no Trinity Sunday, the place of that Festival being taken by the " First Sunday after Pentecost." Succeeding Sundays follow with the same reckoning as far as the " Sunday before Advent." Octaves are attached to the Feasts, except to " All Angels ; " but strange to say, the use of the Proper Prefaces for the Feasts of Easter, Ascension, and Pentecost, is authorized on the Sunday succeeding each of those Festivals, but not on the other days within the Octave.

There is a special Lectionary, calculated for Matins, Forenoons, Afternoons, and Vespers, throughout the year. The series of Lessons for the Forenoon Service is arranged for two successive years; the Lessons for the other Services are repeated every year. The Psalms are gone through every month in the four Services. "Days of Observance" have their proper Psalms and Lessons.

Proceeding with the Services in the Prayer-book, after the Forenoon Service, the Form for removing the Holy Sacrament, and the Form for the Benediction of Holy Water,[1] we come to the Litany. The Form used is the English Litany with the following alterations:— 1. The invocation of the Ever-Blessed Trinity conjointly is omitted. 2. The three versicles relating to the Sovereign, and those referring to the Royal Family, the Privy Council and the Nobility, and the Magistrates, are left out. 3. A new versicle is inserted praying for the fourfold Ministry, in words taken from Eph. iv. 11, 12. 4. The Collect, "O God, Whose Nature and Property," together with one relating to the Departed Saints and made up from the end of the Prayer for the Church Militant, are introduced before the Prayer of S. Chrysostom. The Litany is to be used "on Wednesdays and Fridays, and on other occasions when appointed." It is therefore not used on Sundays.

[1] A list of the various Offices in the Prayer-book is given in *Appendix IV.*

The other Services, as their titles show, afford considerable variety for times and occasions. We find a fair array of additional Prayers and Thanksgivings, though several of these are well-known Collects for Sundays from the English Prayer-book; for the Collects are not changed every Sunday, as the Epistles and Gospels are, but only every Season.

There are proper Services for all Holy Days, including "the Anniversary of the Separation of the Apostles," and "Prayers for the Three Seasons." These "three Seasons" precede Christmas, Easter, and Pentecost, being respectively, (1) "From the 16th to the 23rd December;" (2) "From the Wednesday preceding to the Wednesday in Passion Week;" (3) "And from the day after the Ascension to the Friday following, both inclusive." We find also "The Form for Consecrating Chrism;" Various Forms to be used in celebrating the Holy Eucharist, as by an Apostle before a Solemn Council, for a Tribe, and others; for Receiving and Dedicating Catechumens, for Baptism, Benediction of new Communicants, Ordination of and Receiving or Inducting the several grades of Ministers; and various Offices for Private Occasions, such as the Benediction of a House, of a Chamber-lodging, and a Ship; Absolution of Penitents, Benediction of Holy Oil. The Order for Anointing the Sick, the Commendation of a Departing Soul, and Prayers on Passing an Altar. The Catechism [1] and the Psalter close the Volume.

Strange to say, there is no Office for the Burial of the

[1] See *Appendix V.*

Dead. This absence of provision for the departed at the time of their departure, over which the Christian Religion sheds such a beautiful and glorious halo of hope, has probably risen from two sources. First, their continual expectation of the Lord has, as has been related, made them almost ignore the possibility of death. And secondly, the smallness and numerical insignificance of the Sect would become thus more apparent, and has therefore restrained them from making special provision for themselves. They fall back upon their true mother Church.

Those Services which have been mentioned appear generally to present the most salient points, on which any one would fix in a description of the Tenets of the Body under consideration. But the Office for the Laying-on of the Apostle's hands demands more consideration, inasmuch as "Sealing," both in the Rite itself, and still more through the vast privileges which it is supposed to confer, constitutes one of the most striking characteristics of the Community.

In anticipation of the Apostolic imposition of hands, Baptismal Vows are solemnly renewed within ten days previously. This Rite, for which a special Office is provided in their Prayer-book, is conducted by the Angel, accompanied by four Priests, and includes the Renewal itself, and a solemn "Benediction of Peace" bestowed by the Angel. But when a Candidate cannot attend on the day appointed, he is allowed to appear personally before the Angel and to renew his vows "by responding to the interrogatories" set forth in the Office.

Upon the day appointed for the Sealing, when the Angel and his attendant Ministers have entered into the Sanctuary, they take their seats, and the Angel proceeds to call over the names of the Candidates. As their names are severally recited, they come within the lower Choir, accompanied by their sponsors. Then the Apostle with his Ministers, after the list is received, kneels in private prayer before the Altar.

After this, the Angel, standing in front of the Candidates, presents them to the Apostle, "that they may receive the Gift of the Holy Ghost." Then the Apostle addresses the Angel and the Candidates, in a prescribed form of words, first reciting the Baptismal Gifts of the latter, that they "have been made children of God, members of Christ, and partakers of the Holy Ghost," then adding that they have come to "be established, strengthened, and settled, by the anointing of the Holy Ghost, which is the sealing of the Lord;" and that, "through the strength and power of the same Spirit, they may be made perfect in Christ Jesus, and complete in all the Will of God." The Apostle also urges them, inasmuch as "this holy Seal, which is the very Seal of God by the Holy Ghost, will also confirm and bind upon the unclean the chain of those sins, which are not put away with indignation and abhorrence," to humble themselves in faith and repentance before Almighty God. Then they all kneel, the Apostle and his attendants turning to the Altar, and the Angel leads the general Confession of sins by the Candidates: after which the Apostle pronounces Absolution and Peace.

A prayer for the validity of the performance of the Rite follows, and then, the introductory part of the Service being completed, the Apostle and Ministers having vested, the Celebration of the Holy Eucharist begins, the Apostle acting as Celebrant. At the Offertory, after the Elements have been placed on the Altar, the Archdeacon brings up the vessel containing the holy Chrism, and the vessel to be used in the administration of the oil. After the Eucharistic part of the Service, which is here and there adapted to the occasion, and before the Administration of the Holy Communion, "the Apostle rises and covers the Holy Sacrament with a veil."

Then the Pastor with him pronounces the invitation, "Let all who are to receive the Blessing of the Lord draw near," and the Candidates are led up by the Angel to "the access of the Sanctuary." First the Apostle, extending his hands over them, says, "The Holy Ghost come upon you, and the power of the Highest overshadow you." Then succeeds a prayer, the Apostle kneeling at the Altar, that the Candidates may receive six Gifts of the Holy Spirit, that they may be sealed with "the seal of the Living God," and have written upon them the "Father's Name, the name of the city of our God," the Lord's "new Name;" and may "follow the Lamb whithersoever He goeth." After which the Apostle lays his hands on each, and signs him or her on the forehead with the Chrism. Then he addresses all, telling them that they are washed, and sanctified, and "anointed with the unction from the Holy One."

And after a few more prayers and a Psalm,[1] the Communion is proceeded with, in which "the newly-confirmed" receive immediately after the Priests and Deacons. So the Service concludes.

§ 12. *Other Doctrines.*

It remains now to add some remarks upon a few Doctrines held by these people, which have not yet passed under review.

Readers of the last section may have noticed the rather slighting manner in which they treat the Doctrine of the Ever-Blessed Trinity. They are not, so far as I can discover, unsound upon this all-important point. Their refusal to follow the Church of England in smaller recognitions of this Doctrine seems to have arisen from their tendency in the early part of their career to take as their guide the Bible, and nothing but the Bible; and so to reject, where they could, even a word which, though it expresses what is amply taught in Holy Scripture, is nevertheless itself not found in the sacred Volume. But the fact of their not laying the stress upon this great Doctrine, which the Members had learnt to lay in their younger years, when in communion with the English Church, marks also a tendency which will receive due notice at the proper time. More remarks are needed upon the subject of the Sacraments. And first of the Holy Eucharist.

It has been already shown that they have adopted

---

[1] Members of the Church of England or other Bodies, who do not intend to enter into full membership, are here allowed to withdraw.

the Doctrine of Eucharistic Sacrifice. There can be no question to any one who has really studied this question, and probed it to the foundations upon which it rests, that they are right. People are led into error in imagining that, if the Doctrine of Eucharistic Sacrifice is acknowledged there must be an iteration of the One Sacrifice made once for all. But it must be remembered, that such a position is really maintained by no true Theologian. The Offering in the Eucharist is the correlative of the Lord's perpetual Offering of His One Sacrifice—the Lamb that has been slain—before the Throne of God, in the true Holy of Holies. The Offerings made by the Church on earth do not one whit more trench upon the peerless unity and dignity of His Offering, than the prayers of His Saints trench upon His Effectual Intercession. The one is in word, the other is in deed. So far Irvingites in their maintenance of a Melchisedec Priesthood are right.

But their carrying out of this Doctrine, as was to be expected in a Religious Community which has attempted to cut out new ways for itself, has led them into error. They speak too much of "proposition" before the Lord, and make the Holy Sacrament partake far too much of the nature of an *opus operatum*. But this error arises more from the want of a complete grasp of the nature of the Doctrine of the Real Presence.

They appear not to understand the Theological distinctions of a Virtual and a Real Presence. Thus in the *Readings on the Liturgy* we read as follows:—" We believe that that bread and that wine, which in their original condition were, so far as we know, without any spiritual properties whatever, are now changed into *certain holy bodies*, which, without losing their former physical conditions—being in that respect unchanged—are now virtually and spiritually, by the power of the Holy Ghost, the Body and Blood of Christ. When we say virtually, we mean more than it is as good as, or to the same effect as, if the Body and Blood of Christ were present. We mean that in power, in efficacy, and virtue —that is to say really and effectually—His Body and Blood are present. When we say spiritually, we mean that they are not present by a *change* of place from heaven to earth, nor after any such manner as is proper to mere matter: but after a spiritual manner, a manner proper to a spiritual and immaterial substance, that is to say, without change or notion of parts; and that this presence is effected through the operation of the Holy Ghost. So that we believe that the Body and Blood of Christ are capable, in fulfilment of the will of God, through the ministry of Christ, and by the power and energy of the Holy Ghost, of being present elsewhere than in the place where are the material substances of His flesh and blood in their ordinary physical condition; and that by reason of His presence the bread and wine are changed into the Sacrament of the Body and Blood of Christ; in which Sacrament, under the outward figures and signs of bread and wine, are present, after a spiritual manner, the Body and Blood of Christ. But what we have said is no explanation of this great spiritual mystery; it *is* a mystery, and we cannot explain it."[1]

There is an evident confusion in the earlier part of this passage between the terms "virtual" and "real," which, as all know who are acquainted with this subject, have widely different meanings. And this confusion is further illustrated by various particulars in the usages of these people towards the Holy Sacrament, which argue a defective sense of the Presence of the Lord therein, and a tendency to regard it in too formal a mode of observance, and more as a matter of religious routine.

All the Congregation of full age partake of the Holy Sacrament. None leave the Church : none who are of sufficient age omit to receive. It can hardly be that every one without exception is always prepared for reception. Again, all who have already communicated sit invariably till their brethren have partaken. Kneeling is not only not the rule, it is positively discountenanced. Again, communicants hasten out of Church as soon as the Service is over. The Author of *Apostolic Lordship* pointed out this irreverent habit to some of the authorities, but found no sympathy—no remedy was suggested or attempted. The fact is that there is a too exclusive consideration of the Consecrated Elements, and far too little attention paid to our Lord in the Eucharist as a Personal Being. That close approach to, and loving though humble communion with Him, which is so inexpressibly dear to those who realize the Holy Sacrament

---

[1] *Readings on the Liturgy*, Vol. I. pp. 165, 166. Italics as in original. See also *Union Review*, LXXI. pp. 44, 45.

in its true Catholic sense, fails of obtaining adequate appreciation in Irvingite teaching or practice. Hence in their reservation of the Sacrament—a custom to be most carefully fenced and protected—these people do not pay that outward reverence, which, moderately and wisely rendered, should be the indispensable adjunct of this practice if it be adopted ; and the Jewish notion of shew-bread, not the Christian Doctrine of the Lord's own Presence, mainly reigns over their use of the reserved Sacrament in their Public Worship.[1]

The practice of communicating begins at an early age. Infants are communicated once, at the age of about two years. When the "apprehension" of children is supposed to be sufficiently advanced and awakened, at about the age of eight or nine, with a wide margin, they become occasional communicants; that is, they communicate upon the four great Feasts. At this time they receive the Benediction of the Angel, which is given to "such as having been fully instructed in the Faith, are about to be received to the Holy Communion." This Rite in practical effect answers to our Confirmation, only that there is no actual Doctrinal similarity, as the gift of the Holy Spirit is not supposed to be therein conveyed. Afterwards, at the age, say, of fourteen,—again with a wide margin, since all depends upon "apprehension,"—the young people become regular Communicants ; and at the age of twenty they may be admitted to the privilege of being Sealed by the hands of the Apostle.

[1] *Readings on the Liturgy*, Vol. I. p. 395. See also throughout the Article in the *Union Review* before quoted, LXXI. pp. 42—47.

The doctrine held on Sealing has been explained in the last Volume.[1] Inasmuch as this ceremony is supposed to convey the inestimable privileges of escape from the Coming Tribulation, and such a proximity to our Lord that the sealed are to "follow Him whithersoever He goeth," it is evident what seeds of danger to the spiritual life both of conferrers and recipients it must contain. Sealing is conferred upon those who have been confirmed by Bishops, not however as involving a denial of the validity of such Confirmation, but from the idea, that Sealing by Apostolic hands brings privileges and blessings which are beyond the power of any Bishop to convey. This Doctrine will receive a closer examination afterwards.

The teaching maintained and given in the Body upon Baptism itself is, as has been said, sound and Catholic. The practice of having sponsors to answer for the child is retained from the English Service. Perhaps an exaggerated stress is laid upon Satanic agency in the prayer that Almighty God will "now and for ever expel all power and wickedness of Satan from the body, soul, and spirit of this child (or person);" and will "for ever preserve him from that wicked enemy, and for ever preserve him from his invasions."

Confirmation is almost wholly abrogated by Sealing. The blessing given by the Angel before becoming communicants includes no supposed gift of the Holy Spirit, not even the Renewal of Baptismal Vows, but only the bestowal of peace. When therefore we read of

[1] Vol. I. pp. 248—254.

Drummond saying that Confirmation is of two kinds, the first by the Angel or Bishop as preparatory to Holy Communion, and secondly, the Sealing by the Apostle, we can only infer that he had an inadequate notion of the true nature of Confirmation.[1]

Private Confession and Absolution are maintained in theory in the "Catholic Apostolic Church." An Office is provided in their Prayer-book for the purpose: but it is to be used only "if the sins confessed be of such a nature, and the person in that state of mind as shall render it fitting." Otherwise the Pastor or Elder "shall give to such a person as may make known to him a burden of sin and a desire for Absolution, as soon as may be, full opportunity for making particular confession of his sins, and upon receiving such confession shall . . . . give the person proper ghostly counsel and advice, and also dismiss him with a blessing." But when private Absolution is to be formally pronounced, the penitent is directed to "use abstinence and fasting." "And any Priest pronouncing Absolution should do so fasting: remembering the words of the Lord, who condemned those that sat in the seat of judgment, for that they laded men with heavy burdens, but touched them not themselves with one of their fingers; and the words of the Apostle, that we should restore them that are overtaken in a spirit of meekness, considering ourselves also: and that we should bear one another's burdens, and so fulfil the law of Christ."[2] This direction, it is

---

[1] Drummond's *Substance of Lectures delivered in the Churches*, p. 358.
[2] *Rubrics to Office.*

evident, must restrain the employment of Private Confession and Absolution, and can only be based upon the intention that it should be only in occasional use. Otherwise, the burden upon a Confessor who had to hear numerous Confessions in a day would become insupportable. As it is such Confessions are rare: and when made they take place after the six o'clock Morning Service. The rule of fasting therefore does not weigh very heavily upon either party.[1]

They also practise Unction, in obedience to S. James' direction, but it is not Extreme Unction. The Anointing is made with much ceremonial dignity by the Elder in charge, who is asssisted by other Elders, and accompanied by the Pastor and Deacon. It is administered only to those, who have some time or other received the Holy Communion. The leading idea of the Rite is supposed to be deliverance from death, which is expected to be accomplished by miraculous agency. It is thus connected with the supposed miraculous cures, which Irving and his friends were thought to have effected at the rise of the movement.

§ 13. *Finance.*

The Body has no endowments. Their churches have been built by means of special offerings, as for example, the Apostles' Chapel in Gordon Square was built by two sisters as a place of intercession "for the Churches of.

---

[1] *Union Review*, LXXI. p. 48; to which I am indebted for several hints throughout this chapter. But I have much more authority for my statements.

Britain," according to the record on a brass which is set up in the Eastern wall of that church. Their Ministry and Services are supported by the Tithes, which, to the great credit of the Members of the Body, are paid regularly and as voluntary offerings. They have no regular offertories, no positive solicitations by word or deed for offerings or gifts of money. Boxes are affixed to the walls near to the doors of churches: and in these are regularly deposited the tenth part of the property wherewith God blesses their people.

At the same time, the principles of the Body on the subject of payment of tithe are exceedingly strict, and are enforced on moral grounds in numerous ways. Those who did not pay would be scouted as unworthy Members, and defrauders of Almighty God by withholding His just due. Nevertheless, the regularity in their offerings, into which there is no scrutiny, and the self-denial which is necessarily implied by those offerings, are worthy of all praise. The special arrangements are given elsewhere,[1] and will not bear epitomizing. The income of Ministers varies from £100 to £300 a year.

Such is the Irvingite system of Doctrine, so far as it varies from the Catholic Doctrine of the Church. It has been elaborated with extreme care, and with very considerable ingenuity. It is a system which, we should not go too far in saying, could not possibly have been made up in the eighteenth century. It will bear study, and is in many points instructive, and suggestive of much truth.

[1] See *Appendix IX*.

CHAPTER II.

GENERAL EXAMINATION.

WE have now passed through the History and the Doctrines of Irvingism, or of the so-called Catholic Apostolic Church. And as the entire Body, both in the Tenets which it maintains and disseminates, and in the career which it has run since its growth about the year 1830,—inclusive of its gradual development, the struggles for very life which it has undergone, the earlier and later phases of its existence, the wild hopefulness of its youth, and the less aspiring calmness of its old age,—is now before us, we are in a position to try it "by the Law and by the Testimony," and examine it as a whole, and in its several parts.

I. The first feature that strikes us is perhaps what has been shown all along the history which has been gradually traced, viz., that Irvingism—to give the system its broader name—is emphatically the child of the earlier half of the nineteenth century. The strength of the system has consisted in the advocacy by it of principles before neglected. Its weakness is shown in an incomplete grasp of those principles, or in an exaggerated stress laid upon them to the exclusion of other modifying truths.

Take for example the Doctrines of the Incarnation, of grace bestowed through the Church, of the necessity of a duly authorized Ministry with plain credentials in unbroken line from the Lord Jesus, of the Catholic Church throughout the world, of the place of the Holy Eucharist in worship as the connecting link with the Atonement, of a regular mode of making offerings out of our substance, of supernatural life in contradistinction to false spiritualism, of true Scriptural Symbolism, and of preparedness for the great Advent :—take any one of these Doctrines or Subjects, which have all received great attention during the present century, counterbalancing the neglect which they generally experienced in the preceding period; and it will be found, that the power which Irvingism has had, has been involved in the maintenance of these, and that its failures have been mixed up with an inability to assert them with moderation, and in not knowing where to stop in the assertion, or how to grasp them thoroughly.

The nineteenth century has been characterized by tendencies in an Ecclesiastical direction. Besides Irvingism, another sect may be taken in illustration which presents several similar features, though Members of this Body have always reasonably regarded it with contempt. Looking back to the stern simplicity of ritual and organization which is so conspicuous in previous post-Reformation sects, the grand ritual and imposing hierarchy of Mormonism—to put out of sight for the moment its abominable drawbacks—help also to reveal the quarter towards which the religious waters of our age have been drifting.

Accordingly, up to perhaps 1830, Irving and his friends were in the forefront of the advance of the religious mind of the period. And even after that, so far as the system which we are considering was really Catholic, for a time it was found in the first ranks. It was the harbinger of the Oxford movement, and in its turn learning from that great advance in the English Church, and being fettered by no traditions strong enough to impede its steps, it rushed on, though with a great internal struggle, and again almost contended for the prize. Hence arose its chief excellence: hence came also that strong opposition which besets all who, in matters round which violent prejudice gathers, move on faster than their age.

But then, what can be said of the system now? It is plainly an anachronism. What was pardonable, and may even have been to a certain extent praiseworthy, thirty or forty years ago, is unmeaning at the present day. How are the Apostles to present the living Church to our Lord on His arrival, when, to say nothing of failure and internal dissension, only two are just alive, one of whom at least is utterly incapacitated? For presenting at our Lord's approach must mean also active preparation for His arrival. For the truth of this teaching, our Lord ought to have come long ago. Time and death have proved these people wrong over and over again. Unfortunately for their position, the Apostles have died, and the Lord has not come. Who of their company in 1832 would have imagined that neither in 1835, nor 1838, nor 1845, nor 1850, nor in 1866, nor in any other of the long years up to 1877, the Lord would not appear? The entire system of prophecy, which is in stern historical fact the foundation of their fabric, depends upon the application of the prophecies in the Revelation to the first French Revolution. That was taken to be without doubt the beginning of the end. And not the beginning of the end in any extended sense, such as the post-fact reconciliations of the present time may represent: but on the score, that the Lord was expected within the life-time of twelve middle-aged men. What is the meaning of an "Apostolic" Church—emphatically, pre-eminently so styled—without Apostles? Or with one wholly incapacitated, and one nearly so? Making all fair allowance, throwing into the other scale all that I generously can, I ask the adherents of this system in all seriousness before our common Lord, whether they are not clinging to the fondling of a past age which no one at the present day would have selected for exaltation?

II. Then again, what a dark shade is cast over this Body by its admitted failure. I say admitted failure, because even the Members of the "Catholic Apostolic Church" acknowledge and lament it.[1] In making a fair

[1] "The Apostles and those with them confess the failure."—*Creation and Redemption* (by the late Mr. Sitwell), p. 365. "It is vain to disguise it from ourselves, that the Ministers whom the Lord has sent to His Church, and His work in their hands, after nearly forty years of expostulation and entreaty, are rejected by His baptized people."—Mr. Cardale, in a "Ministry" at Liverpool in 1871.

estimate of the extent of this failure, we cannot but take into account the high expectations which the lofty pretensions of the Body naturally raised in the early part of its career. The Christian Church in this land was in a sad state,—broken up into fragments,—infected with a dull torpor,—careless of unity,—unconscious in great measure of the truth. The cure for this grievous and hopeless malady was supposed to be specially vouchsafed to these people. Well then, it is an axiom in creation, that means are calculated with reference to their ends. No one would dream of putting the engines of the Great Eastern into a steam-tug; and it would be ridiculous to attempt to navigate that enormous product of Brunel's daring conception with the boilers and machinery of a small river-steamer. Are the special schemes devised by Almighty God in the spiritual world, or the particular contrivances of the Lord in His Church, to be ranked lower than the ordinary laws of nature, and to be supposed to be destitute of well-calculated proportion of cause to effect, and of forces to results? The answer to such a question would best be found in a parallel, the more exact the more valuable, with the phenomenon which is immediately before us. Such a parallel is ready to our hands, and fortunately the various details in it are clear beyond dispute.

We naturally recur for materials of judgment upon so important a question to the early origin of the true Catholic and Apostolic Church. There we find Apostles, Prophets, Evangelists, Pastors and Teachers;—in what relation to one another is nothing to our immediate purpose. There was an outpouring of the Holy Spirit. In short, we find the exact pattern after which these people claim to have made up their system. The Church counted only 120 Members, when she is first presented to our view. But what was the result? Passing by the 3,000 converts of the Day of Pentecost, we come upon a rapid, continual, extended growth. Opposition, coldness, violence had no effect, unless it was that often they appeared to stimulate the development of the amplitude of the Church. Various particular Churches were planted in numerous parts of the civilized world. Apostolic journeys brought marvellous effects. Nothing could quench the zeal of those primitive converts to the Faith of Christ. They left their mark in every place that they frequented; till at last, not to go beyond some forty or forty-five years after the Ascension of the Lord, we gather the following results:—Churches were assembled in Jerusalem and several places in Judea, Samaria, and Galilee; at Damascus and Antioch; at numerous places in Asia Minor, Macedonia, Greece, Dalmatia, and Italy; at Alexandria; in Arabia, Cyprus, Mesopotamia, Chaldea, Parthia, Scythia, and India; probably in France, perhaps in Spain and Britain, and most likely in the northern part of Africa. Indeed the growth of the Church in the centuries immediately succeeding her first rise was so rapid and complete, that we are led to conclude, that we could fill in striking details to the sketch just given, and could extend the outline so as to include more countries, if only our history of the times were more detailed.

Turning now to these modern Apostles and Prophets, what show can they make for their forty and more years of labour? First in 1847 we find apologies for small results, and lamentations over want of success. The Apostles could do so little in their "maimed and weakened" condition. Earnest exhortations are given in order to counteract low spirits and halting faith. The Apostles are "reduced in number and weakened by trials and disappointments."[1] In 1851 they were the smallest of the Sects in England, according to their own returns for the general Census. For a long period their Evangelizing labours were not far from being suspended. Few people in England, comparatively speaking, know even the names of the chief leaders. They are really an obscure Sect. In 1858 all that could be said in a general Appeal was, "Particular Churches have risen up in England, Scotland, Ireland, Germany, France, Switzerland, America; in every place where God's Word is read, and men love to obey it."[2] The Body shows no inherent power of growth and development.

All this want of vigorous life, and this failure in bringing about those very results which were originally looked to by the founders of the Body, and which in their anticipated realization formed the very *raison d'être* of its existence, stands in strong contrast with the claims now put forth. When pretensions are set up of authority

---

[1] *Narrative of Facts*, pp. 84, 110, Postscript, &c., &c.
[2] *Appeal to all who believe in the Lord Jesus Christ* (mostly translated from the French). London: Bosworth and Harrison, 1858, p. 27. The hand of Mr. Drummond is very evident throughout this Tract.

extending throughout the Universal Church, those pretensions cannot be emptied of the meaning necessarily implied in them, by any amount of personal modesty, however sincere, or by any resting of them upon the supposed Will of God. Such pretensions either exist, or they do not. If they are real and well-founded, they must of very necessity have a wide and powerful significance. The analogy of Divine operations positively forbids any other assumption. Consequently, remarks about "idolatrous notions entertained in these days" respecting Apostles, or about any presumed expectation on the part of outsiders of seeing "a halo" round the heads of these "Twelve," unless they are meant in a very restricted sense, savour in the eyes of impartial men of playing at Apostleship.

But it is said, that success comes only at the beginning of a dispensation, not at the end. For "when did the means the Lord used ever succeed in recovering a dispensation that had failed? If they did, the end of it would not come."[1]

In the first place, we may remark that this plea takes for granted the supposition that the end is certainly at hand. Reasons will be given afterwards for concluding, that while no one can say at any time whether the end of the Church may not come immediately, and it is the duty and the wisdom of every one to live in loving hope and reverent fear of the Lord's appearing, yet that dogmatizing upon the subject involves that presumptuous peering into the hidden designs of Almighty God which

[1] *Creation and Redemption*, p. 365.

our Lord rebuked.[1] Argument grounded upon such sandy premises cannot be worth much. But how little does it account for the failure in question. For what does that failure mean? It means, that in an age, full of change, when people are everywhere reviewing traditional tenets, and when therefore they are more than usually open to religious convictions presented to them with high credentials, this Body with a separate Evangelistic agency, and with a flourishing start, has been hardly able, notwithstanding a special interposition of the Lord, and special gifts of the Holy Spirit, according to their claim,—this Body has been hardly able, if it has been able, to keep the place it held before its system was developed.

And more than this. If the Church, as the world in the days of Enoch and Noah, had been moving further and further away from God; and if, as in the time of John the Baptist, it had been refusing more and more to accept the Lord Jesus Christ; then something might be said for the small remnant of the faithful amongst prevailing infidelity and wickedness. But during the period of Irvingite existence, the Church has been more than usually active. Acknowledging the general good lives of Members of the so-called "Catholic Apostolic Church," yet no one would think of comparing in the aggregate the amount of zeal and holiness without and within their pale. To call them the small remnant which the Lord reserves to Himself amidst the sinfulness of the Church could have no other meaning than to make

[1] Acts i. 7.

belief in these Apostles and Prophets the test of salvation, or at least the title to precedence in the Kingdom of Heaven. Here again,—to pass by higher questions,—we should be taking for granted the moot point of our controversy. The fact remains, that over and over again in these days, earnest and good Churchmen, whose only wish has been to learn the Truth of God, and to submit themselves to the yoke of the Lord Jesus Christ, have candidly, and with much prayer for guidance, examined the claims put forward by these people, and have been unable to accept them. It is idle to blink this fact. Had such men as these, who were learned in the Holy Scriptures, and acquainted with the History and the Principles of the Catholic Church, accepted the teaching of Irvingite Evangelists, the Body would have achieved many times its actual success. The battle has been fought over and over again in the study and in the closet, with every advantage which could be demanded for securing acknowledgment of the Truth. That defeat under such circumstances, be it observed, has more often ensued than victory, is a serious item in countervailing proofs.

III. Besides this failure in numerical development, we find another reason to make our decision on a general survey adverse to Irvingite demands, viz., an amount of dulness and deadness extending over the Body, which is fatal to such high spiritual claims.

In the first place, this deadness and dulness are exactly what Irving and his friends did not expect. They were on the look-out for striking spiritual gifts, and the "Baptism by fire." The latter, it is well known, never came; and the exercise of the supposed Prophetical Gifts is now confined within such narrow limits as to constitute something wholly inferior to early hopes and expectations. As a matter of fact, the curtailment of the Prophet's province by Apostolic authority has led to secession, where earnestness and zeal were above suspicion. In fact, as has been shown over and over again in the course of their history, the tendency of the Prophets to outstrip bounds has led to such a restraint of the employment of the so-called Prophetical Gifts, as to make them almost generically different from what they were when they first came into exercise. The result has been a tameness and dulness, which is quite in place in a small sect, but is inconsistent with the claim of directing generally the Church.

This is not the place to examine into the nature of these "Gifts," or to see whether they ever came up to the level of their conception. What we are concerned now to notice is, first, that they have from whatever cause sunk to a still lower level than what they first occupied, and that this descent involves an inconsistency with the spirit, if not with the form, of their early principles; and secondly, that no distinguished altitude has been reached either by individual Members, or by any portion of their Community, which could be in any wise taken to be in harmony with the loftiness of their pretensions.

I know that I shall be met with the reply, that such height of pretension is repudiated by the Heads of this Religious Community; that they only do their best as Almighty God has ordered and enabled them to do; that they do not court publicity. But what is the meaning of authority over the Church of Christ, if those who claim authority are not openly to claim it, openly to exercise it, openly to maintain it? What would be the value of a claim to the throne of England, if the Claimant repudiated the responsibilities and consequences of the claim? But the claim under consideration is not founded on hereditary succession, so that the mantle of a long line of distinguished ancestors might have fallen upon one who is unequal to a part, which has been decorated and ennobled by those who have gone before him. These men have been chosen on account of their special fitness for the work before them:—this they must allege, or retire from the contest. Yet notwithstanding, we search in vain through the records of the Body for any traits of commanding genius, for features of real distinction; in short, for anything of a striking or extraordinary character, that would be in unison with, as it is of necessity demanded by, the lofty ambition of the Sect. Taking their own principles,—ranging in thought over the Church's existence,—having regard to its origin and its presumed close,—searching for the spiritual machinery which is supposed to regulate the retinue of the Son of God on His return, and to affect powerfully the entire Catholic Church,—we expect to find a Body endowed with exceptional holiness, with a superiority of faith and doctrine that unfolds more excellence the more we examine it, with vast and increasing powers of influence and growth, full of intellect and sacred learning,—we expect at the very least a wonderful epitome of the Church of Christ;—we find a respectable, but little, English Sect.

Such are the chief impressions which strike those who carefully examine the pretensions of the so-called Catholic Apostolic Church. And in any sound estimate of the validity of the claims put forward, these are very important considerations, which if not fatal, are at any rate so imperatively strong, as to demand a heavy weight of evidence in the opposite scale to make even an equal balance. Because, if there is admitted failure; if the internal forces, as proved by a long period of operations, are unequal to the production of the results demanded by the principles of the Body; and if their principles, so far as they are peculiar to themselves, are now out of date; must there not be unsoundness somewhere in their system?

So much as this could never be said of the Church of Christ. However small She was, She was always making progress. However humble a position She held at first, She had a marvellous pent-up power within. She has always been, in Her principles, at least upon a level with the advancing flood of public thought, so far as it has ever been really advancing. Her position has ever been such as to command the respect which belongs to greatness.

IV. Passing now in our examination within the Community, we discover various points that arrest our attention. Before entering into particulars we should pay a deserved tribute to the zeal of most of the

Members, their regularity at Public Worship, their sedulous attention to their Religious duties, and their upright lives. These characteristics have been pointed out before, and should be borne in mind throughout an examination. To be impartial, we must look upon both sides. Truth is reached by comprehensive scrutiny.

But there are several dangerous principles in the system which interfere gravely with its operation. The first that strikes us, is the internal dissension that must be perpetuated between Apostles and Prophets. Apostles are the Rulers: but Prophets are the vehicles of Divine speech. It is a transparent inference, that two such divergent influences must tear asunder from one another. If Prophets speak from Heaven, plainly every one must give way, Apostles as well as others. If others decide whether the Prophet speaks from Heaven or not, then Divine Speech is made subject to men who may or may not be Prophets.[1] There is an ingenious and plausible way of reconciling the two principles, but it amounts to what is practically the emasculation of the Prophetical office. Many persons amongst them feel this acutely: it has lost the Body several Members. But we should examine the mode of reconciliation.

" The Holy Ghost does not annihilate or suspend the personality of those who prophesy. The question therefore

[1] This is no mere surmise or logical inference. A claim has actually been advanced for the Apostles, to "control God the Holy Ghost." Whatever the Author might mean as to discrimination of false from true prophecies, or in reference to a supposed administrative action of the great Lord of the Church, it is impossible to remove the charge of blasphemy from these presumptuous words.

with reference to their utterances is whether they give vent to their own thoughts, or to the inspiration of the Holy Ghost. Prophets receive from the Angel, or from some one else who is set over them, the things revealed; they feed upon them in their hearts, and bring them forth in such form as to give light thereon to the Angel and Ministers, and to all the people."

Whether therefore their utterances are in consonance with " things revealed " or not, is decided by the Rulers, that is, by the Apostles. Again, the office of the Prophets is "to give light, not to teach or correct, not to fulfil the duty of Elder, Evangelist, or Pastor."[1]

The history of this Sect shows that it has been found to be absolutely necessary to restrain the Prophets in their career, or they would inevitably have wrecked the vessel. But see how the two institutions clash. In working, the restrictions just mentioned would amount to this: " You may prophesy, but recollect that you shall prophesy as we determine: otherwise your prophecies will be no prophecies at all." In fact, it is difficult to discover what room there is for prophecy of an extraordinary character, when the routine of the Church's life is set in order and perfected.

We shall consider these two subjects more in detail afterwards. The internal struggle is all that catches our eyes in this general survey. The bickerings and struggles in their history show that the two opposing

[1] *Short Discourse on Prophesying and the Ministry of the Prophet in the Christian Church.* Printed for the use of the Churches in England, 1868, pp. 4—6.

principles will not work satisfactorily together. One must succumb: and according to the ordinary course of human affairs, the weaker party goes to the wall.

For there is also another feature to be observed, and that is the iron rule which sways the Body, of which some of those who have come under it assert, that it surpasses the ultramontane imperiousness of the Vatican. It must be borne in mind, that this strength of authority is the natural effect of the system. As long as rule is exercised by men who are taken for only ordinary men, and the ultimate source of their authority is either a Nation or a Community, or else a long-established order of ancient pre-eminence, which seems to have the sanction of Almighty God in the distance, liberty and freedom of speech and action are naturally found, even if they lead by inevitable human degeneracy to self-will and licence. But where a special interposition from Heaven is claimed, and the Lord of the Church is supposed in these latter days, not only to have appointed fresh officers over His people, but to be making His Will continually known through their instrumentality, it is clear that if the Lord speaks, the field of free choice must be so far narrowed, and every word of authority must be enforced by a spiritual power which is literally tremendous. The delicate questions attending a conscientious exercise of free-will, even in minuter points of life and in public matters outside of admitted Revelation, are resolved into the simple virtue of child-like obedience, except in the case of those who wield the sceptre, and have to determine whether God really speaks, or whether it be the voice of man simulating the Divine accents.

So we are again brought back in amazement at the vastness of the authority which these " Apostles " claim. No wonder then, if under an overpowering load of responsibility they make that authority to be even more stiff and unbending than they need make it. No wonder, if they are deficient in that largeness of grasp which was shown by our Lord, when He rebuked a similar spirit in the Pharisees of His time. But when we thus excuse so far, as there seems reason to excuse, the administrators of the system, for showing an imperiousness which is proved by numerous testimonies on the part of those who have suffered from it, we are thrown back upon the system itself. Here is a sad blot, intimately connected with the machinery at work, which makes a serious addition to the drawbacks upon a favourable judgment.

But it is time to take a wider view. Let us suppose that this Body were vastly enlarged, and that the scope of its action included a pressing demand upon the Church and nation for general acceptance. We may see how the system would act.

Each Church, to be complete, should have an Angel, with another in Episcopal orders to assist him, and forty-eight Priests, besides fourteen Deacons of the Church, other Deacons *ad libitum*, Deaconesses, and Under-Deacons, to say nothing of Lay-Assistants. It is true that this complete staff presupposes a body of 3,000 communicants. But then, children must be reckoned among this number; and to estimate the working of any system it is only fair, and indeed it is necessary, to take into account an ideal state of things in which the system would have full play. What a formidable hierarchy there would then be. Fifty Clergy, besides Deacons, for each Church having a full complement! How are the necessary affairs of the world to be carried on, if such complex and unwieldy machinery as this is to be provided? We should have the pre-Reformation times of numerous monasteries and convents over again, with idleness as a powerful inducement for embracing a religious life. Such a vast establishment of honourable and fairly lucrative offices may indeed convey great advantages for making converts to a Body that continues small, by means of the numerous openings offered for reaching a presumed episcopal or priestly rank. But it is evident that if the Body were to reach an advanced stage of development, it must become practically unwieldy in itself, and unsuited to the imperative business of life. We can hardly restrain ourselves from imagining, that a great motive in instituting these several offices was a desire to make berths for as many adherents as possible. Be that as it may, we see herein another drawback, as we proceed in our scrutiny.

There is yet another, which would stand in the way of any wide acceptance of these Tenets. We find a feature in the system which is attractive to many minds, but is repellent to many times as many more. A dreamy mysticism pervades it.

Take, as an instance of this, the symbolism which is

traced all through Scripture, and which is supposed to represent Irvingite Tenets. For example :—" The stone which Jacob set up and named Bethel, the house of God, where he saw the ladder on which the angels ascended and descended, even the Body of the Lord Jesus Christ Himself (John i. 51), before he departed to seek his wife: this stone he anointed with oil (Gen. xxviii.). So at the first foundations of the Church at Pentecost, the bride which Jesus had been seeking, He now having gone to a far country, in which He is waiting for both bride and kingdom, the Church received an anointing. On Jacob's return from seeking his wife, he came again to Bethel, erected a stone, and anointed it: indicating a purification of the Church at the close, as well as at the beginning of the dispensation (Gen. xxviii.)."[1] It is true that almost in the same breath the author adds : " Symbols are not proofs, nor can the meaning of any symbol be proved. They strengthen faith in facts proved from other sources, but by themselves they can prove nothing, because their meaning has to be discovered not in themselves, but in other Scriptures." Most sound and good: but take away symbolical proof, and what weak support will be left for many Irvingite points of belief. The passage quoted above is the very first part of the proof of the Restoration of the Church. The symbolical part of Scripture is most beautiful: it is essential to the free play of the dogmatic poetry of the Church. But none the less is it above many minds: and to place it in the forefront of evidence, as in this system it must necessarily

[1] *Appeal to a'l who believe*, p. 20.

be, is to envelope Divine Truth with a mystic covering, which must deter a vast number of people.

But be it again observed that these people have no choice. Symbolism and mysticism are almost the air which they spiritually breathe; their system is full of it. To such an extent do they deal in symbolical intricacies, ingenious contrivances, nets of complication, subtleties, balancings, mystifications, concealments, as to make practically a border between themselves and the rest of mankind, which it is in the highest degree unlikely that the latter will ever cross. For the truth of this statement I appeal confidently to those who have had intimate experience of the working of Irvingism. Though distinctly the blame must be cast upon the unsound system, which its adherents try to prop up by frail supports, I am far from wishing to bring any accusation against individuals, the earnestness of many of whom we cannot but respect. The system must bear the responsibility; and here I find a serious symptom of unsoundness.

We have now from a general view of Irvingism discovered several points which, if not fatal to the peculiar claims made by the adherents of it, form at the least very strong presumptions against its acceptance. At this point we are met by certain pleas put forward in its favour, the consideration of which will carry us further on into the heart of the subject.

CHAPTER III.

EVIDENCE AND CATHOLICITY.

HAVING got all these counts of an accusation, each of which seems to rest upon grounds, which if not irrefragable are yet very difficult of removal, the question naturally occurs, what would the Members of the Body themselves advance in answer to them. It is not perhaps easy to anticipate exactly what course would be pursued by an adversary, at a particular stage in a controversy. But the following argument is pleaded frequently and with much earnestness and vigour. If I fail to represent it favourably enough, it is not from want of desire to do it full justice.

"All this method of judging upon so sacred a matter is wholly out of place. Spiritual things are spiritually discerned. It is not from an outside estimate, by examination of fringes, or appendages, or appearance, that any trustworthy inference can be drawn. This is Divine action, and can only be known by those who are in the midst of all that goes on. These are the operations of 'The Spirit of truth: Whom the world cannot receive, because it seeth Him not, neither knoweth Him.' The mind must be purified from worldly tendencies and

Intellectual Judgment.

judgments, in order to be in a posture to receive the Lord's message. Pride of intellect, not the humility of God's children, is inseparably attached to inexorable reasoning. Let people go into the centre of the Lord's work, with docile hearts, as earnest seekers after truth, and they will see that all this handling and examination of the husk and shell is mere superficial trifling; that the kernel is pure and supernatural, and that there is found an answer to all cavils."

Now if we take away the element of truth in which this reasoning is wrapped, and by which it is recommended, we shall find two factors, viz., that we must not use our intellects to enquire whether a presumed Revelation is really Divine or not, and secondly, that the outside of religion may be objectionable whilst the inside may be Divine and holy. We had best consider these two factors in order.

Are then the maintainers of God's Revelation to take their stand upon the principle, that the things of God are only spiritually discerned, and that man's intellect is to be shut out from all consideration of them? Is every honest seeker after Truth to be told that he must not think, or question, or scrutinize, or investigate, with caution, and prudence, and care?

We should be on our guard against any ambiguity here. We learn in the Bible that "the wisdom of this world is foolishness with God;" that we should judge not "as man's wisdom teacheth, but as the Holy Ghost teacheth;" that "the natural man receiveth not the things of the Spirit of God." There is therefore plainly a meaning in which the use of the intellect is excluded from Holy subjects. But that is not the employment of true intellectual power, but of debased intellect.

And we must carry our admissions further. The debased use of the intellect in sacred matters is an abuse into which it is not hard to slide. When any one commences an investigation by saying or thinking, that under no circumstances would he acknowledge the subject of his investigation; when he is governed by an overmastering prejudice, or by a persistent incapacity for reverence, or for devotion of himself; or when he is deficient in the finer and higher powers of judgment; then, and so far as these exist, there is the use of debased intellect in things spiritual, which is reprobated in the Bible. The reason is plain. If a man has made up his mind irrevocably before he enters upon the examination; if he is devoid of the feelings which the love and goodness of God would properly evoke; if he is too much influenced by self-indulgence or supposed worldly interest to be ready to answer the demands upon him which the religious questions before him if proved would make; if he is unable to apprehend the delicate distinctions which are plain and evident to minds accustomed to such investigations:—just as mathematical calculations are beyond those who are no mathematicians, colours are undistinguishable to the colour-blind, and beautiful melodies and harmonies are unappreciated by those who have no musical taste:—then such prejudice, or want of reverence, or incapacity for self-devotion or for spiritual apprehension, must argue a practically foregone conclusion, and render the examination nugatory, and, if the case be well-grounded, positively injurious.

But we must also acknowledge another point. The best and highest, and by far the most satisfactory manner of recognizing God's Truth,—indeed the manner which is essential to the Christian,—is to discern it with the spirit and to embrace it. No other evidence is so strong. The heart and life are thus brought near to God's Revelation, the intellect bows down to His Heavenly Teaching, the Spirit "discerns" and flies to His Sacred Treasure.

But here the case is different. It is whether the sanctified intellect of Christians, who are anxious to learn all God's Holy Truth, may not carefully weigh the grounds upon which it is proposed to their acceptance. Nay more: whether they are not in prudence, in reverence to Him Who has committed His revealed Truth to the keeping of His People in His Church, out of anxiety to do nothing wrong, bound to make as careful an examination as they can of all the features presented to their view.

When the question, thus cleared of overlying and really extraneous matter, is thus before us, there can be no real doubt about the answer. The intellect is God's gift to us, and next to the Spirit which He has given us, His noblest gift. All evidences coincide in His Sacred Truth. If we were to admit for a moment that the truest and strongest intellects of the world were not with the Christian Faith, we should allow that God's Holy Revelation was unreasonable and incongruous. Supposing any new dogma claiming Divine authority were pressed upon the acceptance of Members of the so-called "Catholic Apostolic Church," they of course, or those who are in authority amongst them, would jealously scrutinize all its features, to see whether it was inconsistent with the analogy of the Faith, whether it had the signs of Truth, or not. Such is the purpose of the present enquiry, in which all particulars and all aspects are placed before the reader, to enable him with caution, humility, and godly fear, to form his own judgment thereupon.

But then, secondly, are we to grant that the obvious details of Religion,—the husk and shell, if it may be,—are not to be examined, and have no germane connection with the kernel and inner life? "To the Law and to the Testimony." "By their fruits ye shall know them." Does this refer solely to Christian deeds, and to the lives of the professors of any creed? Has it not also a wider meaning? What characteristic of our Lord's Teaching was more remarkable, than the thoroughness with which it extended all over the lives and thoughts and Tenets of His Members? It seems needless here to linger over so well-known a truth. To wrap up His Faith in a covering of a different character, would be plainly to dishonour the sacred deposit by a glaring contrast. If upholders of any system were really to maintain such a defence as this is when stripped of its disguises, the rest would naturally beg to be saved from their friends. It is clear that no Member of this Religious Body can seriously justify such a plea.

We may therefore move onwards upon our way so

Are Outsiders unable to form Opinions? 101

far unmolested. No bar can with justice be put in the way of a fair examination, if conducted with moderation, submission, and with an honest and earnest desire for truth.

But, say objectors, "you must not go on so fast. It is impossible for any one who does not hear our Evangelists speak, and come into our churches and join with us, to form any trustworthy judgment upon this matter. You do not really see and know what is going on. You are like some one who at a distance has watched a race, and without being able to see the several competitors, tries to tell the story of the start, the vicissitudes, and the final struggle. And beyond this parallel, the Christian Church advances reasons of her own against you. By the law of the Incarnation personal agency has been made the means of spreading God's Truth and Blessings. It is not by the mere influence of books, but by the action of man upon man, that the Faith is fairly represented and promoted."

There is again here an element of truth, and a considerable amount of misapplication. Is it really contended seriously, that no one can judge about Irvingite doctrine by the light of the voluminous literature which has gathered round this subject during the last forty years? That if to this be added also careful enquiry in many quarters, including discussion with some of the chief Evangelists in the Body, besides others, it is impossible to come to a right conclusion? See what narrow grounds of support are left. If the verdict collected from their literature and this enquiry be against them, how little remains behind to reassure a doubter, or convince one who has been thus led astray! Is it true, or is it not true, that for more than forty years past, this cause has been advocated in the midst of this England of ours, with no inconsiderable ability, and with an earnestness which—at least in a part of that time—no one could challenge? The system itself has a definite objective character, which can be explained as well in writing as orally, and can be examined at least as well in the study or the closet as under the persuasive influence of the tongue of an Evangelist. In the present day, when writing is so common, it is nothing less than preposterous to imagine that the advocates of these opinions, who have shown no lack of ability, have been unable to expound them adequately to the world in their numerous publications. We cannot indeed wonder at people who are sincerely convinced themselves, and are pained at finding how little their publications effect for them, clinging to such a refuge as this. But it is really a refuge: and the very fact of putting forward such a defence shows the poverty of weapons remaining in the armoury.

I fear that these may seem strong words, and may appear to betoken a ruthless logic. I ask my reader to weigh them carefully, and to judge whether the conclusion is not involved in the premises. If it be so, is it not our duty to advance to it?

We are now confronted with a positive argument of a constructive nature, which may be put effectively in the following form:—" You have quoted our Lord's words, in which He says, 'By their fruits ye shall know them.' Be so good as to apply this text to our Body. The excellent character of our Members is well known, and you have yourself acknowledged it. Their regularity in attending Public Worship is celebrated: it is a theme of comment at public meetings.[1] Their earnestness in the affairs of the Body is remarkable. They are in constant expectation of the Lord's Advent. They are absorbed in the thought of religion. Self-denial amongst them is very striking. No glaring sins such as are known often, alas! amongst professing Christians can be laid to their charge, nor any unbelief in the Sacraments, or in any of the general Doctrines of the Christian Religion. They are thus the 'crown in the Lord of the rejoicing' of the Apostles. Surely then these fruits must betoken a tree planted, watered, and tended by the Lord. If not, these prophesyings and this teaching must come from Satan. Surely that is out of the question. It is monstrous to suppose that Satan could thus be the Author of holiness, of Catholic teaching, of large-minded moderation, of attempts to unite the rended Church, and to present Her to the Lord at His appearing. For be good enough to look especially at the Catholic character of the 'Catholic Apostolic Church.' We include the whole of Christendom within our purview. We use no such un-Catholic expression as 'the Church of England;' we have no secular alliance with the

[1] It was referred to by the Right Hon. J. G. Hubbard, M.P., at a meeting at Birmingham in the autumn of 1876, in a speech which was printed and sent round to Members of the National Society by the courtesy of its distinguished Author.

State; we allow no usurpation of universal sway by a single Bishop of a Church. We are pre-eminently Catholic: and as Catholicity cannot possibly come from the Author of quarrels and war, see here a conspicuous proof of the Divine Origin of our system."

There are here in the main three different pleas, which are more effective when combined together as the co-factors of a powerful argument than if they were taken singly. They are these:—The good character of all Members of the Body is a certain proof of her Divine origin: she must necessarily come either from Almighty God or, if not, from Satan, the latter horn of which dilemma is absurd: the Catholicity also of the Body proves that she is from God. Perhaps, in arguing, I may be allowed to change the order here given, and to begin with the second of these three allegations.

It is strongly urged, then, that manifestations amongst these Religionists have been such, that the authorship must be found either in Heaven or Hell. Here I must observe, that the collocation of these two terms, and still more the bringing the Author of sin into such close proximity to the Name of Almighty God, demands an expression of reverence, and of a humble hope that it may be pardoned from a consideration of the exigencies of argument. To resume: the supernatural element, it is thought, is found so unquestionably in the prophesyings, in the general management of the Body, and in this history throughout, that the source of all must be looked for in that dread power which is engaged in sullying and perverting the good plans of Almighty

God, if it is not to be found in the Love of the Lord for His Church and people. The nature of these prophesyings is supposed to be unearthly, as it claims to be. If the Lord does not really speak in them, it must be awful blasphemy, the work of His enemy. There is no middle course.

Now, in the first place, I must here be allowed to claim the liberty which belongs to every man of interpreting my own meaning. I can accept no such dilemma. I believe, and I think that I have shown, that the whole course of the history of these people—not from any colouring of mine, but from the plain witness of facts about which is no question—teaches us that their system has mainly arisen from the assertion of truths and principles which had fallen into not only undeserved, but rather into grievous neglect. There has been in this assertion, as I maintain, exaggeration and misinterpretation, and the assumption of an utterly false position. And so far as these abuses are concerned, we must trace the working of the Author of all the confusion which has marred the fair work of the Lord. But in the main I believe that this has been a well-meant attempt to remedy patent evils in the Church.

The Reformation, doubtless, introduced many advantages. For bringing the Bible into the homes and hearts of the people we can never, I hold, be too thankful; nor for the demonstration then made of the necessity of personal faith and holiness in the case of every single individual, which greatly overflowed the bounds of Protestantism. And it seems probable, that the

Catholic Church in the future will have more reason to be grateful than even we have for the stand made against a despotism, which was inevitably narrowing the Western Church, and had revolutionized her ancient constitution. In England, too, we professedly fall back upon the old lines of Doctrine and practice.

But no one who is alive to the lessons of these days can refuse to admit that the clipping and pruning was carried too far. The mental apprehension of Catholic Doctrine which prevailed at the time was, generally speaking, too superficial and restricted. And when to the bequests of those days we add the inevitable consequences of the insular position of our country, and the more than insular state at one time of the Branch of the Church amongst us, there is no wonder, that when the Reformation-period was becoming effete, and its power was dying out, there should be much of the building of the Church which required re-construction. Truths which had sunk into oblivion or neglect were to be re-asserted. Principles were to be applied, not to the society of the sixteenth or seventeenth centuries, but to the exigencies of the present and the future. No wonder if many with the best intention of repairing built unwisely. No wonder if Irvingites could find cracks in the walls, or holes in the roof, or rotten timbers, or awkward communication, much more easily than they could discover the right way of planning and conducting the needful repairs.

Of course then, as far as they have been led a wrong way, we must acknowledge the operation of evil. But in all that is good, in the earnest waiting for the Coming of the Lord Jesus Christ, in their attempt in common with very many others to induce people to make the expectation of the Great Advent a moving principle in life, and in their desire to unite the Church, and to recover a more perfect machinery in her action, and a more primitive method of worship according to ancient principles and practices—here I believe that we see the Hand of God working in this generation.

And having thus explained my own belief, and the grounds for arriving at it, I venture to put the question to my readers, whether it be not well-founded. Is it really a fair issue, to hang the question upon the horns of such a dilemma? Generally speaking, when any one proposes to us a dilemma, we are inclined to suspect that he is more clever in arguing than trustworthy in convincing. If we find parts of a system which, among much that is good, are positively objectionable in our sight, is there no other opening left to us, than to condemn everything wholesale, and to suppose that it is a piece of repulsive wickedness, devised in and sent out from Hell?

Such is, when nakedly stated, the real question. Doubtless, in this instance, the so-called prophesyings seem to many to exhibit undeniably signs of supernatural agency. Into this question we shall enter, when the course of our examination leads us to enquire into the so-called spiritual gifts. Referring onwards to that chapter for the consideration of this important Tenet, I must now content myself with repeating, that the mixture of truth and excellence with error, which we have already discovered in the course of this treatise, forces us to refer the origin of the system which we are discussing mainly to a general movement in the Religious world, whereby the sacred features of the entire Catholic Faith are being elucidated, and the fragments into which the Universal Church has been shivered are now being gradually influenced by the forces of mutual attraction, instead of being driven further asunder by the discordant elements of hostile repulsion.

These considerations also point out the answer which we must make to the plea, that the excellence of life in the Members of this Body proves that the system is true. No one can gainsay the principle that the tree is known by its fruits, even if we could divest it of the authority to which we all alike bow down. But we are constrained to ask, what is to be included under "the fruits"? Nearly all the comments in this book, if not all, have been based upon this very principle. What is the growth or waning life of the Body but the "fruit" of the soundness or the unsoundness of its Doctrine, and of the presence or the absence of the Divine blessing upon the labours of its Members? What is the Liturgy and mode of worship, but fruit which shows the healthiness or weakness of its general principles? What is the working of the Apostolic College, but an evidence to the wisdom or unwisdom of the original institution? What is the difficulty experienced in restraining the Prophets, but a strong suggestion that practice has revealed serious miscalculations in the theory propounded? These questions might easily be increased.

And if stress is laid upon personal goodness of life alone, then the argument would prove too much. Because in that case Wesley and his friends, the Moravians of his time, and numerous other sects, would all be proved to be right,—a conclusion which Irvingites are too well acquainted with the necessity of the unity of the faith to admit. So that this argument about the tree being known by its fruits yields the following results. If we are at liberty to follow a narrow application of the rule, and to scrutinize solely the manner in which the Members of the so-called Catholic Apostolic Church carry out their own principles, and act in ordinary life, then our verdict upon this particular must be in their favour. But upon this principle we must also pronounce various other Bodies of religionists to have been right; such as the Montanists, Members of the Society of Friends, Plymouth Brethren, and many others. But if we apply the rule widely and generally, as indeed we are obliged to do, then we find the system to be amply condemned. The entire history of the Community supplies weights which must be placed in the opposite scale. The failure of the Apostolic College, the weakness of the Prophets, and the restrictions which it has been found necessary to place over them, the want of growth manifested by the Body, the lack of success in making up the Members of the sealed, the disagreement with Catholic rules and traditions, and the various drawbacks which their career has revealed, must all be taken into account, and furnish a formidable array of fruits whose taste is not sweet but bitter.

We need not therefore linger any longer upon this

fact or in the argument under discussion. The last, which concerns the assumption of Catholicity by the so-called Catholic Apostolic Church, will demand a much longer examination.

This has been a very favourite argument during what may be called the second period of their history. "This work is no sectarian work," is the conclusion of a chapter in the *Narrative of Events*: [1] and the words are repeated in the next chapter, and a supposed proof of them is added, which is rested upon their large-hearted aims, and their liberal and moderate treatment of other Christians. So in numerous other places, in published works [2] and in oral persuasion, the presumed Catholicity of the Body is contrasted with descents from this high principle in the English and Roman Communions, and is adduced and pressed as a strong engine of influence to those who are outside, and to many within their Communion.

Now, acknowledging with commendation and gratitude the several Catholic tendencies of these people, nevertheless I venture to assert that their supposed Catholicity, as a really dominant principle, is a pure delusion. And I do so upon the following grounds, which I submit with confidence will bear out fully that assertion.

We must first enter briefly into the domain of the leading elementary essentials of belief upon the subjects of religion.

What is the standard of ultimate appeal for every

[1] Chapter vii. p. 111.
[2] See, e.g., *Creation and Redemption*, pp. 346—354.

one of us in questions of belief? Do we refer, professedly or practically, to the words of the Bible, to the decisions or well-authenticated teaching of the Catholic Church, or to the reasoning of the mind of man? Here we have three chief standards, on coincidence with one or more of which the decision must rest. Of these the Protestant accepts solely the Bible, according to the well-known saying of Chillingworth, that "the Bible, and the Bible only, is the religion of Protestants." And he points to inconsistencies in Romanist Doctrine with the teaching of the Bible, as his justification for adhering to the written Word, which can never be developed or altered. The Roman Catholic again, pointing out that the books of the Bible are clearly not didactic treatises, but generally written to those who were well acquainted with Christian Doctrine before those books were indited, and that the Church therefore both possessed and taught her deposit of Divine Truth before the New Testament was yet in existence, holds that these books are writings of the Church, and that the Church therefore is above what has issued from itself, and is the sole decider as to what Faith is, and what it is not, both in general and in its several particulars. The Rationalist—to use a generic term of wide comprehension—judges, at least in all ultimate cases of appeal, by man's own powers of reasoning, holding that it is impossible that anything can exist as a truth which contains inconsistency, or is not warranted by the premises, or violates justice or the law of mutual kindness, or is at variance with known realities.

Such are the three standards. In the Church of

England, whilst we never for a moment would go against any principles of morality, or just reasoning, which we maintain are ensured by our standards of proof, we refer for Religious Doctrine both to the Church and to the Bible. We admit entirely that the Faith was committed to the Church wholly independently of any written Word in the New Testament, which was not then in existence; and that the earliest Christians held their belief without reference to the several books, which were not recognized till many years afterwards, as constituting a whole possessed of authority, and then only by the sanction of the Church. Still, knowing the flux and movement of earthly things, we believe that under God's Providence the Written Word was inspired, in order to keep the Church firm to her moorings. So we accept both, the Bible witnessing to the Church, and the Church maintaining and interpreting the Bible. The two come to us together bringing a Testimony which must always be consistent. If there is doubt about the Doctrines of the Church, we turn to the Bible for confirmation and proof. If we cannot understand any of the hard passages in the Bible, we survey them under the light of the Church's teaching, and are thereby prevented from wandering into any new and alluring paths of error.

It appears therefore that there are two theories of Catholicity abroad. For Catholicity means the acceptance of the Doctrines of the Catholic Church,—submission to the authority of the Catholic Church as the decider about the nature of the Faith which has been committed to her charge by our Lord. Now the authority of the Catholic Church can be only taken by itself, or in combination with one or other, or with both, of the two remaining standards. There is positively, as is evident, no other way of taking it.

How the Catholic Church could be combined with reason, to the exclusion of the Bible, as a standard, is hard to see. And indeed, if the expressed Tenets of the Catholic Church are sought for, it is not easy to discover how mere reasoning could possibly be introduced, except as implied in the axiom that the Catholic Faith cannot but be, and actually is, only reasonable, and as a guide to find out Tenets which, as is taken for granted by implication, cannot violate any law of reason.

It is clear therefore, that by a process of exhaustion, we are driven back upon the Roman and English theories of Catholicity. It is not within the scope of my purpose now to compare or examine these. Our object is to weigh the plea of Catholicity made for Irvingism.

The question then is a simple one. Is the Doctrine of the Catholic Church, as ascertained either from the documents of the Church alone, or from them in conjunction with the Bible, or is it not, the standard of appeal in the Irvingite Body?

If the answer is yes, they are not sectarians, they really have Catholicity. If the reply is in the negative, it is idle to insist upon mere fringes and appendages and appearance, and to pretend to what they have not got. The truth of a claim like this, which, if it means anything, must permeate the life, and regulate the sources of the spiritual existence of the Body, is not proved by points of ritual, or by the acceptance of separate Doctrines, or even by a spirit of comprehensiveness reaching to the very boundaries of the Universal Church. Because a false system might simulate Catholic life in separate particulars of more or less importance, and might by a bastard comprehensiveness try to thrust itself into the extensive heritage of the Church of Christ.

But the tests are mainly two. First, does the Body in question submit itself to the Catholic Rule of Faith, not only as declared in the Three Creeds, but in the documents of her authoritative Councils, and besides this, in her ascertained life, while she was as yet undivided by vast schisms? But even this question, if it meets with a sufficient reply, will not satisfy the needs of the case. There must be a further question, whether the unbroken life of the Catholic Church has been handed on to the Body under examination. A plant that grows on another tree is called a parasite. The true parts of the tree are only those which have unbroken connection with the roots, and into which the sap runs through the regular channels up from the roots. The indispensable condition of such an union of a particular Church with the Catholic Church, is evidently a duly authorized Ministry, deriving credentials and titles in uninterrupted succession through the first Apostles from the Lord Himself. For how else can there be union? How else can there be authority in the Church, except as conferred outwardly and openly? And outwardly and openly according to His orders and directions, by the agency of those whom He appointed and authorized? If scrupulous, honest, and sincere obedience in His outward arrangements is paid to Him, He is sure to bless such action inwardly by His Holy Spirit.

These then being elementary principles of Catholicism, which must commend themselves to all who bring impartial minds to the investigation, how far does the system of the "Catholic Apostolic Church" square with them?

First as to Doctrine. When the leading Tenets of the Body were ascertained and embraced, before the Apostles went on their great evangelizing tour, was it a decisive question with them, whether the Catholic Church approved or sanctioned their dogmas respecting restored Apostles and Prophets, or not? On the contrary, does not the course of their history, as detailed even by themselves, show that their great idea of Catholicity was an after-thought; that after the fashion of Protestant sects, they first sat down with the Bible in hand, hoping to discover what the Church had not discovered, and eager to construct their own theories of doctrine and discipline out of undiscovered truths by mining below the surface of Holy Scripture, and by collecting treasures which they thought had escaped notice? What was the meaning of those assemblies at Albury, where the so-called Apostles and Prophets met together daily, and read through the Bible from beginning to end, except that illumination would come to them amidst the darkness that enveloped the Church, and that they would thus shed a new light for which they were indebted to no Councils or

Fathers of the Church, or to existing or preceding Catholic life?

When they acted otherwise, be it remembered that their building was mainly raised. And if they were then led by this new line of study, and by a sense of the responsibilities which they had assumed, into the region of Catholic Principle, and thenceforward discarded to a great extent their Protestant bricks, and mostly used Catholic stone to complete their edifice, and to case the lower part of it, which now exhibited too common an appearance to their chastened taste, they cannot therefore escape the imputations, unless in deed and in effect they discard the Doctrines, which were the results of their earlier career. Are they ready even now to say, that if the Tenet of the Restored Apostolate has no warranty in the teaching of the Catholic Church, they are ready to give it up?

Here is a plain issue. Here would be a test of the reality of their claim to a Catholic character. For if they are unwilling thus to submit to Church authority, it is clear that they are only one amongst the many Sects, however they may attempt to veil their sectarianism in their own eyes, and in the eyes of other people.

But these people have also another difficulty. How can they show that theirs is not essentially a new life, separate from and independent of the life of the Catholic Church? It is true that their Apostles acknowledge the correctness, and allow the validity, of the authority which duly ordained Bishops, Priests, and Deacons derive in unbroken succession from our Lord through His Apostles.

But the argument here depends, not upon their attitude towards others, but upon the nature of their own office. They admit that, according to their own explanation, a new start was supposed to be made when Mr. Cardale and his friends were appointed and separated. But what a break in the Catholic transmission of spiritual blessings in the Church, to find not one Bishop amongst the new "Apostles," only two Priests on whom Episcopal hands had been placed, and the rest, with the exception of one in Presbyterian orders, English gentlemen who had passed their time in politics, or in some other secular occupation. We must remember too that none put their hands on these Apostles, who had been authorized by any external authority. The Angels who separated these Apostles had been themselves appointed by these Apostles. There was an abyss between them and the old sequence: a new sequence of Ministers was supposed to be introduced. How alien to all Catholic principle were such proceedings!

It is quite open to these men to adduce any arguments which they fancy they find in the Bible, or in the depths of their own reason: but Catholic arguments,— never. We cannot but put up our hands in amazement, when we find them so oblivious of the sectarian character of their past history, as to seek to parade a few Catholic weapons, as if they constituted the complete armoury of the Universal Church.

Indeed, they cannot defend their opinion about the necessity of a Fourfold Ministry, without passing by implication a sweeping condemnation over every century of the Church's existence, except a few years in the first. If they were to maintain, that, so to speak, they out-Catholic Catholics, we could understand their position, however much we might demur to their arguments. But when it is as clear as the day, that they form an essentially new Body, and when upon their disputed Tenets—for we are not now concerned with what they hold in common with the Church—they ignore the authority of the Catholic Church, it is time for them to remove this plea from their defence of their position, lest they continue, however unwittingly, to practise deception upon themselves and others.

CHAPTER IV.

APOSTLES.

WE have now completed our general survey of the Religious System, which has been and is now being offered to the acceptance of people of this generation. And without going further, we are led upon sure grounds to the following result:—that no well-instructed Churchman, who has learnt what is implied in the Three Creeds, and especially has been brought thoroughly to understand the meaning of the Article which tells about the Holy Catholic Church, could in the face of this general evidence accept the guidance of these new Apostles.

They come to us with the very loftiest pretensions. No men in the Church have been, as they assert, invested with such authority since St. John died. They bring with them, as they say, the cure of all the diseases which have afflicted and paralyzed the Church, and torn her asunder into numerous parts. Not only so; they have worked for more than forty years, proclaiming the Lord's immediate Coming, and professedly preparing the Church to meet Him, on the grounds that it was their duty to present Her to Him when He comes with His brilliant retinue upon earth.

Yet at the present time all the Apostles have retired except one, or at most two, though the Lord has not come. Their efforts have ended in failure. Numerous Christians, at least as learned in Holy Scripture and in religious lore, and as holy and earnest as any of them or their adherents, have rejected them. Their teaching and life are alien to the Catholic Church. They have tendencies within their Body which are irreconcilable or difficult of reconciliation. They have an unwieldy mechanism. There is a dulness and deadness about the action of their elaborate system which is referrible to their separation from the true Church. Taking all these points into consideration, it is evident that no well-educated Churchman at the present day could admit their advances.

But it is time now to bring our examination to bear upon the several parts of Irvingism. And first of all, the central Tenet of the Restored Apostolate demands our attention. For if these Apostles be indeed true Apostles, they ought to be received. If they are only pretenders, then the whole system of which they are the mainstay falls and crumbles into dust.

The grounds upon which they appeal to us to submit to their sway have been already explained.[1] The Tenet of a Fourfold Ministry rests upon the two passages in St. Paul's Epistles to the Corinthians and Ephesians, and upon divers types and symbols, and a supposed

[1] See above, Vol. II. chap. I. §§ 5, 6.

adaptation of provinces in the nature of the work to be done, and of internal faculties recognized in Psychology. The Restored Apostolate is upheld by reference to the twenty-four Elders in the Revelation round the Throne, by the validity of their appointment as attested by Prophetic Voice from Heaven, and of their separation by the Church, after the pattern of St. Paul and St. Barnabas, and by the work which they have executed, their large-hearted zeal, and their wisdom in government. There is also another argument grounded upon the supposed necessity of the case, inasmuch as these Apostles are supposed to appear at the end of the dispensation to close the Church's period with advantage, and to present Her to the Lord when He arrives.

We may now consider the value of these credentials.

And first of the passages quoted from the Bible as bearing upon this immediate subject. The two passages are these :—

Καὶ αὐτὸς ἔδωκε τοὺς μὲν ἀποστόλους, τοὺς δὲ προφήτας, τοὺς δὲ εὐαγγελιστὰς, τοὺς δὲ ποιμένας καὶ διδασκάλους,

πρὸς τὸν καταρτισμὸν τῶν ἁγίων, εἰς ἔργον διακονίας, εἰς οἰκοδομὴν τοῦ σώματος τοῦ Χριστοῦ.—Eph. iv. 11, 12.

"And He gave some, Apostles ; and some, Prophets ; and some, Evangelists ; and some, Pastors and Teachers;

" For the perfecting of the saints, for the work of the ministry, for the edifying of the Body of Christ."— *English Version.*

Καὶ οὓς μὲν ἔθετο ὁ Θεὸς ἐν τῇ ἐκκλησίᾳ· πρῶτον ἀποστόλους,[1]

---

[1] Observe, as Alford in this passage remarks, that it is not τοὺς ἀποστόλους, as of a definite number, but without the article, as including other

δεύτερον προφήτας, τρίτον διδασκάλους, ἔπειτα δυνάμεις, εἶτα χαρίσματα ἰαμάτων, ἀντιλήψεις, κυβερνήσεις, γένη γλωσσῶν. —1 Cor. xii. 28.

" And God hath set some in the Church, first Apostles, secondarily Prophets, thirdly Teachers, after that miracles, then gifts of healings, helps, governments, diversities of tongues."—*English Version.*

I pass by the types and symbols with a few preliminary remarks, because in a passage already quoted Mr. Drummond said that "symbols are not proofs ; nor can the meaning of any symbol be proved."[1] Indeed symbols and types are of so uncertain and impalpable a nature, that they can bear by themselves the stress of no argument, though they afford valuable confirmation to anything that has been already proved.

Besides this general remark, the symbols or types in question really afford no sound footing. The four beasts of Ezekiel and the four living creatures of the Apocalypse have generally been interpreted of the four Evangelists, or the four Gospels. And indeed, what is there in the Church, which is so worthy to be thus represented as the four Gospels? Instead of witnessing to the Lord for only some 150 years, as these people would have us suppose, they have been the manifestations of Him for well-nigh eighteen centuries. This interpretation is attested by an unbroken line of expounders beginning with St. Irenæus, and con-

"apostles" besides the Twelve. On this inclusive meaning of the word see next chapter. In the earliest ages of the Church, the word was applied, as is well known, to many others besides the Twelve Apostles of our Lord.

[1] *Appeal to all that believe*, p. 21.

Inconsistency in Scriptural Testimony. 123

tinuing through St. Ambrose, St. Jerome, and St. Gregory. And it is accepted in the later ages of the Church, which, as increasing years have the more separated them from primitive times, have learnt to value in proportion this imperishable record with its fourfold history of our Lord's life. The four streams of Paradise, the four colours on the tabernacle, the four standards of the host of Israel, the four spirits of the earth, and such like, are evidently capable of other interpretation at least as apt as that which applies them to a Fourfold Ministry. We therefore turn to the consideration of the two passages above.

And first, is it so clear that St. Paul meant to speak of an organic part of the Church's constitution? The second passage does not coincide with the first; for in the latter instance we read of only three kinds of Ministers, not of four; for (διδασκάλους) "teachers" are there put in the third place, not in the fourth. It is strange then that the passage in the Epistle to the Ephesians should be the only one to teach this Doctrine, if it is one which is of such vast importance as Irvingites represent.

But is it again so certain that the Apostle intends in these passages to speak of a distinct difference of office? May he not refer with quite as much propriety to a difference of function? These people themselves allow a man to hold two offices, as Messrs. Cardale and Drummond were supposed to be Prophets as well as Apostles. Now in the second of the two passages St. Paul includes in his list not four, but *eight* functions.

There is nothing here of the sharply-cut preciseness of the Doctrine, which these people try to rear upon these passages. Indeed the absence of precision which marks the free and flowing speech of the eloquent Apostle, is shown in the words immediately succeeding the second passage.

Μὴ πάντες ἀπόστολοι; μὴ πάντες προφῆται; μὴ πάντες διδάσκαλοι; μὴ πάντες δυνάμεις;

Μὴ πάντες χαρίσματα ἔχουσιν ἰαμάτων; μὴ πάντες γλώσσαις λαλοῦσι; μὴ πάντες διερμηνεύουσι;

"Are all Apostles? Are all Prophets? Are all Teachers? Are all Workers of Miracles?

"Have all the gifts of healing? Do all speak with tongues? Do all interpret?"—*English Version.*

The Apostle, it will be observed, here deviates from the course which he first followed. He omits reference to "Helps" (ἀντιλήψεις) and to "Governments" (κυβερνήσεις), and introduces "Interpreters," with what exact reference is not quite clear; so that from his expressions alone it would seem most probable that he was not speaking with scientific precision, but following the free flow of his easy style.

The tendency of evidence then on a close examination of the passages goes to show, that St. Paul had no intention of putting forth exact dogmatic truth when he penned them. He spoke as he did in the Epistle to the Romans, where he said :—

"Having then gifts differing according to the grace that is given to us, whether prophecy (let us prophesy), according to the proportion of faith;

"Or ministry, let us wait on our ministering: or he that teacheth, on teaching;

"Or he that exhorteth, on exhortation; he that giveth (let him do it), with simplicity; he that ruleth, with diligence; he that sheweth mercy, with cheerfulness."[1]

Upon what a slender Biblical foundation of passages directly expressing it does this Tenet rest. But even this foundation is absolutely taken away, without any question whatever in the eyes of a Catholic-minded man. The interpretation which these people try thus to foist upon these words has absolutely no authority at all from the Church. If we were to grant, as the foregoing considerations certainly forbid us to do, that the balance of evidence lay evenly between the two interpretations, who that acknowledges Catholic authority would not say that this was exactly a case which would be decided according to that authority? Yet in all the references made by Members of the Catholic Apostolic Church to this subject, I cannot find a single one which makes any claim whatever for any Council, Liturgy, or writer of ancient repute, taking the view of these words which they attempt to support.

With reference to the twenty-four Elders in the Revelation who are represented as being round the LAMB of God, what reason is there to conclude that they represent (1) St. Peter and the Eleven with him, and (2) Mr. Cardale and his eleven Friends? Where are St. Paul and St. Barnabas? Why should they be left out?

---

[1] Róm. xii. 6—8.

Who in the eyes of Christians has been more illustrious than St. Paul? Or was Mr. Mackenzie allowed to be faithless to make way for him? If so, what about St. Barnabas? or the symmetrical division into Jewish and Gentile Apostles?

But again I set one passage against another. In the twenty-first chapter of Revelation we are told about the "New Jerusalem." It is represented as having twelve gates—not twenty-four—with twelve angels stationed at them, and the names written on them of the twelve tribes of Israel. There are no tribes of any Gentiles mentioned. And the wall of the city has twelve foundations, upon which are written the names of the twelve Apostles of the Lamb. Observe that this passage occurs towards the end of the book, where all would be presumed to be mentioned in the grand consummation. Yet the number twelve comes over and over again, beyond the passage which I have described as well as in it. When the Apostles are mentioned, we do not read of twenty-four, but of a sternly exclusive Twelve. If the former passage were supposed to exclude St. Paul and St. Barnabas, according to an application which at the least was doubtful, how are not Mr. Cardale and his Friends shown here by the clearest inference that their presumptuous claims are grounded upon no certain warrant of God's Word?

Again, in the Old Testament we do not hear anything of two numbers of twelve, or a total of twenty-four,[1]

---

[1] Except Numbers vii. 88, "twenty and four bullocks;" 2 Sam. xxi. 20, the Philistine giant who had twelve fingers and twelve toes; 1 Kings xv.

which might bear a typical meaning, though according to the claim here advanced we should expect such a type to be given. But we are told of the twelve Patriarchs, the twelve tribes, the twelve spies, the twelve jewels in the High-Priest's breast-plate, besides minor instances in which the same number was included in an order, such as for sacrifice, with reference to the stones taken up out of Jordan, or the brazen bulls taken away by Nebuchadnezzar.

If it be urged that St. Paul speaks of the Church being "built upon the foundation of the Apostles and Prophets, Jesus Christ Himself being the Head Cornerstone," the reply is ready, that it is not necessary for us to have recourse to new Apostles and Prophets, to find a most real application of the Apostle's words.

The Scriptural arguments therefore in favour of a Fourfold Ministry or a Restored Apostolate are too feeble to supply a basis fit to support a Doctrine of such importance, as this would have if it were established. The subsidiary arguments derived from a supposed difference of province coinciding with Apostles, Prophets, Evangelists, and Pastors respectively, or from an imaginary fourfold division of the faculties of the human mind, are of too fanciful a nature to stand by themselves against strong counter-arguments. Indeed the psychological division in the latter case appears to be defective, since, passing over the fact that no distinction is made between Reason and Understanding, we find no notice taken of

---

33, Baasha's reign; Haggai ii. 18, "four-and-twentieth day of the ninth month."

the Passions or Desires. It is clear that dogmatic statements cannot rest upon such insecure speculations.

It is time therefore to take a more general view of the chief arguments which are put forward by such men as Mr. Drummond. Be it remembered, that the question is, whether these restored Apostles are really Apostles or are not. Have they satisfactory credentials?

Now we are not left in doubt as to what credentials have been required for Apostles. There are two chief specimens to our hand in Holy Writ, the original Twelve, and St. Paul. I will take them in order.

Great stress is laid in these discussions upon the wonderful events of the great Day of Pentecost. That was doubtless a marvellous occasion: and it will require a closer scrutiny when we come to the subject of prophecy. The effect of the gifts of the Holy Spirit was most striking. The immediate addition of 3,000 souls to the small company of the Apostles showed what a miracle had been wrought. And the amazing growth of the infant Church proved the extraordinary power of that more than world-wide Spirit, which was humanly speaking pent-up in the small Community at Jerusalem.

But there was a particular in the account which is at first sight small, but is really of great importance. The manifestation was visible. "Cloven tongues appeared as of fire, and sat upon each of them." This visibility of the gifts was strictly according to the law of the Incarnation, and is their safeguard against having their peerless privileges invaded by supposed imitations.

I wish to draw particular attention to this feature in the account, because Irvingites have learnt the existence of this law of the Incarnation, and, if I mistake not, do not know how to apply it. Inasmuch as the Blessed Son of God did not redeem us by a mere spiritual movement from Heaven, but by outwardly assuming man's nature, He thereby inaugurated a system, according to the laws of which something outward and definite is presented to our senses, to which a Spiritual Grace and Blessing is attached. Hence the outward arrangements of the Church: hence the Sacraments: hence all externals. And the better appreciation of this law in the present century has led to a serious diminution of number amongst the "Society of Friends." Members of the "Catholic Apostolic Church" know this truth generally; but they do not yet understand entirely the application of the law, its co-extensiveness with the Life of the Church, and the limitation of it by the Spiritual Essence and Action of Almighty God. The entire circle of the Doctrine of the Universal Church is the only sure guide to this knowledge.

Well then, the Apostles had this outward Ordination or Consecration. But was this their only credential?

It is remarkable that the names of all the Apostles are never mentioned together in the Bible records of events after the great Day of Pentecost. We know them from the lists which are given in the earlier accounts; so that we are sent back to the appointment which was made by our Lord Himself.

Indeed if we were concerned with the events of

the Day of Pentecost alone, there would be no reason for singling out the Apostolic College from the rest of the Church. The Holy Spirit descended upon all of those who were assembled together. A cloven tongue "sat upon each one of them" (ἐκάθισέ τε ἐφ' ἕνα ἕκαστον αὐτῶν). And as if to exclude the notion that the Pentecostal gifts were confined to any order or caste amongst them, it is said that they were "all together with one accord in the same place," and "all of them were filled with the Holy Ghost." If they were all there, it must mean all the 120 who were assembled at the election of St. Matthias, since the words used on both occasions are mainly the same, except that in the latter case the universality of their meeting is denoted by a stronger word.[1] It is therefore a perfectly gratuitous assertion that the Holy Ghost descended only upon the Apostles, on the assumption that otherwise God, in the very act of founding His Church, would have disregarded a law of Her being, that the Holy Ghost passes through the Apostles to the other Members.[2] As an argument this pleading is of course valueless, because it is based entirely upon a *petitio principii*—the assumed truth of the controverted point. But beyond that, the idea is simply without foundation, since the parallelism of the passages, and the continuity of the narrative, plainly show that all of those who were present at the election of St. Matthias were in the assembly on the Day of Pentecost,

---

[1] ἅπαντες—not πάντες.
[2] This argument is quoted by Mr. Grant in *Apostolic Lordship*, p. 63. The author of the argument was really Mr. Cardale in one of his "Ministries." See Mr. Grant's argument.

and that the Holy Ghost sat upon every one without exception.

We must therefore look elsewhere for the main credentials of the Twelve Apostles, as Apostles, and not as Members of rank in the Church. And we fall back naturally upon their converse with the Lord. It was the Ten—for Judas Iscariot had fallen and St. Thomas was absent—to whom He said, "Receive ye the Holy Ghost : whosesoever sins ye remit, they are remitted to them ; and whosesoever sins ye retain, they are retained."[1] No doubt has been cast upon the participation of St. Thomas in the Grace of this Ordination, which was therefore probably repeated to him ; and the case of St. Matthias stands by itself. But the original appointment of the Twelve upon the mountain reveals the primary source of their credentials. On that occasion, they were openly designated and made Apostles. It was a clear, definite, public act. And their position was maintained by their constant association with the Lord, who habitually treated them as Apostles, and sent them all out on an Apostolic journey about a year before He suffered.

Accordingly, there never was any question as to whether they were Apostles or not, either singly or conjointly, any more than there is any doubt as to whether our present gracious Queen is the Sovereign of England, or the Emperor Alexander the Czar of Russia. They were duly appointed by our Lord, when He was present on earth outwardly in the flesh. And accordingly, such outward acts, dating from His own outward

[1] St. John xx. 22, 23.

acts, and from those alone, have ever been considered to be essential to any appointment to the Ministry in His Church. To do otherwise would be to break a fundamental law of His Incarnation.

It is indeed very remarkable, that the entire foundation of the Church, and the provision for its transmission to future ages, was effected by directions given to certain chosen men. Unlike Mohammed, or Buddha, or Zoroaster, or even Moses, our Lord was not an author. He did not see fit to assume any literary character. He only left a Form of Prayer, and the recollection of oral discourses, and private *viva voce* Teaching. He delivered no written code of laws: He drew up no treatise. His Disciples treasured up His sayings, and in course of time published them to the world. It appears that these were by degrees, including also the chief scenes of His career, reduced by the frequent intercourse between His followers into recognized and authoritative stories, which were repeated by believers in almost identical words, and that this cabala, having been the more easily formed owing to Jewish reverence for sacred things, became the groundwork at least of the three Synoptic Gospels, if not of that of St. John. But it is much the most probable, to say the very least, considering the nature of things and the events of subsequent history, that our Lord added to His public Teaching exact directions to His Apostles about the organization of the Church, the order of Public Worship, and Dogmatic Truth.[1] And it is

---

[1] He did not tell them till after His Resurrection τὰ περὶ τῆς βασιλείας τοῦ Θεοῦ, and particulars have not been recorded.

this which gave to the Apostles, whose credentials present no possible flaw, the eminent position which they held, connecting the Church with the Lord,—a position which from the principles of the Incarnation it is simply impossible that any other men should hold, till He personally appears on earth.

So that for the true title of the Twelve Apostles, and their credentials for their office, we must have recourse, not to the events of the Day of Pentecost, strong confirmation as those events gave to the validity of the appointment, but to the choice of them made personally by our Lord, and to their personal association with the Lord. After they were once chosen, and the fact of the choice was made public,—whatever were the outward signs of the accomplishment and conveyance of the choice, of which we know nothing,—thenceforward there was no room for questioning. They were Apostles till death, unless they fell like Judas. Their qualification for holding their office was derived from their personal converse with the Lord: because they thus learnt what was necessary for becoming, according to the Revelation, the twelve foundations of the New Jerusalem.[1] Thus, too, further confirmation is derived from the wonderful success which attended their labours. The extent of that success has been described, so far as it was shown during their life-time. The advance made in the centuries immediately succeeding their death added to the testimony already borne to their faithfulness and wisdom. And indeed throughout the ages of the existence

[1] Rev. xxi. 14.

of the Catholic Church, their names have always been mentioned with peculiar honour. So that their position, though they were after all only men with like passions as we are, though full of Divine Grace, is unassailed and indeed unassailable.

Before we estimate the value of the credentials which are claimed for Mr. Cardale and his Friends, we must consider also the title of St. Paul to the Apostleship which he held. This is a very remarkable case, because his appointment was not outwardly notified, like that of the Twelve: nor was he designated by our Lord in the days when He was in the flesh. It was long therefore before he was recognized as an Apostle.

Before searching into St. Paul's credentials, we should take note of his outward circumstances as he comes before our eyes. In many respects, his figure stands towering above all his associates and colleagues. His own record of his labours, which was wrung from him through impediments placed before him in his work, declares what he went through. He stands at the head of the Gentile Church, not only on account of having founded more local Churches than any one else, but also from the stand which he made and the victory which he won for Gentile liberty. He was actually the author of fourteen[1] out of the twenty-seven books of the New Testament, and as is probable virtually the author of two more. If an exception was to be made

---

[1] I include the Epistle to the Hebrews, because the evidence in favour of the authorship of no one else seems to me to approach in strength the evidence, internal and external, in favour of its having been written by St. Paul. But this is not essential to my argument.

in favour of any one, St. Paul would assuredly be the favoured man.

Now it should be remembered that St. Paul was never included in the Twelve, unless it be true, as has been supposed, that he was the successor of St. James, when the latter had suffered martyrdom at the hands of Herod Agrippa. He stands, according to general opinion and according to every other except the improbable hypothesis just mentioned, upon a different platform from that which is occupied by St. Peter, St. John, and the remaining Ten. How then did he become an Apostle?

Now we should observe first the great stress which he lays upon his Apostleship, and upon the fact that he was not called to be an Apostle by man, but by God. In every single Epistle, except those to the Philippians, both to the Thessalonians, to Philemon, and the Treatise addressed to the Hebrews, he uses introductory words to this effect: "Paul, called to be an Apostle"—"by the Will of God"—"according to the commandment of God"—"and of Jesus Christ"—"not of man nor by man, but by Jesus Christ and God."[1] It is clear therefore that he claimed to have received his office direct from God and the Lord Jesus Christ.

But we must advance a step further. St. Paul sets also the greatest store by the fact that he had actually seen the Lord. "Am I not an Apostle?"—he says to the Corinthians[2]—"am I not free? Have I not seen

---

[1] See beginnings of the nine Epistles, and Gal. i. 12, ii. 7—9; Eph. iii. 8; 1 Tim. ii. 7; 2 Tim. 1—11.   [2] 1 Cor. ix. 1.

Christ Jesus our Lord? Are not ye my work in the Lord? If I be not an Apostle unto others, yet doubtless I am to you: for the seal of my Apostleship are ye in the Lord." This passage is very noticeable, first, because it shows the meaning of his Apostleship, as the Father of the Gentiles in the Faith; and secondly, because it reveals the ground of his claim to the Apostleship, viz., a personal meeting with the Lord Jesus Christ, and an actual mission emanating directly from Him. "Last of all"—he says in another place,[1] speaking of the Lord's appearances after the Resurrection,—" He was seen of me also, as of one born out of due time.[2] For I am the least of all the Apostles, that am not meet to be called an Apostle, because I persecuted the Church of God. But by the Grace of God I am what I am: and His Grace which was bestowed upon me was not in vain; but I laboured more abundantly than they all: yet not I, but the Grace of God that was with me." So that we must take his having actually seen the Lord, as a strong element in the credentials of his Apostleship.

The question then presents itself, *when* and *how* St. Paul received his appointment thus directly from the Lord Himself. There are four possible occasions, viz., his first call, his vision in the Temple, the time when he

[1] 1 Cor. xv. 8—10.
[2] ὡσπερεὶ τῷ ἐκτρώματι. The Irvingite interpretation of this is given above. Vol. I. p. 164. It is evident from the context, that St. Paul is comparing his own case with that of the Apostles. To them, whose birth as Apostles was regular, He appeared all together. To St. Paul, as "τὸ ἔκτρωμα," for the article is used, He appeared by Himself and last of all. Again, if St. Paul is τὸ ἔκτρωμα of the Family—remark the article—where does St. Barnabas come?

was caught up to the third Heaven, and we may perhaps include, though it does not answer the conditions at which we have reached, the occasion when he was sent forth by the Church at Antioch.

1. We may perhaps comprise within his call the three years of his sojourn in Arabia, before and after which he appears to have preached at Damascus. His appointment appears to have now commenced. For first, the Lord says to Ananias, " he is a vessel of choice to me, to bear My Name before the Gentiles "[1] (σκεῦος ἐκλογῆς μοι ἐστὶν οὗτος). Again, from the Lord's words to St. Paul himself: " I have appeared to thee for this purpose, to make thee a minister and a witness both of these things which thou hast seen, and of those things in the which *I will appear* unto thee ; delivering thee from the Gentiles unto whom now *I send* thee." From some of the references to the scene on the road, such as Ananias' words, " the Lord who appeared to thee" (ὁ ὀφθεὶς σοὶ),[2] and St. Barnabas' declaration " how he had seen the Lord on the way "[3] (εἶδε τὸν Κύριον), it seems clear that St. Paul really did see the Lord on that occasion, a particular which we should not gather from the account itself of the event.

There was therefore in this event one of the necessary elements of a true sending forth of an Apostle. The prior condition that the Lord Himself was present at an interview with him was satisfied. But did He then actually send St. Paul ? The few hints which are supplied seem to reply satisfactorily in the negative. First

[1] Acts ix. 15.   [2] v. 17.   [3] v. 27.

there is the future "I will show him"[1] (ὑποδείξω); this was said to Ananias after the event. Next the sequel proves that our Lord did really appear to St. Paul afterwards; and it seems in the highest degree unlikely, that all in a moment an unbaptized persecutor of the Church should be advanced by a leap over Sacraments to the head of the Gentile Church. We are therefore brought to the conclusion, that if there was any other more favourable occasion, which contained less objection, this first Appearance of the Lord would give way to that. Indeed another Appearance is promised in this one: "in the things in the which I will appear[2] unto thee" (ὧν τε ὀφθήσομαί σοι). For the words "the Gentiles unto whom now I send thee"[3] (ἀποστέλλω), need give us no difficulty. All scholars are acquainted with the incomplete meaning of the present tense in Greek, relating to current events, at the time to which the verb refers, in the process of being accomplished. In one of the parallel passages,[4] St. Paul says that the Lord told him to go into Damascus, where it should be told him what was appointed him to do—words not quite consistent with a completed Apostolic mission. So that ἀποστέλλω will mean, "to whom I am now in the course of sending you."

2. We next come to the trance in the Temple. The whole account of it, as given by himself,[5] is evidently connected intimately with his Apostolic appointment or mission. In this trance or ecstasy (ἐκστάσει) he both saw and heard the Lord. So that the prior condition is

---

[1] Acts ix. 16. [2] xxvi. 16. [3] v. 17.
[4] xxii. 10. [5] v. 17—21.

unquestionably found in the occurrence. The words which relate to his appointment are, "Depart: for I will send thee far hence to the Gentiles" (πορεύου· ὅτι ἐγὼ εἰς ἔθνη μακρὰν ἐξαποστελλῶ σε). Now at first sight this speech seems to shut out entirely any present appointment. And it is decisive against St. Paul being thenceforward an Apostle in the way in which St. Peter and St. John were, after the Lord chose them upon the mountain. Yet in the expression we find both a negative and a positive element. Negatively, St. Paul is ordered not to act as an Apostle till he is at some future occasion authorized so to act. Positively, it is declared that at such a future occasion he would be an Apostle (ἀπόστολος).

The time when he was caught up to the third Heaven can hardly be the time of his appointment, from the very mysterious and indefinite account which he himself gives of it. He was to all appearance jealously anxious about his title to the Apostolate, and would hardly have omitted an opportunity of bringing out, even amidst other unutterable sights and sounds, anything which added to his authority, and therefore to his power of spreading Salvation. At first sight this event appears to be that of the "ecstasy" in the Temple, and the same interval, "fourteen years before," seems to confirm that view. But in the first case,—if I am right in taking for granted that the visit to Jerusalem described at the end of the first chapter of the Epistle to the Galatians is the same as that in which the "ecstasy" occurred,— the fourteen years dated back from the Council of Jerusalem. In the present case, the fourteen years count back from the composition of the Second Epistle to the Corinthians. So that this is merely another of a not very uncommon class of curious coincidences.

3. The Imposition of Hands at Antioch remains for examination. Here it would appear that the Antiochian Church must have acted with the full concurrence of the Church at Jerusalem headed by the Twelve Apostles; for we hear of continual communication between the two. St. Paul and St. Barnabas had lately visited Jerusalem: prophets went to and fro.[1] Besides which, we never hear of any question being entertained about the act of the Church at Antioch, and the Council of Jerusalem[2] afterwards confirmed, and single Apostles also,[3] what the two Gentile Apostles had done in consequence of their Ordination or Mission.

On the occasion itself we find, first, an order given by the Holy Ghost to separate Barnabas and Saul. This order recites the previous call[4] ($\tilde{o}$ προσκέκλημαι αὐτούς). Then comes the imposition of hands. So that (1) the two Apostles could not enter upon their work till they were thus formally separated; (2) the imposition of hands was made (*a*) after a previous call, and (*b*) under the express orders of the Holy Spirit.

Such then was St. Paul's appointment to the Apostleship. It included three acts, done upon three several occasions. First there was the Call made with startling and powerful effect, when Saul was in mid career of

---

[1] Acts xi. 27.
[2] xv.
[3] Gal. ii. 9; Acts xviii. 23, xxi. 18—20.
[4] Acts xiii. 2—4.

fanatical persecution. The Call is obeyed, and the amazed man surrenders himself to the Lord's Guidance. After three years, the appointment is virtually made by the Lord Himself, but only to take effect several years after, when and according as the Lord should choose. Then the heads of a local Church ordain or consecrate him by express command of the Holy Spirit, and the validity of this consecration or ordination is recognized by the Apostolic College. The latter act of the appointment coincides with ordinary Ordination, because there is the previous Call and the subsequent imposition of hands; only that on this occasion a special command was given by the Holy Spirit. What makes St. Paul's case extraordinary are his two interviews with the Lord, resulting in his Call, and in his virtual, though not actual, Appointment.

Two cases of Apostolic appointments remain, those of St. Matthias and of St. Barnabas. The qualification of the former was his having "companied with" the other Apostles. But how? Merely to enjoy their society, or to reap the benefits of doing as they did? No: it was "while the Lord Jesus went in and out among them," so that he might tell "of that which was from the beginning, which he had seen with his eyes, which he had looked upon, and his hands had handled, of the Word of Life," and especially "might be a witness with" the rest "of the Resurrection." We should observe that the number Twelve had been fixed before, and that his colleagues received him by co-optation in obedience to Divine lot.

St. Barnabas appears to have been called an Apostle more by courtesy, and because he participated in the act of appointment, by virtue of which St. Paul entered upon his Office. So far as any distinction between Bishops and himself is concerned, we cannot find anything to justify it, except that the Holy Ghost definitely ordered his appointment, and he is one of the fathers in the main of the Gentile Church. It is not certain that he participated in that actual sight of the Lord, especially after His Resurrection, upon which St. Paul lays such repeated stress, and which was regarded as essential to the appointment of St. Matthias. At the same time, he is said to have been one of the Seventy; and it is quite possible that he may have enjoyed this qualification. ' If his actual acquaintance with the Lord was notorious, there was no need for him to speak of it, as St. Paul was obliged to do in his own case. At all events, no argument can be grounded upon his Apostleship, since the nature of it is so little known to us. The term Apostle was loosely applied, as will be shown afterwards.

These then are the Scriptural materials for judgment in the case of any claims to Apostleship in later days. We are now in a position to see, how far the credentials of Mr. Cardale and his Friends come up to the credentials of men whose title is indisputable.

The true credentials are evidently four in number, viz.:—1. appointment by our Lord in person; 2. an outward act of ordination; 3. acceptance by the Church; 4. justifying success. The only exceptions to this are St. Barnabas, of whom we really know nothing, certainly not enough to warrant our denying anything about him; and St. Matthias, whose election and appointment was made to fill up a vacancy in the Lord's own Twelve, and perhaps—for here we cannot deny it—in obedience to some private direction which has not been recorded. His appointment had the united authority of the Eleven remaining Apostles.

Of these four credentials, Mr. Cardale and his eleven Friends can lay claim really to only one, and that in a way which is more than dubious. They have never seen the Lord: they make no pretence to any direct appointment at His own lips. They have never been accepted by the Church, or by those who have authority in it in succession from the Apostles, an authority which they themselves recognize. As for any success to bring justification after the event,—why "the Apostles and those with them confess the failure."[1] They are therefore thrown back upon their mode of appointment, in which the case of St. Paul has been imitated. Before I examine this, some more words are due upon the subject of the credentials of the Twelve Apostles of our Lord.

By the establishment of their unquestionable claim to actual appointment at His Hands, the question of evidence is removed from them to Him. No one met St. Peter or St. John with the objection, "I do not believe in your Apostleship," because the fact was undoubted, and unimpeachable. They stood or fell with the Lord. They converted people to belief in Him, not to adherence to themselves. So that the

[1] *Creation and Redemption*, p. 365.

grounds of their preaching were generically different from the substance of this new evangelizing. Nor is St. Paul's case unlike theirs. He had the authority of the Twelve to appeal to, and the fact of his own appointment by men who were authorized themselves, besides having his own personal testimony to bear about the Lord whom he had actually seen more than once.

But to proceed to the claim to ordination made by Mr. Cardale and his Friends. There was first a private conviction and a supposed Call and appointment by the Holy Spirit through Prophets. These will be examined afterwards. Next there was a solemn imposition of hands by the seven Angels of the Churches in London, as representing all the Angels of the Church, and the Church itself. This requires a careful scrutiny.

Who were these Angels, and what was their Title to Episcopal Office? They were consecrated or ordained mainly, if not exclusively, by Mr. Cardale and Mr. Drummond. So they ordained Mr. Cardale and his Friends, and Mr. Cardale and his Friends ordained them. Where is the primary source of authority? "No man taketh this honour upon himself but he that was ordained of God, as was Aaron." Aaron was consecrated by Moses, who was sent by the Voice of God, and had seen Him. The Apostles dated their Apostleship from the Lord. "As My Father hath sent Me, even so send I you." The Irvingites move in a vicious circle, the only support of which is the supposed voice of the Prophets without any outward authorization, the absence

Destitute of Catholic Authority. 145

of which, as I have shown, wholly contravenes the principles of the Incarnation.

But again, what was the Church, which by its officers "separated" these Apostles? Did that Church derive its authority directly, openly, incontrovertibly from our Lord? We have seen that the Church at Antioch,—to quote the parallel most favourable to the Irvingites,—did so derive their authority, and that their act was afterwards confirmed and adopted by the Universal Church. But what was the case with these people in July, 1835? They were in open schism with the Catholic Church, however it might be taken to be represented. They had set up altars of their own. They owned no allegiance, and asked for no authorization. They had no Priesthood in succession from the Lord. They were a diminutive Body, calling themselves the Church. In virtue of what? Solely upon the strength of a claim to direct Prophetic communications, by means of which they asserted that the Lord Himself had come to take charge of His Church by an immediate Personal Rule. In consequence of these prophetic claims, they had been disowned by other Christian Bodies, and left to themselves.

That is to say, they assert in effect that a fresh beginning has been made in the Church of Christ. When we ask for the proof of this, we are referred first to the Prophetic gifts, which I shall examine afterwards, and next to the various signs of a Divine Presence which are scattered up and down their history and present life. It is not necessary to repeat all that has been plainly proved respecting these fruits of the tree which has been thus planted. But a few more evidences must be unfolded.

First, with respect to the assertion, that each Apostle had, previously to the Prophet's call, a private conviction that he was designated to the Apostolate. Some doubts are thrown upon the nature of this private conviction by the refusal of Mr. David Dow to act, after he had been named by the so-called Prophetic voice. Besides that, such private convictions have been common amongst founders of Sects and other people throughout Christian history. So that any reliance upon such inward impressions, which history has shown again and again to have been sources of mistake and error, is out of the question. The organization of the Catholic Church rests upon a much clearer, firmer, and sounder basis. She surrenders such sandy foundations, if they are to be made foundations, to Sectarianism.

Next, as to the Prophets. We cannot help thinking that when the Apostles had mounted up to their own commanding eminence by their help, they threw down the ladder by which they ascended. Else, what was the effect of that wholesale abrogation of prophecies in 1840? What has been the treatment of Prophets ever since? What is the meaning of forbidding prophecies to possess any validity till they are confirmed by those in authority? What is meant, when it is said that Prophets must not "suppose themselves to be set for giving light to the Apostles and to the Church Universal?"[1] That they must not imagine "that they

[1] *Ministry*, by Mr. Cardale, p. 8.

are set, not merely to give utterance to joy for the light given to the Church, but themselves to give light"?[1] And what is the import of such expressions as the following? "The word of a Prophet! My dear sir, it has become almost a proverb. The Prophets are a dreamy, do-nothing kind of people—the word of a Prophet!" Again—"If we were all like the Prophets, given up to devotions and meditations, not much work would be done." And further—"The Prophets! they are all mad!"[2] So that we have the authority of the entire later period of Irvingism for discrediting the Prophets, who are really the sole foundations of this building.[3]

But we must remark some more points respecting the Apostles. They stand before us self-condemned, and condemned by the witness of their own people. When they were appointed, the expectation was strongly cherished, and mounted up to a firm belief, that they would all survive, and be ready conjointly to present the Church to the Lord when He comes. Besides which, all of them held that the dissent of a single Apostle was fatal to the validity of united Apostolic action. How were these Tenets verified by facts? First, all are dead except two; and secondly, Apostle Mackenzie retired from them in 1840, and never afterwards joined in their councils. So that the Apostolic College, as an unanimous

[1] *Ministry*, by Mr. Cardale, p. 8. *Apostolic Lordship*, p. 52.
[2] Grant's *Apostolic Lordship*, p. 51. The two first were the speeches of an Evangelist, the last of "another Minister."
[3] "If there is anything wrong with Taplin," said one of their leading Evangelists, "all is wrong."

Body, according to the laws of its foundation, died in 1840, or about five years after it was founded. This absolute defection was strengthened by the discontinuance of Mr. Dalton for several years to act with them.

Again, the history of the Sealing is both instructive, and would be decisive in the eyes of most men against claims advanced with such a' show of directly Divine Authority. It will be remembered, that after the passage in the Revelation, a definite number of 144,000 was fixed, 12,000 to each tribe; and it was determined that each Apostle must seal his proportionate number. The glaring failure, for it can be called no less, of this scheme is its own refutation, which must recoil upon the authors of it. I do not now want to comment upon the strange assumption, which makes a small Body of Christians the monopolizers of the privileges beyond price or estimate, which are supposed to be secured by the Sealing; nor to linger upon the extravagant and grossly irreverent idea, which makes acceptance of a few men the title to precedence in the Kingdom of Heaven, instead of the degree of devotion to the Lord Jesus Christ and to God, as evidenced by holiness of life. It is enough to observe, that most of the Apostles have died without sealing any, or at least only a few, or a few comparatively. This fact alone is a sufficient condemnation. And that it has been felt to be so by the Members of the Body, it will be remembered that the strange and hardly conceivable notion arose, that the Apostles who had died before completing their work would finish it in the next world. This notion again, being self-condemned, not only on account of the extravagance of it, but because Sealing in the next world could not deliver people from the "great tribulation" in this, has, as I have related, vanished out of sight. So that the Apostles are now passing away, whilst in only one Tribe the number of Sealed can be anything like approaching the required total, whilst in seven or eight more the reckoning is almost or entirely at zero.

"By their fruits ye shall know them: do men gather grapes of thorns, or figs of thistles?" Is such a plan, so carried out, so destitute of promised results, so propped up by an unworthy expedient, veritably the Lord's doing? Who, judging impartially, comparing spiritual things with spiritual, fresh from the records of the true Apostles of the Lord, can possibly say that this is indeed a vintage of grapes, or a harvest of figs?

To pass on to another point. We have seen that Mr. Cardale and his Friends are wholly destitute of Catholic Authority: we may now go further. Not to insist upon the truth, that no authority, not dating visibly from the Lord through His Apostles, has ever been recognized in the Church Catholic; not now to take cognizance of the open schism of which these men are guilty;—our attention should be drawn to a very remarkable feature in their theory.

It has been more than once explained, that these people consider, that Apostles are essential to the well-being of the Church; that twelve Jewish Apostles were sent at the commencement of the Church's career; that twelve Gentile Apostles were to wind it up, so to speak, when the Lord comes; that a beginning was made in the second Twelve by the appointment of St. Paul and St. Barnabas; but that the faith of the Church was not sufficient, and so that the Church continued in decadence from that time till Michaelmas, 1832, when Mr. Cardale was appointed.

Now it will be observed at once, that this theory implies that the so-called Catholic Apostolic Church is bereft of the sanction of more than seventeen centuries of the Church's existence. Upon any principles recognizing the Church as a Divine Institution, founded by our Lord, what corollary could be more damaging? More than seventeen centuries, during which zeal has been more or less earnest, or even at times enthusiastic, during part of which the ablest intellects in the world, often combined with rare purity of heart, have been engaged in learning and verifying God's revealed Truth, nevertheless are said to have passed in unconscious ignorance of what these men think they have discovered. In fact, they blot seventeen centuries out of the history of the Church, and still call themselves Catholics.

For we must be careful to weigh the real effect of this absence of more than seventeen centuries of Catholic teaching from their testimonials. Absence means not merely omission, but condemnation. If seventeen men were to go into a church, and carefully for hours examine it, is it conceivable that it would be necessary for an eighteenth to enter, in order to discover the altar? For we must remember that according to Irvingite belief, the Apostolate is the most important part of the constitution of the Church. "When Apostles," said Mr. Cardale in a "Ministry," "were taken away from the Church, they being the link which united Christ the Head of His Church to His Body, it fell like a dead earthly thing to the ground."[1] How is it possible, that the Church could have been so " dead " to all knowledge of her state, that she did not know the difference between being joined by a link to the Lord of Glory, and grovelling in the dust?

Yet no Member of this Body can quote proofs of their theory from any Church writer of repute, or from any of her Liturgies or Prayers. It is inconceivable, that the greatest possible blessings should be lying within the reach of faith, being at the same time attached to part of God's Revelation, and yet that during all that long period no prayer should be offered regularly and publicly in the authorized forms of the Church, embodying an earnest desire for the bestowal of the condition upon which alone they could be obtained. The absence therefore of all such teaching from formularies and treatises constitutes in itself another grave condemnation, which by its own unaided weight is sufficient to invalidate utterly the claims of these men. The fact is undoubted. No reply has been made to this charge; nor, unless I am greatly mistaken, can be made.

There is therefore only one conclusion, viz., that this is an essentially Protestant Sect, implicitly condemned by the Catholic Church, founded upon the presumptuous notion, that some 1800 years after our Lord's time, a few men could sit down with the Bible in their hands, and

[1] Grant's *Apostolic Lordship*, p. 66.

invent their own system from the hints which they found, and could then desert the old paths, and follow new-fangled fancies.

The present age also, in the ruthless advance of time, now finds these people in the very difficulties which they say beset the Church at the end of the lives of our Lord's Apostles. What will they do when Mr. Woodhouse dies, but leave successors behind them? Not Apostles, for that by their own theory is impossible, since the twenty-four places are all filled; but they can be no more than the delegates of these Twelve men, just as the Bishops were the delegates of the Apostles. The ceaseless march of time has solved the Gordian knot, if such it may for a moment be termed. How upon their peculiar theory there can be an Apostolic Church without Apostles, it is really impossible to see. If they call their successors "Apostolic men," that is very much what the early Church did. They are acting the drama over again, only in a narrow corner, and without the same undoubted authority. If the early Church "fell to the ground as a dead thing" on the death of St. John, this Body must do the same when Mr. Woodhouse is taken away. They must succeed to all the disadvantages of the early Church, without enjoying her youthful strength and her marvellous growth.

But strange to say, Irvingites are not content with even this decisive view of the· question. Thinking to establish their own system by revealing a flaw in the opposing one, they insist that when the Apostles of our Lord died, they left no successors to themselves.

Bishops, say they, are not the successors to the Apostles. For in the first place, an Apostle must be sent directly from the Lord Jesus Christ, a Bishop is not. 2. There is no proof that the Apostles transmitted their powers. 3. An equal cannot appoint an equal: an officer can only be appointed by his superior. 4. The Offices of Apostles and Bishops are distinct: an Apostle is an universal Bishop of the Church, whereas a Bishop's authority is only local; the authority of Apostles being necessary to hold together in union the entire Church. Each of these four arguments has been actually urged to me on the Catholic Apostolic side.

This is so important a question, that it is necessary to consider it by itself. With reference to other opinions which are entertained now-a-days, as well as having regard to those which are under consideration, it may be well to exhibit the main heads of the evidence which, as is well known to theologians, establishes the claim of Bishops to be considered the successors of the Apostles.

CHAPTER V.

BISHOPS THE SUCCESSORS OF THE APOSTLES.

EFORE diving into the depths of the subject of this chapter, it will be well to examine the four pillars of the argument against us, in order that we may see what we really have to combat.

That there is an important difference between Apostles and Bishops, and that the former alone were sent directly by our Lord Jesus Christ, it would ill become the author of this treatise to deny. For it is precisely one of the charges already brought against these new Apostles, that they pretend to be sent directly from the Lord Jesus Christ, but are found upon a close examination not to be so sent. To be sent directly is to be sent by Him Personally, that is, after visible and audible ntercourse with Him in Person. In the present case, there is no pretence put forward of such personal intercourse. The allegation is, that these men were sent by the Lord Jesus Christ, speaking by the Holy Ghost, Who again spoke through a Prophet. That is, where there ought, from the admitted meaning of the Office in question, to be no intervening channel, there are actually two, as maintained, viz., the Holy Spirit and the Prophet.

But if we examine the other side, this argument which is advanced by these people is really true of Catholic Apostles and Bishops as contrasted with one another. Apostles are those in the line of succession who are in immediate contact with the Lord, while Bishops are not. This is exactly the point of difference between them. Apostles were "not of man, nor by man, but by Jesus Christ." Bishops were outwardly by Apostles handing on the succession which they themselves had received.

So that we may dismiss the first of these four arguments, inasmuch as being perfectly true, it is really destructive of Irvingite claims, and favours the Catholic Doctrine.

The second argument is the main subject of this chapter, but the third had better form part of our preliminary investigation. Can equals ordain equals? No, says the Irvingite, because it is only a superior who can bestow power: an equal cannot give plenary authority to an equal.

There is a speciousness about this plea, which occasionally imposes upon people. It is quite true in all subordinate Offices. A priest cannot ordain a priest, an officer in the army can only appoint non-commissioned officers, a judge cannot make another judge, but can authorize his own clerks.

But it is not true of the highest sources of authority. The grandfather of the present Emperor of Austria abdicated and appointed the Emperor Francis Joseph, and no one seriously questioned the validity of the act. Before him, the celebrated Emperor Charles V. abdicated in favour of his son Philip II. A father, as the head of his family, can bestow his estates, and all his possessions which are not granted him from the Sovereign, such as his title, upon whom he pleases.

This dictum is therefore true of all the subordinate positions of life, so far as they are subordinate; but it is not true of the highest of all. And for the following reasons:—Because if the supreme authority could not hand on position, power, or property to a successor, they could not be handed on at all. And secondly, because the supreme authority thus acting, whether by solitary impulse, or with the concurrence, help, or confirmation of the Body Politic or the Body Catholic, is presumed so to act, not in personal independence, but in a representative character.

It is therefore wholly a mistake, and a very grave mistake, to imagine that Bishops are able of their own free-will, or of their personal or arbitrary choice, to appoint other Bishops. They do so, not as equals investing equals, but as men entrusted with a solemn responsibility by the Lord, and acting as representatives of the Church, or rather of Him—and thus handing on a high Office which they have been ordered so to hand on, but only under certain conditions and in a fixed and authorized manner. Just as in all Sacraments, the Bishop or Priest simply does as he has been commanded, and God the Holy Ghost, we are sure, bestows the Grace which has been promised to attend such simple obedience. To import personal questions of dignity, or ambition, or caste, or what not, into what is merely a careful observance of the Lord's commands, secured from neglect or abuse by there being a duly authorized set of men to maintain it, is simply irrelevant and pernicious. I do not make this implied charge upon Members of the Catholic Apostolic Church except in very pale hue; but, especially as they have virtually surrendered by acknowledging up to a certain point the validity of Episcopal Succession, it is not necessary to linger longer upon the difficulty which they urge about a supposed impossibility of equals ordaining equals.

We must now consider the last of these four arguments, viz., that the Office of an Apostle and a Bishop is different, inasmuch as a Bishop has jurisdiction only over a local Church, whereas Apostles have universal rule—not confined to cities or districts—over the entire Church of Christ. In urging this plea, these people go on to say, that inasmuch as there is such a plain distinction of province between the two Offices, the loss to the Church of one, and that the higher of the two, has been clearly apparent. And inasmuch as the Church has been bereft of the Ministry which was meant to hold together in unity her several parts, she has naturally and necessarily lost cohesion, and schisms in consequence have rended her asunder.

Now we may readily acknowledge, that there is sketched out here a plain distinction of province which is intellectually discernible. And if we were now founding the Catholic Church, it would be quite open to any one to argue that a constitution which recognized this distinction would be the best to adopt, although a closer consideration of the question would show that the difficulty would be better met in another way. But we are concerned in this nineteenth century, not with the inquiry as to what measures might best be adopted in the main organization of the Church, but in investigating as to this organization what have actually been the most prominent parts in it. We have to consider, whether the Church when she reached her full development had Apostles as well as Bishops; whether in her original constitution a fourfold or threefold Ministry was contemplated and set on foot; whether the Apostles died out without successors, or whether the Bishops of the period immediately after their demise succeeded to them; and lastly, whether any provision, and if so, what provision, has been made for the universal government of the Church, as apart from the local administration of Dioceses.

Before entering upon the evidence which makes up the proof of all this, two observations are necessary upon the nature of the proof offered to us.

In the first place, it is a proof derived partly from the Bible, and partly from the testimony of ecclesiastical writers of the earliest ages. If any one imagines that such a proof must be derived from the Bible alone, he entirely misapprehends the nature of the case before us. And for two strong reasons. How can the Bible, which was written before the Apostles went to their rest tell us what happened after they were removed from the Church? St. John, the last survivor of them, was in his writings singularly undidactic upon questions of Church organization and discipline. Again, it is absurd to suppose that the New Testament within the confined limits of a few treatises and letters, not written with a primary intent to teach all about the doctrines and discipline of the Church, should not omit numerous matters of interest, and indeed of importance, which might be gathered from other sources. It is simply a preposterous idea, that an exhaustive and exclusive knowledge of the state of the Church in the Apostles' days can be obtained by merely putting together dark hints and scraps of information scattered up and down the books of the New Testament. Whatever comes to us upon this subject from other trustworthy writings, which is consonant with the language and spirit of the Bible, if established by sufficient evidence, claims our belief, even if it is not *de fide*,—to be required of every man as necessary to salvation. Indeed so well was this truth understood in times much nearer than ours to the Apostolic age, that we find it laid down that "what is held by the Universal Church, not from innovations of Councils, but by unbroken tradition, is rightly believed to have been handed down no otherwise than by Apostolic authority." [1] Really to deny this Canon of Church Evidence, is to refuse to hear the witness of the Holy Catholic Church.

[1] "Quod Universa tenet Ecclesia, nec conciliis institutum sed semper retentum est, non nisi auctoritate Apostolica traditum rectissime creditur." —*August. contra Donatist.*, lib. iv. cap. 24.

The second observation is, that in the ensuing proof that Bishops are the successors of the Apostles, no attempt is made to show that there has been a valid succession of some sort, because Irvingites acknowledge this. They do not gainsay the belief that the first Bishops were validly ordained by St. Peter, St. James, St. Paul, and other of the Apostles by means of imposition of hands, or that the succession has descended without flaw or break to our own days. The only question is, whether the Bishops who came after the Apostles were of a lower order than the Apostles, or formed the continuance of the same line of Ministry. We may now proceed to the proof itself.

We find a probability that there would be a three-fold Ministry in the Christian Church, set forth in the fact that there were three ranks of Ministers amongst the Jews. The High-Priests—for as in the instances of Eleazar and Ithamar, of Zadok and Abiathar, Zadok and Ahimelech, and Annas and Caiaphas, there were always two—the ordinary Priests, and the Levites made up this triple order. And if we search into the origin of this arrangement, we shall not find it in any fanciful resemblance, as in the case of the four living creatures, which have been always taken to typify the four Evangelists, nor again of the four rivers of Paradise, but in the evident carrying out in the Church of the time that perfection of number which finds its highest exemplification in the Ever-Blessed Trinity in Unity. This fact of course affords only a presumption that in the Christian Church there would probably be found a three-fold

Ministry.[1] But inasmuch as the main principles of the two Dispensations, of which one was preparatory to the other and both issued from Heaven, might be expected to be the same, and inasmuch as in point of fact the members of both are addressed under the same title of "a royal priesthood,"[2] we may with reason assign a greater weight to this presumption than we could with justice do to mere signs or symbols.

But if symbols are required, they are ready to our hand. The Ever-Blessed Trinity have impressed Their number all over the provinces of Creation and Grace. The number itself implies unity as well as plurality, priority even amidst equality. But the number four has no such characteristic, but rather implies division and independence. The four rivers of Paradise flowed in four distinct directions. If they had one origin it was independent of them. The four Evangelists give us versions of the Gospel each of which possesses separate and peculiar merits, and rests upon its own foundation. From the sons of Noah, through the period of the Patriarchs, in the enactments of the law, and throughout the general history of the Old Testament, the number three is found much oftener than the number which Irvingites are so forward to honour. There are three parts of man's nature, body, soul, and spirit: and there are three Christian graces, faith, hope, and charity. The

---

[1] "Ut sciamus traditiones apostolicas sumptas de Veteri Testamento; quod Aaron et filii ejus atque Levitæ in templo fuerunt, hoc sibi episcopi, presbyteri et diaconi, vindicent in ecclesia."—*Hieronymus ad Evangelum Presbyterum*, i. 1083 (Migne).

[2] Ex. xix. 5, 6; coll. 1 Pet. ii. 5, 9; Rev. i. 6, v. 10.

English Constitution and an army in the field present each a triad. The number three is the ground-work of most architectural combinations, the leading secret of symmetry, the best passport to associated action. But considerations of this kind, though of some weight when balanced against similar considerations, are too vague and general to establish any point of doctrine or discipline.

The three-fold Ministry is represented even in the germinal state of the Church of our Lord's days. Our Lord Himself, Who alone ordained, the Twelve Apostles, and the Seventy Disciples, make up the triple rank. They had indeed been typified by the twelve chief princes, and the seventy elders, who under Moses governed the Children of Israel. When the Lord ascended into Heaven, it would appear that the two Orders, that were now left on earth, were each advanced a step by His Resurrection-act of bestowing the Holy Ghost upon His Apostles, and possibly by some other unrecorded rite—unless Ordination was involved in the Mission of them all before His Ascension, or else by the general descent of the Holy Spirit on the Day of Pentecost. But at all events, after the Ordination of the Seven Deacons, we find three Orders in existence. These will now require a separate notice.

The Apostles had evidently special privileges or duties, which are proved by the Sacred Volume to include the following acts. They ordained, as in the case of the Deacons and Elders.[1] They confirmed, as

---

[1] Acts vi. 3, xiv. 23.

in Samaria and at Ephesus.[1] They ruled the Church,[2] though with the help of the Elders.[3] They charged the Elders, as St. Paul did the Elders of Ephesus.[4] Excommunication was also pronounced by them, as is shown in the instance of the incestuous person at Corinth.[5]

In the history of the Acts of the Apostles Elders seem to come unexpectedly upon us. We suddenly find them in the Church, and as if they had been for some time in possession.[6] St. Paul and St. Barnabas ordain Elders in every Church towards the end of their first journey.[7] Elders join with the Apostles in the Council of Jerusalem.[8] They are found at Ephesus[9] and various other places. They assist St. James in the audience which he gave St. Paul at the end of the third journey of the latter Apostle. They are plainly a distinct order, and considering that we hear in the Acts of the Apostles and in the Epistles nothing about the Seventy, we cannot be wrong in supposing that the origin of their order was made in the last year of our Lord's Ministry and at His Hands. Otherwise He would be the institutor of an ephemeral Ministry, and His Apostles of a perpetual.

Deacons are found, besides the ordination of the Seven, also at Philippi,[10] at Ephesus,[11] and in other places.[12]

---

[1] Acts viii. 14—17, xix. 1—6.
[2] 2 Cor. xi. 2, 20, 34; Ep. to Titus; 1 Cor. xvi. 1; 2 Cor. xiii. 2, 3, xiv. 27—29, 34, 35, 37; 1 Tim. i. 3, 4, iii. 15, iv. 11, 12, v. 11, 14, 19—22, vi. 13, 14.   [3] Acts xv. 6, &c.
[4] xx. 17—35.   [5] 1 Cor. v.; 2 Thess. iii. 4, 6, 14; 1 Tim. i. 20.
[6] Acts xi. 30.   [7] xiv. 23.   [8] xv. 6, &c.
[9] Acts xx. 17; 1 Tim. v. 1, 2, 19; Tit. i. 5; 1 Pet. v. 1, 5.
[10] Phil. i. 1.   [11] 1 Tim. iii. 8, 10.
[12] 1 Pet. iv. 10, 11, διακονοῦντες, διακονεῖ.

We know the names of some, as Epaphras,[1] Tychicus,[2] and Archippus.[3] Their office was evidently partly secular in distributing alms, and partly religious for preaching and baptizing.

The three Orders are found in Jerusalem, Ephesus,[4] and, according to general opinion, at Philippi.[5]

Thus much is evident in Apostolic times. We have now to see how these three Offices were handed on. Did the Apostles die out without leaving any legitimate successors, or did Bishops gradually rise up, and then duly enter upon the places of their Chiefs when the latter were taken away to be nearer Christ?

Now we must bear in mind that the Church was in a rudimentary state of organization in those early days. It could not be expected that all things would settle down at first into the regular order which they assumed afterwards. Our Lord had taught His Apostles many things which they did not understand[6] at the time, and which for a period slipped from their memories.[7] These dormant recollections were revived, and understanding about them was bestowed according as the needs of the Church called them forth, under the inspiring influence of the Holy Spirit. But the gradual development of

---

[1] Col. i. 7, διάκονος.   [2] Col. iv. 7, διάκονος ; Eph. vi. 21.
[3] Col. iv. 17, διακονίαν.   [4] 1 Tim. iii., v.
[5] Epaphroditus is thought to have been Bishop (ἀπόστολος) of Philippi, Phil. ii. 25, i. 1. Τόν δέ γε μακάριον 'Επαφρόδιτον ἐν τῇ αὐτῇ ἐπιστολῇ ἀπόστολον αὐτῶν κέκληκεν· ὑμῶν γάρ, φησὶν, ἀπόστολον, καὶ συνεργὸν τῆς χρείας μου. Σαφῶς τοίνυν ἐδίδαξεν, ὡς τὴν ἐπισκοπικὴν οἰκονομίαν αὐτὸς ἐπεπίστευτο ἔχων ἀποστόλου προσηγορίαν.—*Theodoret, in Epist. ad Philipp.*, i.
[6] St. John xiii. 7.   [7] St. John xiv. 26.

the Church, in constitution as well as in numbers, was gradually worked out in a human way, and according to the ordinary rules of earthly things.

There was the usual indistinctness of Terms. Common Terms in daily use were employed to designate new Offices and acts of worship, and only received their peculiar technical meaning as time passed on.

Thus the name "Deacon," which properly means minister, and is often rendered by "minister" in our English Version,[1] is applied to our Lord,[2] and to St. Timothy.[3] "The terms Elder or Presbyter, and Bishop are used indiscriminately of the second order in the Ministry[4] as equivalent terms, the one of office and the other of age, as the Fathers repeatedly tell us; or it may be (as has been conjectured) the former a Gentile, the latter a Jewish name."[5] And in like manner the appellation of Apostle is variously applied.

The word itself means simply an "emissary," and is thus used appropriately of our Lord, the foretold "Shiloh," who said of Himself, "As My Father hath sent Me, even so send I you."[6] It is applied also to St. Barnabas,[7] to Epaphroditus,[8] to some brethren of St. Paul, perhaps St. Luke and St. Timothy,[9] and as seems probable, to Andronicus and even to Junia,[10] and perhaps also in another place to Silas and Timothy.[11] If we come

[1] See e.g. Matt. xx. 26; Rom. xiii. 4; 2 Cor. xi. 15, &c.
[2] Rom. xv. 8.   [3] 1 Thess. iii. 2.   [4] e.g. Acts xx. 18, 28.
[5] Haddan's *Apostolical Succession*, p. 74.
[6] Heb. iii. 1; St. John xx. 21, ἀπέσταλκε.
[7] Acts xiv. 14, coll. xi. 22.   [8] Phil. ii. 25.
[9] 2 Cor. viii. 23; 18, 19, 22; i. 1.   [10] Rom. xvi. 7.
[11] 1 Thess. ii. 6; coll. i. 1.

to view the word as one which was merely affixed to those who were definitely sent forth,—as indeed the Seventy were,[1] though in the short account of them given in St. Luke we do not hear of this name being given them,—then, although the Apostles might possess it preeminently, we are nevertheless not surprised to find it employed in other cases, where a high office might be held, or even where it merely designated, as probably in the end of the Epistle to the Romans, the general company of those who were sent with the glad tidings and means of salvation. In this sense our English Version translates the word, " Neither is he that is sent greater than he that sent him." [2]

This vagueness in the application of the title "Apostle" continued after Scriptural times. Thus Ignatius disclaims speaking as an Apostle, though it was competent to him to do so.[3] Eusebius states that several of our Lord's disciples were called Apostles besides the Twelve.[4] In the interpretation of the passages which speak of Epaphroditus as an Apostle, and Timothy, Archippus, and the rest, it was taken as a principle that the name was in a wider sense applied to all who were sent by our Lord, and not to the chosen Twelve alone. " Apostles of the Churches," says Theophylact, gathering up in later times the information scattered through earlier years, "that is, those who were sent and appointed by the Churches."[5] The name is attributed to the Seventy[6]

[1] St. Luke x. 1, ἀπίστειλεν.
[2] οὐδὲ ἀπόστολος μείζων τοῦ πέμψαντος αὐτόν. St. John xiii. 16.
[3] *Ep. ad Trall.*, § 3 ; *Ad Rom.*, § 4.   [4] *Eccles. Hist.*, i. 12.
[5] Theophylact on 2 Cor. viii. 23.   [6] Suicer on the word 'Ἀπόστολος, 3.

by others besides Eusebius, and indeed he represents a custom in the use of the word. So that, although peculiar honour was paid to the Twelve as having been chosen by our Lord, and placed at the head of the Church, and designated by a name which set forth their special mission, yet they were not supposed to be so fenced off from the rest of the Church as to bear a name which could not be used of any besides themselves.[1]

But the Apostles were also Bishops, and exercised local, as well as general Episcopal powers. The general voice of Catholic Antiquity points out St. James the Less as Bishop of Jerusalem. St. Peter is said by St. Jerome[2] to have been the first Bishop of Antioch, and after that to have held the first bishopric of Rome. Whether this was so or not, or whether, as Epiphanius[3] says, he divided the bishopric of Rome with St. Paul, at least it marks the general belief that the Apostles were also Bishops of churches or dioceses. "The Apostles are Bishops," says St. Ambrose.[4] And in earlier times St. Cyprian asserts, that "Deacons ought to remember that the Lord chose Apostles, that is, Bishops and Prelates."[5] "In the earliest days," writes Theodoret, "they called those Apostles who are now named Bishops,[6] and those who are now called Bishops they named Apostles: but as time advanced, they left the name of Apostles to

---

[1] "Döllinger's expression, that the Episcopate was from the first latent in the Apostolate."—Haddan's *Apostolical Succession*, p. 80.
[2] *Catal. Scriptorum Ecclesiasticorum in Petro*, i. 262.
[3] *Advers. Hæres.*, i., *Hæres.*, 27.   [4] In Ephes. cap. iv. 354.
[5] *Episcopos et præpositos*, lib. iii. epist. 9 (or ep. 3, p. 6).
[6] Theodoret on 1 Tim. iii.

those who were truly Apostles, and applied the appellation of Bishops to those who were of old called Apostles." No doubt some of these latter expressions are used of the general position of the Apostles, rather than of any local post which they undertook. Still, besides the instance of St. James, they undoubtedly express the opinion of Catholic Antiquity, that during the infancy of the Church the Apostles were in the place of Bishops, and if they did not in the rudimentary state of the Church's constitution remain permanently at any one place, nevertheless they did often exercise locally Episcopal powers.

We may now advance a step further, and show that the Apostles appointed Bishops in various places. Of this there is no doubt. St. Timothy was the first Bishop of Ephesus, St. Titus of Crete, and were both appointed by St. Paul.¹ Linus, mentioned by St. Paul in his Second Epistle to St. Timothy, was appointed by St. Peter Bishop of Rome. Dionysius the Areopagite was the first Bishop of Athens. Euodius succeeded St. Peter at Antioch. Annianus came after St. Mark at Alexandria. St. James was followed at Jerusalem by Symeon. And St. John consecrated Bishops in several places in the neighbourhood of Ephesus. The general appointment of Bishops by the Apostles can really meet with no doubt, if historical evidence is at all trustworthy. And we may remark, that in view of death, and on consideration for the needs of the Church, this is exactly what we should have expected those who were entrusted with the management of the Catholic Body to have done. The natural presumption would be, that the men thus appointed would be their successors. Is it possible that they were not really so?

Here again the early writers of Catholic Antiquity, who ought to be able to know what occurred of importance in their own time, supply us with positive assertions. Clement of Rome, who is mentioned by St. Paul,[1] and was Bishop of that city after Linus, and was therefore in a position to judge, tells us distinctly that the Apostles appointed the Bishops as their successors. "Our Apostles" he says, " knew through our Lord Jesus Christ that there would be disputes about the name of the episcopacy. Therefore having perfect foreknowledge, they appointed the aforesaid Bishops, and committed to them the order of succession,[2] so that if they themselves were taken to their rest, other approved men might succeed to their Ministry. Those therefore who were appointed by the Apostles, or afterwards by other men of reputation with the consent of the whole Church, and who ministered blamelessly and humbly to the flock of Christ, and received frequent witness to their faithfulness from all, are rightly judged by us not to have lost their Ministry." Here it is plainly shown, first, that the Bishops appointed their own successors, secondly, that these successors succeeded to the Apostles' Ministry, and thirdly, that those successors, by virtue of the power conferred on them, in their turn appointed others to succeed them. Can we resist the inference, that Clement had his own

[1] Phil. iv. 3.
[2] μεταξὺ ἐπινομήν.—Compare Haddan's *Apostolical Succession*, p. 106. *S. Clementis ad Corinthios*, § 44.

call foremost in view, remembering that he was ordained by Linus, and Linus by St. Peter and probably St. Paul?

But Clement's testimony does not stand alone. The next of the Apostolic Fathers, St. Ignatius, though he does not speak so unmistakably to the point under examination as St. Clement, nevertheless reiterates emphatic witness in the same direction. "Do nothing without the Bishop," he urges again and again, so as to excite wonder, did we not recollect that, while Bishops had all the responsibility of the Apostles, they could not present the claims to obedience which their predecessors had, who had been entrusted with the management of the Church by the Lord in Person. "Wherever the Bishop appears," he adds in one place, "there let the multitude of believers be present; just as, wherever Christ Jesus is, there the Catholic Church is present."[1] He had said just before, "Let all follow the Bishop, as Jesus Christ follows His Father,"—a saying which would be meaningless, if Bishops held subordinate offices.

Again, in the middle of the second century, Hegesippus, after mentioning the roll of Bishops in several places, adds: "In fact in every line of succession, and in every city that custom prevails, which is proclaimed by the law, the prophets, and the Lord."[2]

But we shall find more precise expressions if possible than those of Ignatius or Hegesippus, as we trace the testimony further down. Irenæus, who lived later[3]

---

[1] *S. Ignatii ad Smyrnoos*, § 8.   [2] Hegesippus in Eusebius, iv. 22.
[3] Ignatius suffered martyrdom in A.D. 115. Hegesippus flourished about A.D. 152. St. Irenæus succeeded Pothinus as Bishop of Lyons in A.D. 177.

in the second century, says: "We can reckon up those who were made Bishops in the Churches by the Apostles, and their successors as far as our own times. If the Apostles had known any hidden mysteries, which they taught to the initiated secretly and apart from the rest of their converts, they would deliver them above all to those men into whose keeping they committed the Churches themselves. For they wanted those men to be thoroughly perfect and unreprovable in every way, whom they left too as their successors, bequeathing to them their own place of teaching."[1] And again: "The true acknowledgment of this is in accordance with the teaching of the Apostles, as is also the ancient constitution of the Church throughout the world according to the succession of the Bishops, to whom they delivered the Churches in each several place."[2] How could the constitution of the Church throughout the world under Bishops be in accordance with the teaching of the Apostles, if it were a mutilated constitution? The first quotation requires no comment.

Or again, take Tertullian, in the opening of the next century. "Let them exhibit the origin of their Churches, let them trace the succession of their Bishops in descent one after another from the beginning, so that the first had as ordainer and predecessor one of the Apostles, or some apostolic man, who had been a faithful companion

---

[1] "Quos et successores relinquebant, suum ipsorum locum magisterii tradentes."—*Iren. ad. Hæres.*, iii. 3.

[2] *Irenæus ad. Hæres.*, iv. 63 (33, Migne). See also c. 43. "His, qui successionem habent ab apostolis, sicut ostendimus, qui cum episcopatus successione," &c.

of the Apostles. In this way the Apostolic Churches present their rolls; just as the Church of Smyrna had Polycarp placed there by St. John; as the Church of Rome shows Clement ordained by St. Peter; as the rest also point to men who were made Bishops by the Apostles, and hand on in their turn the line of apostolic descent."[1] Again: "The chief Priest has the right of bestowing baptism, that is the Bishop."[2] How could a bishop be called with justice "the chief Priest"—*summus sacerdos*—if he ought to have an Apostle over him?

Later on in the same century, we come upon a remarkable testimony borne by the Council of Carthage in 256 A.D. The Bishops there assembled say: "The intention of our Lord Jesus Christ is plain when He sent His Apostles, and gave into their hands alone the power which had been given Him by His Father; to whom we have succeeded, governing the Church of God by the same power, and baptizing faithful believers."[3] St. Cyprian, who presided at that Council, speaks in his writings of the Bishops "who succeed the Apostles by successive ordination."[4] Again: "We ought to take pains to hold fast the unity given by the Lord and handed on by the Apostles to us their successors."

Again, Firmilian in a letter to Cyprian says: "The power therefore of remitting sins was given to the Apostles, and to the Churches which they constituted by virtue of their mission from Christ, and to the Bishops

---

[1] *Tertullian. De Præscript. Hæret.*, xxxii. Cf. cc. xxxvi., xxxvii.
[2] *Tertullian. De Baptism.*, xvii.
[3] See also *Firmilian*, ep. 75, *ap. Cypr.*, p. 225.
[4] *St. Cyprian ad Florent.*, ep. lxix. (Migne), 4, "vicaria ordinatione."

who succeeded to them by successive ordination. But the enemies of the One Catholic Church in which we are placed, and the adversaries of us who have succeeded to the Apostles . . . . what else are they than Korah, Dathan, and Abiram?"[1]

We have now descended through the sparse Christian writers of the time down to about 200 years after the life-time of the Apostles, or to little more than a century and half after St. John's death. We may add to these testimonies the frequent witness of Eusebius, when in collecting with laborious accuracy the records of the time, he speaks of the "earliest succession to the Apostles,"[2] and often alludes to Bishops as being appointed in various stages of succession to the Apostles. And what affords the strongest confirmation to the argument is, that amidst all these passages, and a large number of others which allude to general doctrine of Apostolical Succession, but not specially to that particular point of it which is now under consideration, not one word is found which can be said to afford a proof that Bishops were in their time lower officers than the Apostles, or that the Church had lost the chief order of her Ministry when the Apostles were taken to their rest.

The case might well be allowed to depend solely

[1] *Firmilian ad S. Cyprianum*, xii.
[2] *Euseb.*, ii. 22, iii. 4, heading of chapter, περὶ τῆς πρώτης τῶν ἀποστόλων διαδοχῆς.—Cf. end of the same chapter. The words which he uses are διαδέχεται and διαδοχή, the same that he applies to the succession of one Emperor of Rome to another. See too iii. 36, τῆς κατ' Ἀντιόχειαν Πέτρου διαδοχῆς, 37, τῆς τῶν ἀποστόλων διαδοχῆς, τὴν πρώτην τῶν ἀποστόλων διαδοχὴν; iv. 1, πέμπτην ἀπὸ Πέτρου καὶ Παύλου διαδοχὴν; 5, ἕβδομος ἀπὸ τῶν ἀποστόλων διαδέχεται, &c.

upon the testimony which has been already adduced. But we cannot neglect that of the Universal Church of all ages.

Bishops have always been treated as the supreme rulers of the Church. The idea that they are subordinate, and that there ought to be Apostles over their heads, has not indeed been condemned at Councils, simply because the question has never been mooted. Councils have only rejected error that has been from time to time pressed upon the acceptance of the Church. Nobody has presented this Tenet to the consideration of the assembled Church, and it has accordingly received no notice. But her leading Doctors, whose names are held in never-ceasing remembrance, have used language which though not aimed at the supposition which Irvingites have advanced, is nevertheless destructive of it.

For example, St. Augustine says: "The Apostles begat thee: they were sent forth in person, they preached in person, they were themselves thy fathers. But could they be for ever with us in the flesh? And if one of them said, 'I have a desire to depart and be with Christ, which is far better: nevertheless to abide in the flesh is more needful for you,' he said so indeed, but how long was it in his power to abide here? Could he have done so to the present time? Could he have stayed beyond this age? Is the Church then deserted by their departure? God forbid. 'Instead of thy fathers thou shalt have children.' What is the meaning of this, 'Instead of thy fathers thou shalt have children?' The Apostles were sent as thy fathers: instead of the Apostles, children have been born to thee, and made Bishops. For where were those Bishops born, who are now scattered through the world? The Church herself calls them fathers, she herself bare them, and she herself placed them in the seats of the Fathers."[1]

St. Jerome, commenting upon the same passage in the forty-fifth Psalm, writes: "'Instead of thy fathers thou shalt have children.' The Apostles were thy fathers, thou Church, because they begat thee. But now, because they have retired from the world, thou hast instead of them Bishops for sons, because they were made so by thee. They are also thy fathers, because they exercise rule over thee. 'Thou wilt make them princes in all lands.' Christ put His Saints over all nations. For in the name of God the Gospel was spread to all the boundaries of the world, over which the princes of the Church, that is, the Bishops, were set up."[2] In another place writing against the Montanists, who like the Irvingites had degraded Bishops, he says: "Amongst us Bishops occupy the place of the Apostles."[3] And again, speaking of Bishops: "They all," he says, "are the Apostles' successors."[4]

Such has been the universal doctrine. "In the Bishop," says St. Ambrose, "all orders are comprised: for he is the first Priest, that is, the chief of the Priests."[5]

---

[1] S. Augustine in Psalm xlv. 16. See also his Epistle *ad Fratres Madaurenses* (xlii). "Christiana Societas per sedes Apostolorum et successiones Episcoporum certa per orbem propagatione diffunditur."
[2] Hieron. in Psalm xlv. 16.
[3] *Hieron. ad Marcellam adv. Montanum*, ii. 128.
[4] *Hieron.* ep. 85 (101), § 1.   [5] Com. in Eph. iv. 11.

St. Chrysostom says of St. Paul that he was "entrusted with the whole world;" and uses similar words of St. Timothy, that he was "entrusted with the supremacy of the world," and of the office of a Bishop, that it is "a work of supremacy."[1]

And Optatus in his work against the Donatists makes indeed four orders in the Church, but under an arrangement which excludes Apostles as holding a rank by themselves: "There are four classes in the Church, viz., Bishops, Priests, Deacons, and the Faithful."[2] Again: "Why should I speak of the laity, who at that time possessed no dignity in the Church? Why of numerous servitors? why thirdly of Deacons, why of Priests, who occupy the second rank in the Priesthood? There were even Bishops, the very heads and princes in everything, who impiously gave up to the flames the copies of God's law."[3] What does the expression so frequently found amongst Ecclesiastical writers—"Apostolic Sees" (*sedes Apostolicæ*)—mean, but that their holders were supposed by the entire Christian world to sit in the seats of the Apostles? Or passing onwards to the ninth century, we find Amalarius[4] quoting a passage from St. Ambrose which says, that "those who are now named Bishops were originally called Apostles."

Now what is the purport of all this evidence? Why, plainly this. It was an universal tradition in the Church, never questioned, never brought into dispute, that the

---

[1] Hom. xvii., p. 241; Hom. vi., Adv. Jud., p. 541. In 1 Tim. Hom. x. προστασίαν.
[2] *Optatus adv. Parmenianum De Schismate Donatistaram*, ii. p. 54.
[3] Id. i. p. 14.   [4] *Amalarius De Offic. Eccles.*, ii. 13.

Apostles of our Lord, in obedience to the commands which they had received from the Lord Himself, appointed their successors before their death.

As St. Augustine has told us in the passage already quoted, there was a considerable unwritten tradition which the Apostles handed down. They had enjoyed the inestimable advantage of religious and theological training under the immediate care of our Lord. What was necessary, they wrote down under the inspiring guidance of the Holy Spirit. But that this was not even a tithe of the whole, the remarkable words of the latest survivor amongst them, as if anticipating the narrow views of later generations, teach us infallibly.[1] How we may prove as much as can be ascertained of this body of tradition, is told us by St. Augustine. It is found embedded in the teaching, not of particular Churches, still less in the unattested sayings of individual men, but in the consentient Doctrine of the Universal Church. It is therefore enshrined in her Constitution, her Liturgies, her Divine life. And while the utmost care and caution are employed in searching for and checking the details of this tradition, the fact is clear that Bishops did succeed to the Apostles,—not by usurpation, not unforeseenly, not unintentionally,—but by express provision, in obedience to the Lord's own directions, and with plenary Apostolic Authority.

This fact, thus attested by Catholic tradition, derives also, as we have seen, a very powerful confirmation from Holy Writ. When in the full light of what the Church

[1] St. John xxi. 25.

has taught us, we read the Bible, we find witness borne to its validity, in the arrangements of the law foreshadowing the Gospel, in the provisions made by our Lord during His life-time, in the Constitution so far as it is made known to us of the infantine Church, and in the ordinations made by St. Paul and the other Apostles. So that, especially since no countervailing evidence can be brought forward which does not crumble in the grasp, the fact of Bishops succeeding to Apostles is settled as strongly, as any historical fact can be expected to be established.

Yet the Church has ever, as the difference of name shows, distinguished between Bishops and Apostles. The first Apostles wielded an authority which Bishops never can employ: they enjoy a dignity in the remembrance of the Church, which can never be conceded to Bishops however eminent for learning or piety. The cause is evident. Not merely from the fact of their association with our Lord, but from the fruits of that intercourse, they had a message to deliver which they alone could define,—fresh from the fount of salvation. Vast as had been the honour involved in their intercourse, it was not barren. They are called by a name peculiar to themselves, because they were able beyond all other men to say, whether our Lord had really taught anything which might happen to fall under dispute, or whether it was alien to His Revelation. Nor is St. Paul to be exempted from the sweep of this distinction. His peculiar message was the admission of the Gentiles, and the acceptance and delivery of this message in obedience to our

Lord's Personal commands constitutes His title to Apostleship.

And if any questioning still lingers on the subject of local and universal rule, it must be remembered, that very soon in the early ages of the Church the Episcopate was naturally developed to meet the need. In the words of St. Chrysostom, Bishops were supposed to be "appointed to the provostship of the world."[1] And St. Cyprian often speaks of there being but one Bishopric in the Church, of which every Bishop has a share, so as to have an interest in the whole. He speaks of this as being a diffusive power, which resided in the entire College of Bishops.[2] Accordingly, we are soon told of Dioceses being consolidated into Provinces with Primates or Metropolitans at their head.[3] And in course of time, Provinces were included under Patriarchates, with a Superior holding the title of Archbishop, Ex-arch, and later on as it seems, of Patriarch.[4] So that, as the Church grew, there was a natural development of the Episcopal order in correspondence with her requirements.

But to pursue this part of the present enquiry further would be to enter upon a wide field of information. It is enough to point out, that the fancied distinction between Bishops as having only a local jurisdiction, and

---

[1] τὴν τῆς οἰκουμένης προστασίαν ἐγκεχειρισμένος.—Hom. vi., ad Jud. i. p. 542. See also Gregory Nazianzen in Laud. Athanasii, xxi. p. 377. Basil, ep. 72, ad Athanasium.

[2] Cyprian De Unitate Ecclesiæ. Episcopatus unus est, cujus a singulis in solidum pars tenetur.—Bingham, Orig. Eccles., ii. 5.

[3] There were signs of them as early as the second century.—Bingham, ii. 16, § 4.   [4] Bingham, ii. 17.

Apostles as possessing universal authority, is without warrant either from Holy Scripture, or from the teaching or traditions of the Church. Bishops succeeding into the places of the Apostles, as has been proved, inherited both their local and their universal sway. Bishops of course are taken here as an entire order, as Apostles cannot be taken singly, but as constituting one College. The great Councils of Nice, Constantinople, and the rest, afford unmistakable evidence to the position here maintained.

How then, it may be asked, when the evidence is so strong that Bishops were the successors of the Apostles, could these people assert so firmly that such a position could not be proved? The answer is, that first, the question has not been seriously argued on the Catholic side, and secondly, that a superficial view has confirmed them in their erroneous supposition. The majority appear to have been content with the broad assertion in the Letter written in answer to the Articles in the *Old Church Porch*. The passage runs as follows:—

"In the next place we maintain that, in point of fact, you can bring us no proof that Apostles did appoint their successors. You can bring proof that they appointed men to be Bishops, which Bishops *became* their successors: but you can bring no proof that Apostles *appointed* them to be their successors. In Scripture you *know* that there are none. There is not a syllable in any of the words of our Lord, or in the writings of His Apostles, which can be distorted into the remotest hint even of the removal of Apostles, still less that Bishops were appointed to succeed them. Neither can you show from Scripture, that authority was at any time given to the Apostles to appoint successors to themselves. This being the case, it is very difficult to conceive how any statement, not contained in Holy Scripture, can avail to prove that Apostles had any such authority: and it requires the most explicit statements, and from persons testifying of their own personal knowledge, to prove that any such appointment was ever made. Now there is no such testimony in existence anywhere. There is no account in any author, inspired or uninspired, of any formal act by which Apostles constituted Bishops to be their successors in the Office of Apostleship—no notice that any such act ever took place. I am aware, I believe, of all the passages from St. Clement downwards to the end of the fourth century, which could be alleged as bearing upon this point: they are all written in vindication of the existing priesthood and episcopacy, against sedition or schism, or else in vindication against heresy, of the Doctrine handed down from the Apostles through the Bishops. And the Fathers do this (naturally and most truly) on the ground that the then existing Ministers had been duly admitted to their Offices according to the ordinances of the Apostles ($\grave{\epsilon}\pi\iota\nu o\mu\grave{\eta}\nu$, as St. Clement has it), and that when the Apostles departed, they left Bishops their successors; which, as a matter of fact, I have not the slightest idea of disputing."[1]

Coming fresh from the perusal of the testimonies just quoted from the works of the early Fathers, one is struck

---

[1] *Letter*, &c., pp. 24, 25. The italics are in the original.

with amazement at the hardihood of some of these assertions. St. Clement tells us that the Apostles, with a foreknowledge of future difficulties, appointed Bishops with a power of later succession to succeed to their Ministry. After we have passed by St. Ignatius' assertions of the dignity of Bishops, and Hegesippus' declaration of the unbroken continuity of custom, St. Irenæus tells us, that the Apostles committed the Churches to certain men, and left them as their successors. After hearing Tertullian's evidence in confirmation, we listen to the Council of Carthage announcing, that they as Bishops have succeeded to the Apostles and governed the Church by the same power as the latter did, and we are told both by Firmilian and by Cyprian, that the Bishops succeeded the Apostles by successive ordinations. And all this testimony is welded together and strengthened by Eusebius, who reiterates again and again phrases expressing the fact that Bishops were the successors to the Apostles. And it has been shown that Holy Scripture, which was written before the deaths of the Apostles, foreshadows this arrangement in many ways, and affords no proof of the theory set up against the Catholic Doctrine. How then can the author of this Letter put forward so gratuitous an assertion?

He says, first, that although the Bishops became the successors of the Apostles, the latter never appointed them; and secondly, that there is nothing in Holy Scripture to show that the Apostles had the authority to appoint their own successors; and that "it requires the most explicit statements, and from persons testifying of their own personal knowledge, to prove that any such appointment was made." The first of these is simply contrary to the express assertions of St. Clement, the Council of Carthage, and others. And with respect to the second, the absence from Holy Scripture of any such express authorization is by no means fatal to its existence. Could Mr. Cardale bring forward any passage from Holy Scripture stating that the Apostles had no such authority?

When our Lord sent them forth, He contemplated a continuance of His Church "to the end of the world," and told His Apostles that He would be with them till then. So that the burden of proof lies upon those who maintain, that the Apostles and the Church had no power to provide for the perpetual government of the Church. St. John too declares, that the Apostles knew very many things which had not been written down: and St. Augustine expresses the opinion of the Church, in saying that some of these were enshrined in her universal and unanimous traditions. The Apostles taught by deed as well as by word; in the habits, laws, Liturgies, and the parts of the Constitution of the Church which they instituted or regulated. To suppose that the Church of the first three centuries was so ignorant of her own Constitution, as not to know whether the Bishops succeeded to the Apostles plenarily or not; or so dishonest, as to conceal the fact if they succeeded only upon a lower platform, is so insulting to the Primitive Church, that we should have imagined it must have proceeded from those who have no veneration for her, not from people who maintain and glory in the honoured title Catholic. While many passages run right against the statement just quoted, no Irvingite can bring forward a single passage which proves either that the Apostles had no authority to transmit their powers, or that the Bishops who as a matter of fact succeeded them, were not their true successors upon an even line.

So that the idea that an order of Apostles is essential to the integrity of the Church's Constitution, meets with no support from Ecclesiastical authority, and indeed stands condemned by the tacit or declared opinion of the Church in all ages of her history. We have already seen, that the Scriptural authority upon which it has been supposed by Irvingites to rest is purely imaginary, and is counterbalanced by much stronger testimony upon the other side. In fact this Tenet is a baseless figment supported only by an imagination which has laid hold of one passage which seemed to suggest the conception, wrested a few others from their natural signification, and has attempted to prop up this reasoning by plausible arguments, which when closely examined, melt away before the view. Whereas the failure which has from the first attended these so-called Apostles, the inconsistencies revealed in their action, and the fact that they have passed away from the earth before they have finished the work, "which," as they say, "was given them to do," prove that there has been error somewhere, and that they have been induced to believe in what is really not true.

How is it then, people may ask, that this Tenet has ever been entertained and accepted by men of education and earnestness, if the grounds upon which it stands are so unsafe and indeed visionary? The answer to this question appears to be not uninstructive.

For many centuries, there has been a tendency in the Western Church to exaggerate the position and power of individual agents. The origin of this tendency may be discovered in the condition of Europe, when whole countries had been flooded by hordes of barbarian infidels, and learning, faith, and holiness were confined to Churchmen. The truths of Christianity and civilization, in the absence of a spread of literature, could be learned only at the lips of ecclesiastics ; and conversions of large numbers of people, seeming to partake of the miraculous, led minds to overweening conceptions of the capabilities of single men. Bishops and Priests were, for a long period, like beings of a superior order amidst ordinary men.

Hence followed two results. On the one side the Clergy became too highly exalted: and on the other, by the inevitable revulsion of human habits, many people came in course of time to refuse to acknowledge any right at all in the duly ordained clergy to guard the faith, or to teach and govern the Church. Not to insist now upon the wisdom and the necessity of avoiding both extremes, we find at the opening of the present century both these principles at work, viz., neglect of the duly authorized clergy, and undue exaggeration of the power of individual agents.

Hence in the early days of Irvingism, when the adherents of the nascent sect were not led along the old Church ways into Catholic channels, and they were anxiously longing for some new power to reinstate the

Church in her pristine prosperity, they anxiously strained their eyes in the direction of the entrance upon the earth of men endowed with vast spiritual powers. Whether their thoughts took definite shape so far or not, they had an indistinct anticipation, prompted by their longings, of the appearance of twelve spiritual Napoleons. For even in the time of the Macdonalds, and at the first manifestations in Scotland of an appearance of prophecy, these people were praying that Apostles might be sent. Irving's own wonderful success in his earliest preaching in London made several people, who were not close observers, to anticipate marvellous results from his matured strength. So prayers for the coming of Apostles were offered continually, not only by Irvingites, but by many more who never cast in their lot with this Sect.

But such Apostles as they expected never came. Thereupon many persons were sensible enough to perceive that the idea was a delusion, and withdrew from the fellowship of the rest. But these people were afraid, or declined, to draw back; and when no man appeared equal to their needs, or to the pictures which they had drawn, fancied that they themselves had indulged in misconceptions, and made it a point of faith to smother doubt, and to acquiesce in the only course left open, if they were to go on, and to ascribe all to God's Providence. Accordingly, twelve men were appointed, who though men of unexceptionable life, and thoroughly devoted to their work, were both in their capacities and their careers far below the anticipations that had been formed, and utterly unequal to the really grand effort which was demanded of them. Then came failure, weakness, want of unanimity; and collapse was only averted by the determined will of their real leader, the moderation that marked their management, the skill which prompted the formation of their system and the adaptation of it to pressing wants, their steering into a forward place in the spiritual current of the age, and the real religious earnestness which actuated many at least among them.

But at the present time, when only one of these Apostles is really capable of any effort at all, and ten have passed away, how people can believe in Apostles when there is no Apostolic College is strange indeed. Nor less strange is the infatuation, which in spite of strong argument induces them in other respects to hold fast to this Tenet. What answer, it may be asked, do they make, when they are driven victoriously from point to point? In what citadel do they entrench themselves?

"It is the Lord's work. Whatever He does is right, even if He goes contrary to the expectation of man. Does not He 'destroy the wisdom of the wise, and bring to nothing the understanding of the prudent?' The Apostles have been appointed from Heaven. That one fact is sufficient."

So that we are now brought to the only argument which has not been already overthrown in this work, the validity of the appointment of these Apostles by the voices of the Prophets. Did these Prophets after all really speak from Heaven?

An examination into this question will form the subject of the next two chapters.

CHAPTER VI.

PROPHETICAL GIFTS.

BEFORE we commence an examination into the nature of Irvingite prophecies, it will be well to gather some fruits of experience from the history of the Church. While Doctrines comprehended in the Christian heritage have found a home in some part at least of the Catholic Church, after they have been expelled temporarily from elsewhere, heresies and mistakes have occurred again and again, and history has repeated itself in the several returns of an exploded error.

That there were Christian Prophets in the first ages of the Church as distinct from those of the Jewish period, has been shown already,[1] and may be easily proved from the Acts of the Apostles, and from St. Paul's writings, and notably from his First Epistle to the Corinthians. The latter book affords us an insight into the actual operation of the gift of Prophecy in a local Church which was yet in early youth. There was a remarkable enthusiasm, accompanied by an imperfect estimate of the nature of the new Religion, and of the

[1] Above, II. i. § 7.

character of the means of Grace. People who celebrated the Holy Eucharist with such unseemly ceremony as marked the Corinthian assemblies, who formed themselves into sects under the names of Christ, Paul, Cephas, and Apollos, who tolerated with satisfaction the presence of the incestuous man among them, were likely to revel in a self-pleasing possession of spiritual gifts. Accordingly, St. Paul explains the nature of these gifts, and especially of the gifts of Tongues and Prophecy, and endeavours to lead the Corinthians into a proper employment of them.

If therefore we would really understand the true operation of these gifts in the early Church, we must subtract something from the picture of their rudimentary use, which is revealed in this Epistle as existing amongst these neophyte Christians. Still, making all due allowance, we undoubtedly do find prophesying in a prominent place at this time at Corinth: and the Apostle, so far from rebuking the practice, exhorts his correspondents to "covet earnestly" the best gifts. It is true that he keeps them subordinate to Charity, and that the group of gifts includes more than one kind. Miracles, gifts of healing, kinds of tongues are conjoined with the exercise of prophecy.

We need not here linger upon the other evidence of prophesying which is scattered through the later historical parts of the New Testament. It was appropriately summarized in the presentment already given of the arguments for present prophesying advanced by Irvingites.[1] Early Ecclesiastical Writers tell us that these

---
[1] Above, II. i. § 7, pp. 39—41.

gifts of the Holy Spirit, which are usually termed "extraordinary," remained in the Church after the Apostles' period. Quadratus, the author of an Apology which was well known but has unfortunately perished with the exception of a fragment preserved by Eusebius, was associated with the daughters of St. Philip in the possession of prophetical powers.[1] Irenæus tells us of prophesyings and tongues still remaining in the Church in his time. When the echo of the Apostolic age died away, these gifts too died away as a matter of fact. St. Chrysostom expresses the general opinion when he says that many of the Miraculous Gifts had since ceased, such as the Gift of Prophecy, the Gift of Wisdom, the Gift of healing the sick, the Gift of raising the dead, the Gift of Tongues, the Gift of Prayer, which was then distinguished by the name of the Spirit.[2] In advancing this opinion, no Ecclesiastical Writer of repute questions the possibility of the revival of these Gifts in the Church, should it seem good to Almighty God so to restore them. We presume that it will not seem good to Him, unless there is an occasion demanding their employment. For the principle of the Heathen Poet appears unimpeachable even beyond his immediate survey,—

"Nec Deus intersit, nisi dignus Vindice nodus."

Nor should Heaven interfere,
Unless a feat too vast for man be there.

The first claimants to extraordinary spiritual powers

[1] *Euseb.*, iv. 37.
[2] Chrysost. in *Ep. ad Rom.*, viii. 26. See also Bingham, *Orig. Eccl.*, xiii. 6, § 9.

that came up, were the Montanists. About the year 173, A.D., at Ardaba, a village in Phrygia, Montanus, as Eusebius tells us,[1] began to prophesy. He is said to have joined the Church under the idea of rising to a high post of dignity. He affected to speak in the Spirit, and to be suddenly brought into a state of enthusiasm and ecstasy. He spoke in strange tongues in a manner unknown at that time in the Church. This drew to him a crowd of people. Some tried to put a stop to his proceedings, but others were attracted upon the supposition of his utterances being the genuine prophesyings of the Holy Spirit. He was soon joined by two noble ladies, Maximilla and Priscilla, who deserted their husbands, and by a man named Theodotus, and their united efforts drew to them a considerable following. The Bishops of Asia, thinking that some action must be taken, met together, and formally condemned the prophecies of Montanus, and excommunicated those who propagated them. They then followed up their measure by writing, according to the custom of the Church at that time, a full account of all that they had done, and sending it to the Western Churches, which had been out of the reach of united action. Although in some parts of the West the new teaching was at first well received, the ultimate consequence was that the prophecies of Montanus and his followers were generally condemned.

Upon this, finding themselves exposed to the censure of the whole Church, Montanus and his followers separated themselves into a distinct society, and caused a schism.

[1] Euseb., *Hist. Eccles.*, v. 16. Clinton's *Fasti Romani*, A.D. 173.

They adopted the ordinary creed of the Church, except on one main point. They held that the Holy Spirit had spoken directly by Montanus, and had delivered through him a more perfect discipline than had been bestowed through the Apostles. They called themselves the spiritually-minded ($\pi\nu\epsilon\upsilon\mu\alpha\tau\iota\kappa o\iota$), and the opponents of these new revelations carnal-minded ($\psi\upsilon\chi\iota\kappa o\iota$). They condemned second marriages as being impracticable for those who are going to heaven, they forbad flight from persecution, and cast out all who were guilty of notorious crimes without hope of restoration. They encouraged celibacy, allowed divorce, and observed three Lents in the year. We should especially notice here the maintenance of the Catholic Creed by these sectarians, with the exception of their own pet dogma.

Montanism for a time spread widely, and made a large number of converts. Even after Montanus' death, which happened early, they continued as a separate set of Christians, though they split up into various sections, such as the Quinctiliani, Priscilliani, and others, and slid into Sabellian views on the Doctrine of the Trinity. The chief lustre which attended them arose from no less a man than Tertullian becoming a convert to their teaching. Late in life, whether attracted by the austerity of their discipline, or repelled by want of sympathy in others, he adopted their Tenets, and boldly advocated them in many of his treatises. The higher character of the standard which they placed before them, and the yearning for a present Revelation, added to the general orthodoxy of their views, appear to have imposed upon him. It is needless to point out, how Montanism died, and left no defender.

As a principle, general outbursts of prophetical claims are confined to periods of great religious excitement. They require a powerful impetus to set them in motion. Added to this, there must be a strong tendency to the exaltation of the individual, who is thus supposed to be made a vehicle of Divine inspiration. Montanists stand by themselves, as claimants on a large scale in the ancient Church of special gifts of prophecy. Nor do we meet with many others till we reach the approaches to our own era. Various appearances indeed of inhabitants of the next world to holy people, whether technically saints or not, were supposed to have taken place. But we do not meet with the claim of inspiration by the Holy Spirit as regularly and widely put forward, till we come to the period of the Reformation.

The Anabaptists of Münster claimed that they had supernatural powers of foresight by means of dreams and visions. And about that era we hear, amongst others, of Elizabeth Barton the Holy Maid of Kent (1533), of the Celestial Prophets in Germany (1520), of the Ursuline Prophetesses in France (1640); of Christopher Kotter (1625), Christina Poniatowski (1627), Nicholas Drabicius (1657), all connected with the Moravians; besides Hachet Swenckfield, David George, and others. The supposed near approach of the Millennium constituted the staple of much of the prophecies of these people. Millenarianism had been embraced by the Montanists.

The origin of Quakerism was very much like that of Montanism. George Fox thought himself a Prophet with an especial inspiration from Heaven, and the main object of his system was to make all the people of the Society of Friends to be organs, through whom the Holy Ghost was to speak, so that it should not be they that speak, but the Holy Ghost that speaketh in them. It is true that no ecstatic effort is affected, but that all is quiet and self-composed. But in the expectation for the heavenly breeze, in the refusal to speak unless " the Spirit moves them," in the assumption that what is said is uttered under the moving impulse of that Holy Person, we see the Montanist principle again at work.

Towards the end of the same century we meet with enthusiasts of more pronounced character. In the year 1688, A.D., several persons, amounting to some five or six hundred, inhabitants of Dauphiny and Viverais, asserted that they were Prophets, and were inspired by the Holy Ghost. They were of all ages and of both sexes, but were principally young people. Their proceedings were wild and violent. They had strange fits, in which they stretched out their hands and feet, and fell to the ground, beating themselves violently. There they would stay for a long time, affirming that they were in a trance, and saw heaven opened, and the angels moving about, and Paradise. When this agitation of body had continued for some time, they began to prophesy. The burden of their announcement was, " Amend your lives, repent ye; for the end of all things is at hand." They shouted out so loud for mercy that the very hills are said to have resounded. And with their cries were mixed imprecations against the Pope and the Priests, and prophecies of the speedy downfall of the Papacy. They also announced the approach of the Millennial reign of Christ.

These habits and doctrines spread so widely, that through three Dioceses the Papal religion seemed to be all but annihilated. They met however with great opposition from the Church and the Government of France, and in the beginning of the next century they raised the standard of revolt. From the shirt which they wore they were called Camisards, a shirt being in the dialect of Languedoc, *Camisa*. A bloody contest ensued, marked by great cruelty and perfidy towards these unfortunate and misguided people. The war was carried on first under the Marquis de Montreval, and afterwards under no less a general than Marshal Villars. Three of the leaders of the Camisards were burned alive, several others broken on the wheel, and many fled across to England, where they preached their doctrines under the name which was given them of French Prophets. There they were joined by several people, amongst whom was one John Lacy, who published in three parts, amounting together to some 370 pages, a collection of the prophetical warnings which he delivered when in a state of ecstacy.

The movement of the Wesleyans in the eighteenth century, though the direct action of the Holy Spirit upon the soul was recognized and brought out into prominence, nevertheless did not include any direct instances of prophecy to an appreciable extent. Nevertheless, the idea of individual action being prompted by the influence of the Holy Ghost, exercised consciously over the heart, was so strongly and generally propagated, that men's minds were ready for a belief in a general outpouring of the Spirit, at the end of the last century and the beginning of this.

First, perhaps, we meet with the instance of Emmanuel Swedenborg, the son of Jesper Swedborg, Bishop of, Skara in Westrogothia. He was born at Stockholm in January, 1688. The early part of his life was spent in the study of physical science. In 1719 he was ennobled by Queen Ulrica Leonora under the name of Swedenborg, and in course of time he established an European reputation by his numerous treatises upon scientific subjects. These works have been styled "a grand consolidation of human knowledge—an attempt to combine and re-organize the opinions of all the schools of medicine since the days of Hippocrates." But about the age of fifty-eight he assumed a new character. In his own account he says:—"I have been called to a holy office by the Lord, Who most graciously manifested Himself in Person to me His servant in the year 1745, and opened my sight into the spiritual world, endowing me with the gift of conversing with spirits and angels." The event to which these words relate occurred at an inn in London. "A man appeared to him in a strong, shining light and said, 'I am God the Lord, the CREATOR and REDEEMER. I have chosen thee to explain to men the interior and spiritual senses of the sacred writings. I will dictate to thee what thou oughtest to write.'" He immediately returned home, and devoted himself to Hebrew and a diligent study of the Holy Scriptures. After this, he frequently and consistently made and maintained the assertion of his spiritual intercourse.

He does not appear to have laid claim to inspiration, in the sense which prophetical inspiration is ordinarily supposed to bear; but to have imagined that his spiritual sight was opened, so that he witnessed and could describe the action of the spiritual world. Thus in the year 1757, Swedenborg asserts that he saw the first judgment descend upon the Christian Church, after which commenced the descent from the new Heaven of the new Church and her doctrine, signified by the New Jerusalem of the Apocalypse. The system which he introduced was of a somewhat complex character, the only point that comes under our present survey being the claim advanced by him to be a "Seer," endowed with a gift of spiritual intuition, which enabled him to be the channel of a new Revelation.

In course of time, other people went far beyond Swedenborg. As the eighteenth century closed, we fall upon the case of Joanna Southcote, a servant-girl at Exeter. She was subject to paroxysms of weeping, and to trances attended with convulsions. Sometimes she thought that Satan came to her. On other occasions she imagined that she was visited by the Lord. She declared that she received prophecies from the Holy Ghost, and conversed with good spirits, as well as with bad ones. She gave out to her followers sealed papers, which she called her "seals," to protect them in this world and in the next.

At last, in 1814, having from indulgence and want of exercise fallen into a gross habit of body, she gave out that she was pregnant with the "Shiloh," Who was then about to come a second time. The day fixed for the birth was the 19th of October, 1814, and it was to take place at midnight. Large sums of money were subscribed in order that preparations should be made worthy of the Prince of Peace, and amongst other things an expensive cradle was provided. On the night of the 19th of October a large crowd of persons assembled in the street to receive the expected announcement: but the hour of midnight passed over, and the people were only induced to disperse by being informed that Joanna had fallen into a trance. She was then sixty-four years old, and died soon after, on the 26th of December in the same year, having previously declared that "if she was deceived, she was at all events misled by some spirit, either good or evil." Her body was opened after her decease, and the appearance which had deceived her followers, amongst whom was Dr. Reece, a medical man who examined her during her supposed pregnancy, and perhaps herself, was found to have arisen from dropsy. Belief in her remained after her death,—and her followers, who were at first very numerous, continued to exist for a long time,—and has not yet died out.

Somewhat similar to Joanna Southcote and her followers were the Shakers. This Sect professes to believe that our Lord made His second appearance on earth in the person of one Ann Lee, daughter of a Manchester blacksmith. They existed a few years before she joined them in 1758. In 1770 she laid claim to Divine inspiration, and called herself "Ann the Word." Persecution in England drove her and her followers to America, where they settled and flourished. In 1830 they numbered 6,000. Many among them profess to see God, the Lord Jesus, and "Mother Ann." They assert that they are taken into the spiritual world, and there are introduced to good spirits, and even sit at table with Almighty God. Besides their characteristic shaking, they speak in unknown tongues, and use various repulsive ceremonies.

But the most remarkable Sect, which in the present century has taken rise from supposed spiritual manifestation, is that of the Mormons. Joseph Smith, the Prophet of this fanatical body, was born in Sharon, Windsor County, Vermont, in 1805. His story was, that on the 21st of September, 1823, while he was praying to God, a sudden light, like the light of day, only much purer and more glorious in appearance and brightness, burst into his room. In a moment a Personage stood before him, surrounded by a glory exceeding the previous light. On Joseph Smith's enquiring who it was that appeared to him, this Personage announced himself to be an Angel sent to make certain revelations to him. The visit was repeated, and at length disclosures were presented to him, written on plates which looked like gold. They were said to be in Egyptian characters, and bound together in a volume with three rings running through the whole. The characters of the writing were to be interpreted by means of the " Urim and Thummim."

Mormonism therefore arose about the same time as Irvingism. It is true that there is a vulgarity and a coarseness about Mormonism, which is wholly wanting in Irvingite life and teaching. And we cannot be surprised at the soreness which adherents of the latter feel when a comparison is drawn between these two Bodies, nor at the asperity with which they meet the charge of similarity, even when it is brought temperately and distantly against them, as it was by the late admirable Bishop Forbes of Brechin. No doubt Joseph Smith was an illiterate propagator of a new system, besides being guilty of crimes[1] which no one would ever dream of imputing to Members of the Catholic Apostolic Church. Besides that, the polygamy of Mormonism alone, to say nothing of other characteristics, opens a wide and impassable chasm between the two.

No comparison therefore between Irvingism and Mormonism is here intended to be drawn, when we nevertheless notice the same religious currents moving in both cases.[2] First there is the prophetical origin,—the claim made by Joe Smith of a Divine appearance, and of a new revelation. "Unknown tongues" are found

[1] See Article on "Mormonism and the Burial Office" in the *Ecclesiastic* for October, 1850, p. 201.

[2] Though as a matter of fact there was a leakage from Irvingism to Mormonism. One of the Members of the former Body left it, and brought with him to the then nascent Mormonism several Tenets and points of organization which he had learnt amongst his first friends.—Compare *English Review*, xxviii., pp. 262, &c.

amongst these people contemporaneously with the claim made to them by Irvingites in England. Calamy describes the tongues in their case as "syllabical with a distinct heave and breathe between each syllable; but it required attention to distinguish the words."[1] Next we have a system of Priesthood founded upon the Old Testament, the Melchizedechian and the Aaronic, accompanying the outburst of the spirit of prophecy. The earlier converts "saw visions and prophesied, devils were cast out, and the sick healed by the laying on of hands." This reminds us irresistibly of the original claim to miracles made by Irving and his followers. Besides ordinary prophesying, a set day was appointed for the descent of the Holy Spirit, the account of which as given by Dr. Caswall[2] reads like a travesty upon some of the early Irvingite Ceremonies.

Mormons have a large hierarchy. There are the Twelve Apostles, who however were always subordinated to the "Prophet," besides bodies of Seventy Elders called "the Seventies," Bishops, Priests, and Deacons. Again, we find stronger views of the Incarnation prevailing, carried indeed in Mormonism so far as to end in a pronounced anthropomorphism,[3] which is

[1] Blunt's *Dictionary of Sects* (Irvingism).
[2] *Prophet of the Nineteenth Century*, p. 124.
[3] "The true God exists in time and space, and has as much relation to them as man or any other being. He has extension, form, dimension, as well as man,—has body, parts, and passions; can eat, drink, talk, &c., as well as man,—is like man in form, and features, and size; even the wicked have seen Him, when on earth as one of their own species (!) The Father is wholly material; He cannot be in two places at once; all spirits are material; the Holy Ghost is very similar to Spirit of Father and Son,

of course in strong contrast with the orthodoxy of the Catholic Apostolic Church. Great stress is laid upon Baptism,—the Baptism by fire is found in a prominent place,—the sick are anointed with oil, and there is a grand ceremonial.

But the chief point in Mormonism which here comes under notice is the prophetical spirit which is at the very foundation of it. In fact, there was a meeting of three religious currents at the opening of the present century, viz., first, the tendency to look for a new outpouring of the Holy Spirit upon the minds of chosen individuals, apart from the traditionary Indwelling of the Holy Ghost in the Catholic Church; secondly, the yearning for a more perfectly realized continuance of the Incarnation by means of complete Church machinery and worship; and thirdly, a tendency to expect immediately the Second Coming of our Lord Jesus Christ. At present we are concerned with the former of these three; and Mormonism, with the rapid spread of her Doctrines amongst the lower orders here and in America, affords a strong example of a claim to special gifts of prophecy.

Many other instances of this claim have presented themselves during the progress of the present century.

First, Plymouth Brethren believe that the Holy Spirit speaks often amongst them. Perhaps their chief peculiarity, though they share this with Quakers, is, that they have no separate Ministry, but that every " brother " and " sister " may prophesy or preach whenever he or she is

but this (*sic*) is Omnipresent by existing in inexhaustible quantities."— *Ecclesiastic*, Oct. 1850, p. 196.

moved by the Spirit so to do. This Sect also arose about the same time as Irvingism. Almost simultaneously in 1830 at Dublin and Plymouth, some people met together and called themselves " The Brethren," for the addition of " Plymouth " to their name has not been made by themselves, but by the outside world. As in the case of many sectarians, they began operations without the intention of separating from the Church. Their chief founders were a clergyman who had been a barrister, named Darby, from whom they have received the appellation " Darbyites," and a Fellow of Exeter College of the name of Newton. Mr. Darby gave up his ministrations in the Church of Ireland, and having established in Dublin a small Sect under the name of Separatists, came to England, and preaching in several places, organized small societies at Plymouth, Bristol, and elsewhere. The large Orphan Asylum on Ashley Down, near Bristol, owes its origin to Messrs. Craik and Müller who belonged to this persuasion.

Plymouth Brethren have a strong Calvinistic leaven, and enter into speculations often divergent, about the Second Coming of our Lord. In their own phraseology, they are " the Assembly of God," not meeting together by human will, but "gathered to Jesus by the Holy Ghost." Accordingly, they imagine that no human Ministry is necessary, but that they can meet together under directly Divine Presidency, in fulfilment of the promise, " Where two or three meet together in My Name, there am I in the midst of them." The natural sequel of this Doctrine is, that inspiration is capable of being extended to each individual. So that Plymouth Brethren present another instance of the special claim of the Prophetic Spirit made by religionists in this century. They call their system that of the "many-men Ministry," in contradistinction to the "one-man Ministry," which they hold to be characteristic of ordinary congregations.

The same period—so pregnant was it with wild religious movement—saw the rise of another Sect of more extravagant fanaticism. In 1832, Henry James Prince, then a young man of twenty-one years of age, was Home Surgeon to the General Hospital at Bath. Wishing to change his profession, he made an unsuccessful attempt to gain admission at Durham University. After this he went to Lampeter College in March, 1836, and whilst a student there organized a band who went by the name of the "Lampeter Brethren." On leaving Lampeter in 1840, he married an old Roman Catholic lady, and was ordained to the curacy of Charlinch near Bridgewater. Here he gradually adopted the notion that the Holy Spirit had taken entire possession of him, "so as to unite him to Himself." His Rector, Samuel Starkey, became a convert to his views, and when Mr. Prince's wife died, the latter married a sister of Mr. Starkey. Revival meetings were held with great excitement amongst women and children. Prince called himself "The Holy Ghost personified."

These proceedings were brought before the Bishop, and Prince's license was revoked. He then moved to Ipswich and proceeded to form a Sect, being joined by six ladies named Nottidge, and possessed each of a nice little independence. He did not however stay long here, but shifted his quarters to Brighton, and in 1845 to Weymouth. Here he made some converts in the neighbourhood; but in 1847, finding the place too hot for him, he set up a permanent home at Spaxton, called "the Agapemone," or the abode of Love. Some of his own associates at Lampeter joined him, together with Starkey, and some other former clergymen of the Church of England. They lived in much luxury, and at the Great Exhibition in 1851, the former "Evangelical Curate of Charlinch was to be seen driving about Hyde Park in a carriage and four, preceded by hatless outriders, the latter riding uncovered because they were in attendance upon 'the Lord' in the person of Prince."[1] It is not necessary here to repeat the extravagances which this Sect of "Princeites" or "Agapemonites" have successively adopted. Prince is said to have gone even further, to a new Incarnation. Prayer was at one time abolished, "because it would be interfering with the sufficiency of God to save." What has been told of him, viz., that he asserted that he was the personification of the Holy Spirit,—though not without the precedents of the Amalricians in the twelfth century, and the Wilhelmians of the thirteenth,—shows the culminating point of fanatical extravagance, to say the least, which the arrogation of spiritual gifts has reached in the present century. Human presumption could hardly go further. There ought to be some broad lines of demarcation to separate such fanaticism from the legitimate exercise of spiritual gifts.

[1] Blunt's *Dictionary of Sects*.

But the roll of those who have laid claim to an extraordinary Heavenly favour in this century would not be complete, if we omitted various eccentric individuals, and oddities, who have pretended to receive direct communications from above, or to be sent upon special and definite missions, or, as some females have fancied, to be the chosen Bride of our Lord. The strange doings of Mrs. Girling and her followers show, that these spiritual imaginations have not yet ceased to assume novel forms of exhibition.

Having now completed our survey, the first conclusion that strikes us, upon an impartial view of the cases presented, is, that it is impossible that they can be all genuine outpourings of the Holy Spirit. The excesses in some cases, and the varying witness borne, prove to demonstration, that they cannot all proceed from the " One and the self-same Spirit."

This point being settled, for it requires no further comment, the question ensues, how we are to distinguish between genuine and spurious prophecies.

Now the prophetical periods of the Old and New Testaments supply us with materials for estimating the credentials of Prophets. The only firm ground, therefore, is found by drawing from these two sources canons of universal criticism, features which were exhibited in the prophets calling for acceptance of their prophecies by those to whom they severally prophesied. We shall then be in a position to judge whether all or any of these Sects, which have been mentioned as advancing claims, may be admitted as true Prophets, and especially, we shall be furnished with tests to put to the Prophets of the Body under consideration.

Moses may for our purpose be regarded as the first, as he was, excepting of course our Lord Jesus Christ, the most remarkable, of the Prophets. For Abraham, Isaac, and Jacob, though they possessed the characteristics of converse with Divine Beings, which is the peculiarity of the highest class of Prophets, and of becoming the media of prophecies, were Prophets only to themselves and to their own families. And the records of Noah and Enoch are too curt and indistinct for us to gather any precedents for successors in the prophetical line. The account of Moses on the other hand, as detailed by himself, is singularly copious and complete. The salient points in his history are the following :—

Having been marvellously saved from death, he was brought up in the highest school of education then existing, and became "learned in all the wisdom of the Egyptians," and developed great literary and practical talents. Expelled from Egypt, he passed many years in seclusion, which, as we may reasonably infer, were spent in holy and studious pursuits, by means of which he added to his knowledge, followed out deep investigations and matured plans for the government of Israel, should the reins be ever placed in his hands. At length the moment arrived, and the Lord Himself, not one of the inferior Beings of the spiritual world, "appeared" to him. Not that Moses saw the Lord, who has been always taken for the Second Person in the Ever-Blessed Trinity drawing near to men in anticipation of the Incarnation, yet there were visible signs of His Presence and the sound of His Voice.

As soon as Moses received the command to go to the children of Israel, his first reply was, "But, behold, they will not believe me, nor hearken unto my voice: for they will say, The Lord hath not appeared to thee." What then were the credentials with which he was armed, in order to win and force confidence in his mission and compliance with his orders? Miracle following upon miracle, an ascending series of wonders and judgments; for to suit the circumstances of the case, the miracles performed took the nature of judgment rather than of mercy, or, except in the first miracle, of mere marvel.

Not however that Moses was insensible to the value of another kind of proof. When giving directions about putting false Prophets to death, he replies to the question, "If thou shalt say in thine heart, How shall we know the word which the Lord hath not spoken?"—"When a Prophet speaketh in the name of the Lord, if the thing follow not, nor come to pass, that is, the thing which the Lord hath not spoken, but the Prophet hath spoken it presumptuously; thou shalt not be afraid of him." So that we have here a second credential, the fulfilment of the prophecy given. This credential was employed by Almighty God to produce faith in Moses: "This shall be a token unto thee, that I have sent thee: When thou hast brought forth the people out of Egypt, ye shall serve God on this mountain." And Moses could appeal to this credential as the miracles proceeded, because he foretold several of them to Pharaoh.

The spirit of prophecy was also poured out more widely than usual in the days of Moses, as is shown by the Seventy Elders who were enlightened by the Spirit of the Lord so that they might help Moses in governing the people, and " prophesied."[1] But they formed part of the Mosaic economy, they were introduced and accredited by Moses. Therefore they did not come forth by themselves, depending for acceptance upon proof which they supplied. They were fathered by Moses, and could refer to him for credentials. They could rest therefore upon the external signs of prophesying which Eldad and Medad, for example, exhibited, but which were easily simulated by false Prophets.

After the age of Moses, prophecy appears to have been almost silent. The very name of a Prophet did not exist in the ordinary language of the day. Should the heavenly inspiration light for a moment upon any one, or should he be held to possess greater powers of apprehension and judgment than other men, he was called a Seer.[2] " In those days the word of the Lord was precious, there was no open vision."

But a new era opened with Samuel. From a child he enjoyed the incalculable honour of living near to God and of being the medium of Divine utterance. When he grew up, besides prophesying himself, he took measures for keeping up a Body of educated and official Prophets. He established the Schools of the Prophets

---

[1] Numbers xi.   [2] ראה, not נביא.

in various places, where men could be trained for the purposes of prophecy. Of these there appear to have been five or six. Their stations respectively were at Ramah, Bethel, Jericho, Gilgal, perhaps Gibeah, and afterwards Jerusalem. The pupils were called "the Sons of the Prophets;" and they reached the number—occasionally at least, if not always—of several hundreds. For on one occasion Ahab collected 400, independently, as it appears, of those who belonged to the Kingdom of Judah, where there was a College certainly in later times at Jerusalem. About the same time, Obadiah "hid a hundred of them by fifty in a cave, and fed them with bread and water." This was in troublous days.

The chief Prophet of the age seems to have presided over them. Elijah held this office: and before his miraculous ascent into heaven, he anointed Elisha as the "High-Prophet," if he may be so called, in his own stead. In these Schools a regular course of instruction was given, which embraced the following subjects:— music, which formed an important element in public worship, and was closely connected with prophesying —both of which truths are exemplified in the life and career of David; the composition of lyrical poetry, which constitutes the staple of the greater part of the prophetical portion of the Old Testament, amongst which must be ranked the productions of David and Solomon; and finally the laws and institutions of Moses.[1]

---

[1] I must express my obligations to the Ven. Archdeacon Lee on *The Inspiration of Holy Scripture*, pp. 158—167, a work full of learned information.

It is clear therefore, that for our purpose these Prophets must in the main be taken in the lump, not singly and individually. The effusion of the Prophetical Spirit once proved, it was a vast deal easier for any single Prophet to show that he belonged to the band. And it follows that the sixteen Prophets, whose prophecies have descended to us, did not stand alone. For besides them, we hear of Samuel, Gad, Nathan, Ahijah, the Prophet who warned Jeroboam, the old Prophet who dwelt at Bethel, Elijah, Elisha, the Prophet who came to Ahab, Micaiah, the Prophet sent to Amaziah, Oded, Baruch, and others. We are told also of Bodies of Prophets, and of Prophetesses. There was evidently an unbroken series, reaching beyond the return from Captivity.

Therefore to estimate the nature of their credentials, we must take a few eminent specimens. Samuel at the beginning, Elijah and Elisha at a period of general scepticism, Amos not a trained Prophet, Isaiah at a critical point of danger, Ezekiel in a foreign land, Daniel and his fellows amidst unbelievers, will supply us with satisfactory evidence of the nature of a Prophet's credentials. Now in all these instances, besides the internal evidence of coincidence with the course of Divine Revelation, conspicuous purity of thought, and remarkable strength as evinced in the prophecies so far as we are in possession of them, we find also a contemporaneous fulfilment of certain predictions, and events at least partaking of the miraculous, and generally issuing in judgment.

Thus Samuel is introduced with a prophecy of the

fate impending over Eli and his sons, which was soon fulfilled. He afterwards promised success to the Children of Israel against the Philistines at Mizpeh, and accordingly a signal victory with lasting consequences ensued. After the Kingdom was substituted for a Theocracy, he brought down by his prayers, as he foretold, thunder and rain in representation of the judgments of the Lord. He anointed Saul and David, and they were afterwards duly appointed kings. The pregnant words of the brief record lead to the conclusion, that he presented more credentials of his mission than have been recorded in detail.[1]

Elijah, besides privately raising the child of the widow of Zarephath, publicly proved himself to be a true Prophet by bringing down fire from heaven. After this he prophesied a heavy fall of rain after the long drought, that Hazael and Jehu should succeed to the Kingdoms of Syria and Israel respectively and Elisha to the post of chief Prophet, that Ahab should win victories over Benhadad, that dogs should suck the blood of Ahab in Naboth's portion, and his own death.

Elisha performed various smaller miracles, cured Naaman, raised the Shunammite's son, and posthumously an Israelite. He foretold the birth of the Shunammite's child, the wicked intention of Jehoram, the deliverance of Samaria, an approaching famine, the succession of Hazael, and of Jehu, besides victories, and defeats.

The instances of Elijah and Elisha deserve the more attention, because they vindicated their claims against

---

[1] 1 Sam. iii. 20, 21.

scepticism, and cannot be said to have inherited an ascertained and trusted position.

The case of Amos demands enquiry, because he was not brought up as one of the accredited race of Prophets. But to go to the other extreme, and to place him on a par with a man who had to win his acceptance with no precedents or no contemporaries, would be equally untrue to the real circumstances. Amos made his appearance as an alien to the prophetical Body; but that Body was in active existence, and afforded therefore strong moral support to a true claimant. But special credentials were essential. Accordingly, Amos foretold the earthquake two years before, and appealed to this prediction verified by fact for the proof of his mission.[1] He also issued a judgment against Amaziah, the slanderous priest of Bethel, which affords an instance of a fulfilled prediction, and in some sense of a miraculous judgment.

At a critical time Isaiah found it necessary to inspire confidence by a sign, which combined judgment and prediction. The birth of a child, and the deaths of two kings, were surely enough to establish his credit. Yet afterwards he foretold the deliverance of Jerusalem from the investment by Rabshakeh by means of the utter destruction of Sennacherib's host, and by the subsequent death of the Assyrian monarch. He also predicted Hezekiah's recovery from a dangerous illness.

Ezekiel, prophesying to the Jews in Captivity, required also credentials, besides the commanding weight and the moral strength of his prophecies. His prediction of the

[1] Amos ii. 14—16, i. 1 ; Zech. xiv. 5.

siege of Jerusalem with such extraordinary circumstance, and of the destruction of Tyre by Nebuchadnezzar; the judgment pronounced by him against himself in the sudden death of his wife, and against Jerusalem, were supernatural accompaniments of his words, which forced them upon the acceptance of all who were not bereft of spiritual understanding.

The instances of Daniel and the Three Children are more germane to our enquiry, because the scene of their action lay where an appeal to prophetical precedents was impossible. Accordingly, the miraculous deliverance of Shadrach, Meshach, and Abednego from the flames in the sight of all the people, the predictive interpretation of Nebuchadnezzar's dream, and of the writing on the wall, both of which were verified by immediate fulfilment, and the wonderful preservation of Daniel from the lions, supplied credentials which could not be gainsaid by reasonable people.

No reliance can be placed upon Jonah's case, which at first sight seems fit to be cited. And for this reason. The book is evidently a brief account of events, and Jonah's own preaching is given only in the curt summary, "Yet forty days and Nineveh shall be overthrown." What were the arguments which he employed, and what was his method of persuasion, we are not told; yet a miraculous deliverance preceded his preaching, and we can hardly imagine that he did not make use of it, to help him to influence the inhabitants of Nineveh.

The rest of the Prophets, if we may except Jeremiah,

Daniel, Jonah, and the Prophets generally. 215

who threw his ægis of miraculous [1] judgment and verified predictions over the others, were found amongst the accredited band, who contributed grounds of belief, so to speak, to a common fund.

A few words are now necessary to gather up the inference.

The chief source of persuasion lay in the testimony delivered. Had it the water-mark of Heaven? Was it consonant with ascertained Revelation, pure, holy, truthful, consistent, full of moral weight both in itself and in the mode of delivery? If so, it possessed the main essentials for winning its way. But besides this, in order that there might be no mistake, in order that belief might rest, not upon the sands of human opinion, but upon the rock of God's Truth, fulfilled predictions and miracles, often wrought in judgment, were invariably vouchsafed. For Prophets must be taken in the lump, not in individual isolation.

We now pass on to the New Testament. And here we must observe, that inasmuch as prophecy had ceased during a period of some 400 years, stronger evidence was plainly required of the reality of the outbreak, than if the prophetical spirit had continued in action from some acknowledged origin. Although Samuel is spoken of as the first of the Prophets, yet supernatural manifestations

---

[1] Predictions of the fate of Shallum, Jehoiakim, Coniah, and Zedekiah; of Pharaoh-hophra; of the Babylonish Captivity, and the complicated miseries which preceded and characterized the desolation of Jerusalem. Jer. xxii. 11, 12, 18, 19, 24—30, xxxiv. 2—5; 2 Chron. xxxvi. 20; 2 Kings xxv.; Jer. xix. 6, 7, lii. 11, xliv. 30, xiv. 1—12, xxi. 8—10, xix. 6, 7.

had never entirely ceased after the time of Moses. Joshua, Deborah, Gideon, Manoah, Samson, and others, handed on the tradition of heavenly intercourse. The change in Samuel's time, and by Samuel's institutions, was from the Roeh to the Nabi—from the Seer who received impressions from outside and communicated what he saw and heard, to the Prophet who became the vehicle of Divine inspiration, and by means of his natural organs uttered what the Holy Spirit prompted.

We should err, too, if we were to restrict the field of prophecy to foretelling events. Verified predictions are a clear and convincing method of establishing the character of a Prophet: but they form only a portion, and that not the most important portion, of a Prophet's province. The Prophet deals with the supernatural, and declares it. Past, present, and future come beneath his survey. Spiritual mysteries,—important truths about Almighty God and Heaven,—weighty verities respecting human nature and life,—form the region of his intuition, and the topics of the revelation conveyed by him. Faith, which remains as our inheritance bequeathed from times strictly prophetical, is the "evidence of things not seen," as well as "the substance of things hoped for."

John the Baptist laid no claim to prophecy. In ringing tones he bid people repent and believe on Him Who should come after him, declaring himself to be not a Prophet, but only a Voice. What credentials then did our Lord present?

He appealed first to the Old Testament Scriptures,

Our Lord's Credentials.

and to John the Baptist, and then to His miracles and verified predictions. After His first miracle in Cana, "His disciples believed on Him." At His first passover, "many believed in His name when they saw the miracles which He did." Nicodemus acknowledges that He was "a Teacher sent from God," because no one could do the miracles which He did without God being with him. Of Himself He said at a later period, about the end of the great Galilean year [1] of His Ministry, "The blind receive their sight, and the lame walk, the lepers are cleansed, and the deaf hear, the dead are raised up, and the poor have the gospel preached to them." And probably soon after, "The works that I do bear witness of Me, that the Father hath sent Me." Indeed no one can possibly deny that the truth of our Lord's Mission as a Prophet was not amply proved by His miracles, unless he denies the facts of the miracles as miracles.

Of verified predictions He gave not a few. At His first passover in His Ministry, He offered the sign of His Death and Resurrection. He repeated this prophecy afterwards as "the sign of the prophet Jonas." Probably not less than nine times as recorded, He foretold His Passion and Resurrection to His disciples. He announced a

[1] I say this advisedly. It is to me a matter of wonder how in the face of the internal evidence, the Cambridge School of interpreters of the facts of our Lord's Life should restrict our Lord's Galilean Ministry to less than a year, or even, as the learned Bishop of Gloucester and Bristol does, to a few weeks (*Hulsean Lectures*). The proof to the contrary is too long to give here. The Galilean Ministry with its wonderful success was, judging outwardly, the grand feature in our Lord's earthly career. The records of the Gospel are confessedly short (St. John xxi. 25). How for example can we conceive our Lord pronouncing woe against Chorazin, Bethsaida, and Capernaum, for not believing in three weeks?

distinct fact taking place at a distance to the Capernaite nobleman. He used words which were tantamount to a prediction of the resurrection of Jairus' daughter. His prophecy of the rising of Lazarus was clear and plain. He sent forth the Twelve and the Seventy with implied predictions, which were justified by their success. He foretold the miraculous draught of fishes on two occasions, the discovery of the stater in the fish's mouth, the finding of the ass, the fall of St. Peter, and the treachery of Judas. The prophecies which He delivered about events of a later period need not be enumerated here.

From our Lord's time, Prophets continued, as we have seen, in unbroken succession, till after the echo of the Apostles' footsteps had died away. They were therefore introduced by our Lord: and their greatest credentials were derived from Him. The chief proof required was that what they prophesied was a part of His Revelation, and that they themselves were really of His Company. St. John gives a test which was to be applied to each of those who claimed the gift. " Believe not every spirit, but try the spirits whether they are of God: because many false prophets are gone out into the world. Hereby know ye the Spirit of God: Every spirit that confesseth that Jesus Christ is come in the flesh is of God: and every spirit that confesseth not that Jesus Christ is come in the flesh is not of God: and this is that spirit of antichrist, whereof ye have heard that it should come; and even now already is it in the world." This test may have been given by the Apostle with two intentions, either that it should have only a temporary application, or that it should be an universal rule for trying spirits till the end of the present dispensation.

If the words be taken only in their bare literalness, the test might nevertheless be efficacious in those early days, when faith and unbelief were separated by broad lines of demarcation. But in later times, when belief and unbelief are combined together in a thousand ways, a hard and fast rule of curt significance could hardly baffle the forces of evil. If therefore we are to understand the Apostle's formula to bear a perpetual application, we must receive it in a meaning as pregnant as the ways of evil are manifold and mutable. What is that meaning? Evidently a belief in the Doctrine of the Incarnation. But then, the Doctrine of the Incarnation includes all that is involved in the coming of our Lord in the Flesh,—the Revelation which He made, and the means for the salvation of mankind which He established. Accordingly, we enumerate in this short formula, by successive steps, each necessitated by the previous step, the entire circle of Doctrine which has been handed down in the Church by writings, and especially in the Holy Scriptures, and by continuous life. So that the first test to put to a claimant or claimants to the Gift of Prophecy, is whether the utterances put forward as prophecies are consonant with Catholic Truth; whether the profession of belief, verbally and practically, coincides with "the Faith once for all delivered to the saints."

But the early Christian Prophets appealed to more

witness than this. First observe that to all intents and purposes, except that they did not seek any individual exaltation or separate position, the Apostles were Prophets. They had seen the Lord, they were inspired, they declared a Revelation. First then, they all witnessed to the great miracle of the Resurrection, a fact which is especially apposite to them, because their great object was to testify not to themselves, but to the Lord. Next, the miracles of healing the impotent man, of working signs and wonders, of the judgments against Ananias and Sapphira, besides the detection of them, of raising Dorcas and Eutychus, as well as other miracles, brought a powerful testimony to the action of the prophetic Spirit. Besides this, the wonderful descent of the Holy Spirit upon them on the Day of Pentecost, not, as so many of these pretenders to spiritual gifts have supposed, without sensible signs, but with a noise that was heard and fiery tongues that were seen, adds a vast weight of evidence. For this descent was attested not merely by the partakers of the gift, though here we have 120 witnesses instead of one—but by the miraculous consequences of it. People of various countries heard unlearned men speak in numerous languages which they had never before acquired.

Nor were there wanting verified predictions, though in the presence of the testimony from numerous miracles this class of evidence was not so much needed. Here again the prophecies of the Resurrection by our Lord must be especially included, inasmuch as all that the early Christian preachers wanted, was to induce people to believe in Him. His credit once established, theirs would follow, if they ever thought of it. But the prophecies of the deaths of Ananias and Sapphira, those by Agabus of the famine, and of St. Paul's imprisonment, and the one to St. Paul of his being taken to Rome, and several others which were verified in the fulfilment, proved the soundness of the claims of these people to be Prophets.

The examination therefore of the instances of undoubted Prophets as recorded in the Old and New Testaments affords these results. For the credentials of any one Prophet, or set or race of Prophets, who appeal to us for acceptance, we must demand three kinds of testimony, viz., the coincidence of the prophecies delivered with the Faith already revealed, miracles betokening the movement of supernatural inspiration, and predictions verified by the event. For if the first of these were wanting, it might be inferred that Almighty God was the Author of confusion and inconsistency; if there were no miracles, the force exerted would fall short of being supernatural; and if no verified predictions could be produced, the sphere would be only ordinary human.

It is evident at first sight that these characteristics place a large gulf between the real Prophets of the Old and New Testament and their legitimate successors of the first age of the Church on the one side, and on the other the persons put forward as Prophets in the various Sects which have been briefly enumerated. But to enter into any minute examination of the several claims which they advance, is beyond the scope of this treatise, and would be considered unnecessary by the majority of the readers of these pages. It remains now to weigh all that can be brought forward of importance in favour of Irvingite Prophets. Do they belong to the votaries of the Sects condemned? Or are they to be considered as standing upon real and strong grounds when they say that the Lord has indeed spoken by them?

CHAPTER VII.

ARE THESE MEN PROPHETS?

THE enquiry upon which we are about to embark is unfortunately one which must inevitably cause pain to many, who honestly and conscientiously believe that our Lord Jesus Christ really declares His Will through these people who "prophesy" in His Sacred Name. Such people are in the habit of listening reverentially and submissively to what are to them Voices from God. Such an enquiry as this therefore naturally seems to them to be a rude profanation, and indeed to be more than perilously near to that sin against the Holy Ghost, which can never be forgiven.

But we must not obey one precept, or even a cluster of precepts, of Holy Scripture, and pay no regard to others. St. John tells us "to try the spirits whether they are of God." How indeed are false Prophets to be distinguished from true, unless they be subjected to a searching examination? If the Canons by which they are examined are those which Holy Scripture and the Church sanction and authorize, how can we go wrong, always supposing that reverence, moderation, candour, eagerness for truth, and readiness to follow God's Will, however it may be declared, govern our enquiries? While upon this subject it is my duty to shrink from no plainness of speech or of argument, or from a conclusion where such is found to be necessary, I am anxious to say nothing that may needlessly wound, or give offence. Discussion upon the action of God's Most Holy Spirit is one which eminently requires reverence, and caution, and keenness of apprehension, and prayer.

Before entering upon this enquiry, I may point out that the Prophets of the Body under consideration stand in favourable contrast to many that have been mentioned. They are under careful restriction, they are trained for their work, and vulgar inappropriateness is sedulously excluded. They are regularly ordained, and their very prophecies are subjected to a rigorous examination before they are duly received.

We may now go on to examine the credentials which they offer. The results of the last Chapter point out the line which our examination may best take. Accordingly the first question is, whether the prophecies delivered coincide with, or keep within the limits of, "the Faith once delivered to the saints."

Irvingites assert that they do, as a general body of prophetical teaching. All that contravenes the faith, or infringes upon its analogy, they lay aside as being only the production of the man, not the utterance of the Holy Spirit. They point to the manner in which they have revived much Catholic Truth and custom, to their careful maintenance of the Creeds, to the holiness of life inculcated by them, and then infer that such good effects as these could not have been produced by an inexcusable pretension to sacred gifts, or a profane playing with holy things, or blasphemous imposition. The general tendency and character of these spiritual gifts has been far too good to admit of their having been anything else than Divine. If, say they, people instead of arguing would come in a teachable spirit—the spirit of little children which our Lord described so tenderly and sweetly— and thus examine the real phenomenon for themselves, they would see how holy a matter is thus being rudely handled. This is a subject of faith, not at all fit for public, and perhaps heedless, certainly unprofitable, discussion.

Yet, as we have seen, faith in these matters is not made to depend upon impalpable distinctions. We are not expected to put our intellects, so to speak, into our pockets, by Him who gave them to us as most valuable possessions. It was never intended that the way of faith should be made unreasonable, and that its difficulties should be thereby grievously enhanced ; that intelligence should be taken out of the scale of religion, and transferred into the balance of the world. There must be some sure handposts, definitely decipherable, to point out our road when gloom settles over our paths.

So too with respect to the first part of this argument. We may readily allow much that Irvingites advance, and we do so gladly, because it amounts to a clear mitigation of sentence. If there is reason to conclude that they have erred, many doubtless, we may trust that a large majority at the very least, have made the mistake in honesty and sincerity. How far this is so, and how far it is not, an unerring Judgment will decide. We are concerned only with the question,—Do these Prophets speak from God, or have they spoken of themselves?

> Dine hunc ardorem mentibus addunt,
> . . . . an sua cuique Deus fit dira cupido?
> Does God indeed Himself impart
> Such glowing ardour to the heart,
> Or passion surging past control
> Seem all Divine to each one's soul?[1]

The real question therefore with respect to the first Canon is not whether a great part, or indeed by far the greater part of these prophecies, is true to the standard of the Catholic Faith, but whether they all are, that is, all which have been stamped with the seal of the Community's approval. A small amount of error is quite consonant with human excellence, but none can be admitted into Divine utterance. When therefore Dr. McNeile inferred from Mr. Taplin's faulty reading of the Word of God that it could not be the Holy Spirit that read through that human channel, his argument and conclusion were sound and unimpeachable, as relating, that is, to that single utterance. Accordingly, if we find that in any important particulars these prophecies — confining ourselves to those which are acknowledged—offend against the Catholic Faith, we are not only justified in condemning them,—we are

---

[1] *Virg. Æn.*, ix. 184. The English Version is altered from Conington's Translation to suit the dignity of the present subject.

imperatively called upon by our reverence to the Faith to condemn them.

What then can be said, in the first place, of their appointing an order of Apostles, which has not only not been sanctioned, but, as has been shewn, has been excluded, by the teaching of the Catholic Church? The balance of evidence from Holy Scripture has been proved to be against such a theory, as has been propounded by these so-called Prophets. And the witness of the Church, both negative and positive, has been shewn to be unanswerably destructive to its validity; so that, if the Apostles say, that whatever may be the difficulties in the way of our acceptance, we are nevertheless Apostles, because God has declared us to be such through the voice of the Prophets, the answer is evident. Such a supposition is impossible.

> μόνου γάρ αὐτοῦ χὠ Θεὸς στερίσκεται,
> ἀγένητά ποιεῖν ἄσσ' ἂν ᾖ πεπραγμένα.[1]
> One thing alone e'en God Himself can't do,
> To make what's done undone.

It is no curtailment of the power or privileges of Almighty God, but rather a tribute to His inalienable perfections, to say that no inconsistency is possible with Him, whether of word or action. He has "no variableness," nor even "a shadow of turning." Inasmuch therefore as He has declared by the Voice of His Church, implicitly perhaps but unmistakably, that the theory of Apostles as here put out is alien to the "Faith once delivered to the saints," it is evident that those

[1] Agathon in *Aristot. Eth. Nic.*, vi. 2.

who profess to put it forth in His Name cannot be moved or authorized by Him. It is not here denied, that He might send Apostles or Prophets or any other special emissaries whom He might choose. To dogmatize about the future would be presumptuous : we know not what is in the womb of time, or what God may hereafter do; and we should be ready to submit to any regulations or institutions that are really His. Our question now is solely about the theory before us of Apostles and a Fourfold Ministry as essential to the integrity of the Church, with the various details which have been before unfolded. Upon these, the verdict of our first Canon is clear. They cannot be of God; and these therefore must be spurious prophecies, and the deliverers of them cannot be true Prophets.

Have they then any powerful external testimony? Have we reason shewn us by miracles to accord to them our faith? Now the history of Irvingite miracles is remarkable.

At first it appears to have been taken for granted that miracles would naturally attend an outpouring of the Holy Spirit. At the opening of the history of this movement we find a claim advanced of the working of miracles. Margaret Macdonald, Mary Campbell, Elizabeth Fancourt, and others, recovered from illness in a manner which was certainly strange and astonishing. Other cures of the same sort abounded. Miracles in fact were claimed, and were advanced as a proof of the outburst of supernatural power in preparation for our Lord's Advent.

But as time has gone on, this appeal to miracles has been surrendered to such an extent, that we find now carefully-drawn arguments put forward to show that miracles are not necessary to prove the restoration of Apostles and Prophets. Thus in some Discourses delivered in the Catholic and Apostolic Church in Gordon Square, in the year 1856,[1] an elaborate argument is presented in proof of miracles not being required as evidence. In the first Discourse, which asserts that "miracles are not the ordinary credentials of God's Messengers, nor the proper credentials of Apostles in the Christian Church," stress is laid upon the instances of Enoch and Noah, though the Scripture accounts are too short to support any negative arguments. Old Testament miracles are slurred over: no notice is taken of the continuity of the race of Prophets: the great instance of our Lord Himself is utterly unnoticed: and the "signs and wonders" of St. Paul are professedly explained away. But what is most noticeable with reference to our present position is this: at least two Discourses, if the third is not to be included, are devoted to the proof that miracles are not needed as credentials of these new Teachers. What can be a greater proof of their surrender of the appeal to miracles?[2]

Which then are we to follow? The earlier or the later lessons of Irvingism? Are we to conclude that the credentials of these Prophets depend upon miracles,

[1] *On Miracles and Miraculous Powers, Three Discourses delivered in the Catholic and Apostolic Church, Gordon Square.* London: Bosworth and Harrison, &c., &c.

[2] This is now a stock argument with Irvingites in reply to objections.

or are supposed to be independent of such extraneous aid? At all events, there is a shifting of front here, which must weaken any confidence felt in these claims.

If then the allegation of miracles is surrendered, as it appears, beneath the light of increasing experience, these new Prophets fail to satisfy the requirements of our second Canon. They are not attested, as God has always attested His true Prophets, by "signs and wonders." Let there be no mistake here. According to the theory of these people an interval of silence in the prophetical utterance has occurred far exceeding any previous interval, unless it be that between Moses or Abraham and Noah. For 1,600 years, and perhaps more, Prophets, as they say, have ceased from the Church. Precedents tell us, that as in the cases of Moses and our Lord,—for Abraham was not a Prophet to the world generally, only to his own family,—upon a fresh outbreak of the Spirit of prophecy, miracles were abundantly vouchsafed. If then there are here no miracles, the analogy of God's dealings teaches us that there are no Prophets.

But for the purposes of candid judgment, we ought to examine also the miracles for which a claim has been advanced. They are, doubtless, not only unusual, but even astonishing events. Yet upon a close enquiry they are found to be lacking in at least two important features.

The miracles of Moses and of our Lord, of Samuel, of the Prophet who warned Jeroboam, and of Daniel and the others, also of the Apostles, were wrought publicly. The previous conditions of the case, the mode and evidence of the change, and the sequel, were notorious. All was above suspicion, mistake, or doubt. This was not the case with the miracles claimed by these people. The evidence of them rests only upon their own accounts. Now without imputing any intention to deceive, for which at least in the leading cases there seems to be no evidence, we may yet remark that such secrecy is not the case with God's actions. Pharaoh gave involuntary proof by letting the Children of Israel go. The Chief Priests and the Pharisees acknowledged our Lord's miracles, and afterwards "the notable miracle" of St. Peter and St. John. For reasons which are obvious, when Almighty God calls upon His people generally for faith in any manifestation, He addresses them openly by evidence of which all can judge.

But again, none of these so-called miracles are such as could not under peculiar circumstances be effected naturally, without the intervention of any supernatural power. The influence of the mind over the body, especially in diseases of the nerves, or of the spine, which is the source of the nerves, and more particularly in females, is almost inconceivable to those who have not examined it. Accordingly in religious revivals, or in other religious movements where the feelings are wrought up to a high pitch, the concentrated force of feeling and impulse within has been often turned upon a diseased part, and an undoubted and surprising change has been worked, but all by causes strictly natural. Wesley believed that he wrought miracles: so did the Mormons: and so have many other religious enthusiasts. Many, as Miss Fancourt did, have ascribed the power of recovery from disease to simple but powerful faith. But the history of similar religionists has shewn over and over again, that if the idea is conceived, as it was by Irving, that sickness is simply the result of sin, and can therefore be cured by faith, as time wears on, and the terrible force of disease is encountered day by day, this idea is surrendered, and comes to be regarded as an impracticable notion. The troubles of humanity, like the origin of evil, are mysterious, and cannot be explained by our limited powers of judgment. We must wait for the explanation till we pass from the region of dark vision, to where we shall "see face to face."

Of the power of the mind in effecting cures of either a temporary or a permanent nature, the following instances may serve as specimens. The first comes from my own experience: the others from a medical work of acknowledged authority.

Some years ago, a single lady, who had been confined to her bed for some months, was suddenly awakened in the middle of the night by three men coming into her bed-room, one of whom presented a pistol at her head. They demanded of her where her plate was kept, and after taking all that they could find of value in the house, and easily movable, went away. On the next morning, Miss C., instead of lying in bed, got up, and was busily engaged with the help of her friends in searching for traces of the robbery which might lead to the discovery of the guilty men. She continued to move about, and to all appearance had quite recovered her health. When the burglars were tried at the ensuing assizes, she went into court, and gave her evidence with remarkable clearness. Some time after the conviction and condemnation of the men, her health gradually declined, she took again to her bed, and in about a year afterwards she died.

This instance is remarkable, because the subsequent death of Miss C. shewed what her neighbours doubted at the time, that she was really ill when the burglars entered her house. Also because her cure, though it proved to be of temporary duration, was nevertheless to all appearance quite complete at the time. As long as the excitement lasted, and her thoughts were taken off herself, she was in excellent health and spirits. She was at the time many years older than Mary Campbell, or Elizabeth Fancourt, or Margaret Macdonald.

"It is curious enough," says Sir Thomas Watson,[1] "to notice how the mind is apt to become affected in some of these cases. After the patient has been lying supine for some weeks, she *is* unable to stand or walk, simply because she *thinks* she is unable. The instant she makes a fair effort to use her limbs again, she can and does use them. Her condition is reversed. *Potest quia posse videtur.*

"Dr. Corfe, the present Apothecary to the Middlesex Hospital (1847), has no little trouble with patients of this kind; but he generally succeeds in *making* them walk, and in convincing them, as well as himself, that

[1] *Lectures on the Principles and Practice of Physic.* London : Longmans, Green, and Co. Fifth Edition, 1871, p. 725. Italics as in original.

they may do so with impunity. Sometimes, though ordinary authority may not be efficacious in this respect, some stronger influence prevails.

"A lady told me not very long ago, that an acquaintance of hers, a member of a family of distinction, had been lying I know not how long on her back; that position having been prescribed to her by some medical man for a presumed disease of the spine. She lost all power of using her legs; but she got quite fat, as indeed well she might, for her appetite was remarkably sharp, and she lived chiefly upon chicken; and the number of fowls she devoured was incredible. She lived at some little distance from town, and at last Sir Benjamin Brodie was sent for to her. Now Sir Benjamin, to use a vulgar phrase, is *up* to these cases; and he wished her to *try* to walk: but she declared the attempt to do so would kill her. But he was resolute however and had her got out of bed: and in a few days' time she was walking about quite well, and very grateful to him for his judgment and decision. A medical man of less name, or of less determination, would probably have failed.

"Dr. Bright has a good example of a somewhat similar kind, shewing the power of another form of influence. He was asked to see a young lady who had been confined to her bed for nine months. If she attempted to move she was thrown into a paroxysm of agitation, and of excruciating agony, affecting more particularly the abdomen. She had almost lost the use of her lower limbs; and she and her friends seemed to have given up all hope of her restoration. But she presented no appearance of important disease; her countenance bore no marks of visceral mischief; nor was it possible to discover any proof of organic change. Dr. Bright set the case down in his own mind as one of hysteria. She was thought to have derived relief from some stimulating injection, and from certain pills. As her friends were in moderate circumstances, Dr. Bright talked seriously to the mother, and recommended that simple water should be employed for the injection, and that bread pills should be substituted for those the girl had been taking. The mother soon perceived that these means produced the same tranquillizing effects on her daughter which had hitherto been ascribed to the medicine. 'My visits,' he says, 'became less frequent; I was absent a fortnight; on my renewing my visits no change had taken place. I attempted to get her shifted gently from the bed to the sofa, but it was impossible; the paroxysms almost overcame her. Once (after having attended altogether about nine months) I called after an absence of nearly a month; her sister met me at the street door with a smiling face to tell me that our patient was quite well; and on enquiry she related how three mornings before, *under a deep religious impression*, she had completely recovered all her powers; and was sitting up and working and amusing herself as if she were completely convalescent from some ordinary illness.'"

Partly then from the nature of the cures asserted to have been wrought, and partly from the evidence of these people themselves, we may safely conclude that no invincible argument can be constructed in favour of these so-called Prophets from any miracles accompanying the outbreak of "prophecy."

Yet from the last chapter we see how the two, prophecy and miracles, at least in the beginning of a prophetical period, have ever gone hand in hand. And the reason is plain; both are supernatural. The Holy Spirit appearing amongst men and striving with men, shows forth His Power in "signs and wonders" which cannot be gainsayed. He does not make the effort of faith more difficult, than for the sake of men it need be. Faith does not rest upon an undefined basis, and is not intended to sink into credulity.

The third Canon still remains, viz., that the outpouring of prophecy is always proved by a contemporaneous fulfilment of predictions. Where shall we find these fulfilled predictions in the history of Irvingism? Shall we turn to the forty-five prophecies of Mr. Baxter, which are shewn in the *Church's Broken Unity* to have failed of being verified by the event? Shall we point to the numerous predictions of the end of the world, or the Coming of our Lord, which have been successively proved false? Shall we appeal to utterances received and acknowledged by the Community, in which the Twelvefold Unity of the Apostles was urged and promised? Or to the body of speeches, in consequence of which the Apostles were recalled from their evangelization in foreign lands?

But if we cannot find such predictions as shall offer us the evidence of a true foretelling of future events, will these people themselves supply us with such? We do not find references to such proofs in the speeches or writings, with which they seek to evangelize the world.

In the absence then of the production of such instances, and in the presence of various accepted "prophecies" which failed of fulfilment, we are justified in assuming, that these people cannot appeal to fulfilled predictions in support of their prophetical claims.

And finding that our three Canons are thus proved in negative, we cannot but conclude that there is no ground for supposing that these men are real Prophets. Accordingly, the only remaining prop to the Tenet of a Restored Apostolate is taken away, and the Tenet falls hopelessly to the ground.

This position may be still more strengthened by the following considerations :—

1. There is nothing in these so-called prophecies which is—not to say superhuman—eminent for originality, or force, or beauty. They are generally vapid, poor productions, suggesting the idea that they were delivered when the powers of the deliverer were weakened by some over-mastering excitement. They appear more like a distant echo of Old Testament prophecies, or passages from the old Prophets, so to speak, plentifully watered.[1]

---

[1] "I have heard some thousand so-called prophetic utterances, but (with two exceptions) they have contained nothing beyond the ability of any ordinary man to speak. They were largely composed of quotations from Scripture, and all else they contained has been better expressed from the pulpit. The two exceptions were poetical utterances, and although it is beyond the ability of ordinary men to extemporize poetry, the gift is not so rare as to require us to suppose that any other than human agency was concerned in it. The only thing remarkable about these utterances is the

Yet we are surely justified in inferring from the matchless force of the style of the Bible which has stood the criticism of centuries, that if the Holy Spirit really spoke, it would be with a grandeur and strength and beauty, which of themselves, setting aside the supernatural meaning, would enforce attention. After the death of Mr. Drummond, a critic placed side by side his terse and forcible sentences spoken in the House of Commons, and his utterances as a Prophet, and asked which of the two, laying aside the religious character of the latter, would generally be supposed to be the supernatural speech. Various prophetical utterances are to be found scattered through the first of these Volumes; which of these, I ask, or what other Irvingite utterance reported exactly as it was spoken, bears the stamp of Heavenly power?

2. Take again the Irvingite treatment of their own Prophets. First the Prophets were all supreme. Irving was forced to give way to them. By degrees they were brought under subjection. First Cardale and Drummond restrained them. Next they were almost *en masse* silenced at one fell swoop, when the Apostles returned from abroad. Then gradually they were all subdued, so that at the present day the Prophets are but a small power in the Community. What can be a greater sentence of condemnation, virtually passed by these people upon themselves? Experience has shown, that

unnatural way in which they are spoken."—*My Reasons for retiring from the Catholic Apostolic Church*, by H. M. Prior, 1873. (Printed for private distribution.)

cooler reasons must regulate proceedings, rather than the hot impetuosity of these excitable people delivering themselves in the seasons of their strongest excitement. Yet if the Holy Spirit really did speak, such wisdom would govern the utterance, that there would be no grounds for apprehending danger, but only reason for perfect obedience.

3. Again, the strange travesty of the events of the Day of Pentecost adds much to confirm suspicion. True, that the "Unknown Tongues" are now things of the past, and are no longer heard in Catholic Apostolic Churches. But this fact only proves the doubt with which they must be regarded by the Members themselves. For again, why should they be unknown tongues, instead of any of such languages as are spoken and understood? The account of the great Day of Pentecost shews that the languages then miraculously taught were those which were in use by the people who came to the feast. "We do hear them speak in our tongues the wonderful works of God." The plural is used of the Apostles' speech,—other tongues, not another tongue. Fourteen different languages are enumerated,[1] or at least variations in dialect. The force of the miracle would be lost, if what the Apostles said had been unintelligible to the various components of that large concourse of men.

And so the earliest Irvingites read the passage. The first utterance in tongues was supposed to be made

[1] *Church's Broken Unity* (Irvingism), p. 177, &c. ἑτέραις γλώσσαις not ἑτέρᾳ γλώσσῃ, Acts ii. 4. Cf. *Irenæus*, v. 6, 1; iii. 12, 1 (Migne).

in the language of some South Sea Island, and, as has been related, a collection of these utterances was reduced to writing, and was submitted to Dr. Pusey, Dr. Lee, and Sir G. Staunton. At Irving's trial in London before the Scotch Presbytery, the following answer was given :—

"*Question.* You have said that your gifts are different : in what respect do they differ ?

"*Answer.* We speak each a different tongue, and as in the Old Testament Prophets and among the Apostles there is found a diversity of style and character, owing to the medium of their own mind, through which the word passed, although they spoke by one Spirit ; so among our gifts there is the same kind of diversity.

"*Question.* How do you discover the difference between the tongues ?

"*Answer.* In the same manner as we discern the difference between French and Italian, the Turkish or Hindoostanee ; that is, by the ordinary method by which languages are distinguished."

But it is well known that no language has been found to correspond with these uncouth sounds. And accordingly when they were afterwards assailed, the mode of defence adopted implied that the tongues were unknown, and were intended to be and to remain unknown. The objects of them have been declared to be, to attract attention, and to speak to God. " He that speaketh in a tongue speaketh not to man but unto God : for no man heareth, but in the spirit he speaketh mysteries."[1] The

---

[1] 1 Cor. xiv. 2.

whole passage, they urge, implies that when the gift of tongues is used, not only the people are ignorant of the meaning, but the speaker himself often does not understand what he is saying.

The Irvingite interpretation of this passage in St. Paul's Epistle to the Corinthians has been already drawn out.[1] The close resemblance of their system of prophecy to St. Paul's direction in this chapter and in the twelfth of the same Epistle, constitutes what is perhaps the strongest part of their position.

But in the first place, let it be remembered, that even if it be shown that these people do copy this chapter exactly, it does not therefore follow that their Prophets are true Prophets. There was a spirit of prophecy abroad in the Church in St. Paul's days, and we know not whether it may appear some time hence. No one denies the possibility of an outpouring. There may be an animal with all the characteristics of a sea-serpent; but it does not therefore follow, that every creature seen to bear some resemblance to it is really a specimen of that far-famed kind of creature. The present is a question of Divine fact, not of human coincidence.

Secondly, it will be found that these people really misunderstand this important passage. That there were gifts of tongues at Corinth at the time when St. Paul wrote, and probably in other parts of the Church, is clear from his words. There was much evangelizing to be done then, and the calm action of those early Christians was wholly unequal to the strain laid upon it. Hence

[1] Vol. II. 1, § 7, p. 41, &c.

came the need of extraordinary gifts, and especially of gifts bestowed upon them as linguists. But if these gifts were generally granted, is it not likely, is it not certain, that they would be used in practice, in a previous sharpening of weapons and exercising the arms for combat?

That there was an irregular employment of them, is clear from the fact that St. Paul found it necessary to give laws and directions for their use. These Corinthian converts, in their natural exultation upon the possession of a new and remarkable gift, forgot the true end and object of it. Nor did they remember, that the gift of tongues did not necessarily ensure further gifts of interpretation and of prophecy; that, at least frequently, some gifts fell to the lot of some people, some to others.

Irvingites also strain some expressions. When it is said, "He that speaketh in a tongue edifieth himself," it is clear that the tongue cannot be unknown to the speaker, or he would enjoy no edification. "He that speaketh in a tongue edifieth himself. How," says St. Chrysostom, "unless he knows what he says?"[1] But if a Corinthian speak in a tongue before Corinthians, or a Roman in the midst of Romans, or an Alexandrian in an Alexandrian congregation, it is evident that the people present as a body could not understand the speaker, unless he or another interpreted, because the "tongue" was plainly different from the ordinary speech of the people present.

Again, in the passage "If I pray in a tongue,[2] my spirit prayeth, but my understanding is unfruitful," the

---

[1] *Op.* iii. 474. [2] ἐὰν προσεύχωμαι γλώσσῃ, 1 Cor. xiv. 14.

interpretation of the verse turns upon the meaning of the word "unfruitful" (ἄκαρπος). Does it relate to fruitfulness to the individual, or rather to fruitfulness to others? Now immediately afterwards when the Apostle has added, "I will pray with the understanding also, . . . I will sing with the understanding also," he gives as a reason,—"because (ἐπεὶ) if thou blessest with the spirit, how shall he that filleth the place of a private man say Amen at thy giving of thanks, since he knows not what thou sayest? For thou indeed givest thanks well, but the other is not edified." So that it is clear that the Apostle's meaning is, that when any man prays in an unknown tongue, he may make a truly spiritual supplication himself, and realize fully the meaning of his prayer; else how shall it be a prayer at all, unless that may be called prayer which is reasonless, and a mere outreaching of feeling can be called spiritual? But his understanding is without bearing fruit to others, who cannot say Amen, since they know not what it is to which they attach their assent and co-operation. It seems plain therefore, since the latter is the strongest passage which can be quoted on the other side, that tongues are not supposed to be unknown to those who make use of them.

The specimens that we have received of these tongues are indeed little more than such gibberish as almost any one would have at command, if he were willing to indulge in it. Some expressions, like the *amamini, amaminor,* of Mr. Taplin, suggest the ordinary occupations of the utterer. Indeed, although there has been much controversy upon the subject, especially at the time when the practice of such utterances commenced, no words have been introduced to notice, which have been ever likely to contribute dignity to this portion of supposed spiritual utterances. It is therefore only what we should expect, when we find that these tongues have been given up, and that the increasing wisdom of later years has led to their disuse. But then this disuse adds to the witness against them.

There being then so many additional reasons why we should look with more than suspicion upon these prophesyings, are we not obliged to conclude with the utmost certainty, that there is nothing really extraordinary in them? The witness of antiquity, as St. Chrysostom and St. Augustine tell us,[1] is, that the extraordinary gifts of the Holy Spirit ceased soon after the age of the Apostles, but that His ordinary gifts remained. Accordingly prophesying has in such an ordinary sense been left behind.

Yet a deep insight into things spiritual, an unerring theological instinct grounded upon study and prayer, a keen tenderness of vision fostered by a holy life, are gifts which can hardly ever be overvalued by us. Such we should still earnestly covet. The root and substance remain, when the temporary development of a period in

[1] "Τῆς δυνάμεως ἐκείνης οὐδὲ ἴχνος ὑπολέλειπται." — Chrysost. *De Sacerdotio*, vi. 35. Also *De Vera Religione*, 25, tom. i. 763. "Primis temporibus cadebat super credentes Spiritus Sanctus, et loquebantur linguis quas non didicerant, quomodo Spiritus dabat eis pronuntiare. Signa erant tempori opportuna. Oportebat enim ita significari in omnibus linguis Spiritum Sanctum, quia Evangelium Dei per omnes linguas cursurum erat toto orbe terrarum. Significatum est illud et transiit." — August. in *Evangelum Presbyterum* (Evagrium), tom. iii. 868.

the Church which left nothing like itself, has passed away. God the Holy Ghost still animates, more or less powerfully, though in gentle and sober influence, the Temples which He sanctifies, both in the individual souls of the true Members of Christ, and in the Collective Body of the Lord. And so in reading treatises, which like the Apostolical Epistles were addressed, first to Churches of the time, and afterwards to the Universal Church of all ages, a serious question continually arises, whether passages are intended to bear an ephemeral or a perpetual application, — whether they concern only the immediate and primary recipients of the Apostle's words, or those who stand to him in a secondary position. Thus in the present case, whatever relates to extraordinary gifts must concern the Corinthians, and all that bears upon the ordinary gifts of the Holy Spirit which are permanent in their nature, and are left behind when those others are not bestowed, belongs to the Church of all times.

But an interesting question still remains for our consideration. How is it possible that powers merely human should simulate Divine gifts? People who have adopted the views of prophesying here combated, notwithstanding the objections—indeed the fatal objections —lying against them, are nevertheless unable to make up their minds to reject these so-called gifts, because they cannot conceive how they can be anything but Divine.

Such people really little know what human nature can do. For the question is now, not of cunning human nature, which of course all people admit to be capable of any amount of deceit or depravity. But here amongst the Prophets are earnest, straightforward persons, who, especially in a matter so sacred as this, would not for the world deceive their friends and neighbours. Can it be possible for such people unwittingly to be the means of deception?

This is a question which we should hardly suppose could meet with an affirmative answer. And yet a close examination of human nature compels us to say, that such a proceeding is not only quite possible, but, under certain circumstances, exceedingly probable.

For in the first place be it remembered, that these prophesyings—not to speak of the alleged prophesyings of people belonging to other Religious Denominations—confessedly cover not only a large area of utterances taken to be genuine, but also many which are admitted to be false. The latter class are allowed to be wholly human, a Divine claim being put forward only for the former. The exercise of a supreme authority is held to be necessary to distinguish between the two—to stamp the genuine as true coinage, and to cast away the worthless imitations. When so important an advance is made in the admission of an exclusively earthly authorship, more than half the space has really been traversed towards the ascription of the entire body to human origin. The line of demarcation between the human and Divine must be faint indeed, when there is so much difficulty in deciphering it.

But we must trace the internal movements in the

Prophets in order to discover whether it is possible that human nature by itself should be capable of such results.

1. Now few people, as I imagine, are aware of the power of *Concentrated Attention*. Dr. Hammond tells us[1] that a lady under his professional care "for intense nervous headaches, who is of a very impressionable organization, is able at will to produce a pain in any part of her body by steadily fixing her attention upon it. Even the mention," he adds, "in her presence of physical suffering experienced by other persons immediately results in her feeling similar pains to those described in corresponding parts of her own body." The latter feature in this case has frequent parallels. The thought of amputation or of severe suffering will produce corresponding twitches in the same places of the body of an auditor or thinker, if the nervous system in him or her is morbidly over-sensitive, notwithstanding the presence of good and sound sense. Similarly, though not so strikingly, "an observer gazing anxiously out to sea, or across a vast plain, will scarcely ever fail to see the object of which he is in search; an expectant watcher hears every moment the rumbling of wheels, the footstep, or the knock which announces the wished-for or dreaded arrival; and pains, tastes, odours, and even diseases, can frequently thus be originated."[2] It is a fact well known to members of the medical profession, that people who hypochondriacally imagine that they are afflicted

---

[1] *Spiritualism and allied Causes and Conditions of Nervous Derangement*, by William H. Hammond, M.D. London: H. K. Lewis, 1876, p. 27.
[2] Ibid.

with any malady, often end in getting it, even though they were absolutely free from it at first.

This strange power of the human mind over itself is indeed a subject of really awful consideration. The very look, features, and nature, are altered by the action of the inner being. When the internal forces are combined and directed with intense effort upon one focus, we see how much strength is placed by Almighty God under the control of each individual, how on the will depends virtually the construction of our eternal selves, how not only error, folly, and sin, but also health, sickness, and even death, hang upon the exercise of our mental powers.

"In his book on Hypnotism . . . . . Mr. Braid says, that on one occasion he requested four gentlemen to lay their arms upon a table with the palms of their hands upwards, each one to look at the palm of his hand for a few minutes, and at the same time, concentrating his attention on it, to wait for the result. In about five minutes the first, one of the present members of the Royal Academy, stated that he felt a sensation of great cold in the hands; another, who is a very talented author, said that for some time he thought nothing was going to happen, but at last a darting pricking sensation took place from the palm of the hand, as if electric sparks were being drawn from it; the third gentleman, lately mayor of a large borough, said that he felt a very uncomfortable sensation of heat come over his hand; the fourth, secretary to an important association, had become rigidly cataleptic, his arm being firmly fixed to the table.

"I am very sure," Dr. Hammond goes on to say, "with the great John Hunter, that it is impossible for any one to concentrate the attention on any part of the body, without having, as the result, a sensation of some kind originate therein."[1]

These facts, to which numerous others of the same class could easily be added, appear to establish the great power exercised by Concentrated Attention in evoking results imaginary in their origin, but real under continued development. For if results comparatively trifling are produced on the moment, days or months of attention habitually concentrated upon the same point would materially increase those results in an ascending ratio, as time went on, till the highest point was reached. But this consideration carries us on to a further degree, which will best come into investigation when we have added another factor to the agency under review.

2. This factor may perhaps be called *Constructive Objectivity*. There is a tendency in us to take parts of ourselves or some of our own words and actions, and to regard them as if they had some objective existence apart from our own origination or parentage. Many people, whose will is weak, talk as if much of their own nature, and indeed their own doings, were independent of themselves, and were prompted by motive force and governed by laws, over which they themselves had no control.

But we may go a step further. Many people are so desirous of alienating the parentage of their own

---

[1] *Hammond*, p. 29.

actions, that they seek to create some imaginary source of origination outside of their own will, reason, feelings, and passions. They toss up when no one else is concerned, or consult the *Sortes Virgilianæ* or some such suppositive oracle, or count the number of appearances of some chosen phenomenon, or cast the burden of choice upon some other person, or imaginary being or thing. That this tendency is legitimate when not carried out to such extravagances, but when it is guided wisely and calmly, and above all soberly, and is directed towards Almighty God, does not make it less noticeable, or less real and important. Instances of the exercise of it have been far too frequent and common, to need particular illustration here. Enough that this tendency is very common amongst people of a certain class, and that when it is combined with Concentrated Attention its power must be evidently great. It receives material support from several other assistants.

(*a*) Amongst these stands pre-eminently Weakness of Will. In the brain there are two remarkable portions. First what are called the Convolutions, in which part there are a number of beautiful cells, filled with grey matter. This is the region of the Will. Below it lie the Ganglionic Nerves, the seat in the brain of the emotions. In people whose power of self-control is predominant—strong-minded people, as they are commonly called—the grey matter is abundant. The contrary conditions are to be found in weak people, and the Ganglia follow suit. That is to say, they are highly developed in emotional people, and are contracted and feeble in the cold and calm-minded. The balance between these two parts is uneven in lunatics, the hysterical, and the impetuous, to the disadvantage of the higher and ruling province. Generally speaking, in these cases of excess, the grey matter is deficient.[1]

Now it will be found, I believe, that this latter is the usual condition of those people, who amongst Irvingites constitute the Prophets. They have strong emotions but weak wills. So much indeed their writers admit.[2] When then these people, with their strong emotions and feebler powers of self-control, are taught and induced as a Divine duty to construct objectivity, and to concentrate their attention determinedly and habitually upon a longed-for consummation, the desired result does not seem to be far off.

(*b*) They are assisted also by their faculty of imagination, which is usually strong in them, and by a desire for these supposed Spiritual Gifts, in inculcated obedience to St. Paul's command, "Desire spiritual gifts," and by an overpowering sense of the Divine Presence. The two former of these weights which are now added to the scale, are too evident in their operation to need further notice, but a few words must be said upon the sense of the Divine Presence and Inspiration which is apt suddenly to overmaster these Prophets.

Indeed the idea of the proximity of Almighty God to us cannot but be overwhelming. And in these cases,

---

[1] I am indebted for this information which I have attempted to explain to my friend H. Tuckwell, Esq., M.D., of Oxford.

[2] See above, Vol. II. 1, § 5, p. 30.

the Presence is not general, but special. The individual Prophet is selected from amongst the congregation and other people of the world. And further even than this—the Presence is not outward but inward. The imaginary Prophet is supposed to be made the vehicle of Divine utterance. The Holy Spirit is thus thought to be brought wonderfully near, so that there is even an identity of utterance. It will be seen that the moral strength of this consideration, if received with implicit faith, is enough of itself, without any superadded power, to work wonders on a man.

(*c*) Again, such prophesying is preceded by a long period of prayer. The strength of prayer is two-fold. Besides the answer to it which is granted in some way by Almighty God, whether according to the terms of the prayer, or in some manner not contemplated by the offerer but better suited to the case by His Infinite Intelligence, there is also the reflex effect which is shed upon the worshipper. According as he throws himself forward upon the objects of his petition, he becomes morally identified with its fulfilment. So that whenever the object of the prayer is some action, temporary or continued, of the offerer, the prayer materially aids in working out its own realization.

To take parallel instances, how are so-called accomplishments gained, such as playing a musical instrument, drawing, and so forth, except by the exercise of concentrated attention, and the practice which follows upon that exercise? Whether as in Irving's time a company of people assembled daily to unite in supplication for the spiritual gifts, or a single Prophet now-a-days is preparing for his office, it is evident how his daily thought and earnest longings are thus gradually paving the way in him for accomplishing what may be both remarkable and difficult.

(*d*) The force of contagion, or rather of infection, is too well known to require more than slight notice. Outbursts, where the powers of men or women break loose from the self-control which belongs to the Will, are strangely catching. That Hysteria, Epilepsy, or Catalepsy, would extend beyond bounds by the influence of example or infection, were they not sternly repressed, is well known.

(*e*) Still, some people may wonder how the substance of the supposed prophecies is gathered. We should observe that, with small exception, these so-called prophecies are lacking in originality and 'talent. It appears that the Prophets lay hold of what is, so to speak, floating about in the religious atmosphere at the time. These prophecies usually relate to some practical precept, or the acceptance of some supposed truth about which there is doubt or hesitation amongst the Members of the Body. The minds of all are turned in the direction where the solution of their difficulties lies concealed. This may have been partially or virtually discovered by some in the company, who nevertheless hesitated to trust to the glimpse which they have caught through the mist, and perhaps indeed do not realize what they have seen, or dare not trust to their own implicit inference. In a moment of excitement, a flash comes upon the mind of a person with more delicately constructed organization his emotions are roused, he is sure that the idea is communicated by some power not his own, and he gives expression to the feelings or thoughts of all which are vainly seeking shape and utterance.

This short description of what really occurs, and of the several moral factors which variously combine in producing the result, is not meant to be by any means a complete account of this class of striking phenomena. These are merely hints towards the solution of this difficulty upon principles of human nature. Of course these manifestations vary largely. In the "Catholic Apostolic Church" they would evince a much more pronounced character, if they were not regulated by an admirably devised body of rules and customs. Still not the less, when they are carefully examined, will they be found to belong to that large class of cases, of which perhaps the most striking belong to hysteria.

This class includes all those which arise from nervous affections. The nerves are, at least mediately, the springs of physical and moral action. And they have a strong tendency, unless they are kept under firm and habitual control, towards a spasmodic movement which is the parent of morbid disorder, and is itself often caused or intensified by morbid conditions. When therefore the efforts of the central government within us are directed, not towards a restraint of these wild forces, but upon the production of their outbreaks according to a preconceived idea, the realization of which is the object of an earnest longing stimulated by the overwhelming motives of Religion, we can readily see how the result may ensue.

Hence also amongst other conditions of the kind arises Ecstasy. "The patient is lost to all external impressions; but wrapt and absorbed in some object of the imagination. The muscles are sometimes relaxed; sometimes rigid as in slight tetanus: but the loss of voluntary power over them is not complete or universal, for these patients often speak in a very earnest manner, or sing. They are, as the term ἔκστασις imports, out of the body at the time, wholly engrossed in some high contemplation. This state is not uncommon as forming a part of religious insanity; and sometimes it runs into ordinary hysteria. Nervous and susceptible persons are apt to be thrown into these trances under the influence, whatever it be, of mesmerism: and grave authors assure us that the intelligence which then deserts the brain, concentrates itself in the epigastrium; or at the tips of the fingers: that people in that state read letters which are placed on their stomachs, or applied to the soles of their feet; answer oracularly enigmatical questions; discover and declare their own and other persons' internal organic diseases; describe minutely and accurately distant scenes which they have never visited, nor previously heard of; and even foretell future events."[1]

How far to these physical causes a spiritual influence is also superadded, is a question of great mystery. We

[1] Watson's *Lectures*, pp. 737, 738. The author adds, "*Credat Judæus Apella, non ego.*"

are told that Satan transforms himself even into the form of an Angel of Light. The simulation of good characteristics, however far it is carried, short of the elimination of every evil feature, simply proves nothing. When the observation of symptoms strictly human has carried us so far, we had better not venture into the region of the unseen and spiritual.

But it will be said, that to explain away these prophecies upon principles exclusively physiological, is to explain away all prophesying, and to admit principles destructive of everything supernatural.

The answers to this objection are evident.

What has been advanced in explanation of these phenomena has not been advanced in disproof of them. They have been already proved to be wanting in supernatural signs. They do not follow the analogy of God's actual dealings when He has wished to convey a Revelation. All that has been just now brought forward has been said in answer to the question, But if these prophecies are not supernatural, how can you explain them? To show that the enormous monoliths at Stonehenge were brought there and reared by men, would not involve a proof that the boulders on the Jura were not conveyed there by forces beyond any human control.

But again, why should not Theologians employ all the observations of Physiologists? All the Sciences come from One Source, though some are pursued by natural investigation, and one of them is grounded upon special Revelations. Jealousies between them belong to the nursery of human intelligence. We can be only in an elementary stage, so long as Theology shuts her eyes to the deductions of Science, or Physiologists or other Students of Physical Science are so taken up with their own domain as to be unable to look into their neighbours' grounds, or for example because the Will has a separate part of the brain for its functional exercise, to deny the existence of the spiritual part of man.

The case is widely different, when the supposed supernatural judged by the rules of the really supernatural is driven out of the province of Theology. The question then is, where shall this claimant go? Is there room for it within the domain of Physiology? Physiology answers, Yes.

But we must not therefore be so rash as to infer, that supernatural agency, in its usual operations, is to be excluded from the trials of men. The question here is between the ordinary and the extraordinary,—between the exercise of supernatural power in great emergencies, and the common employment of it in the Church or in the world. Because we may explain phenomena according to the results of physiological experience, it would be a most unjustifiable and narrow-minded deduction thence to infer, that spiritual agency does not underlie the outer framework of human activities. Although there is no reason to suppose that the corner occupied by the so-called Catholic Apostolic Church is the chosen arena of salvation in the present century, yet there are no grounds whatever for imagining that the powers of Heaven and Hell leave it unvisited in their ordinary movements upon earth.

The writer of this work again wishes to express his deep sense of the importance, indeed the solemnity of the present investigation. "Try the Spirits" is the Apostolic command: but the province of the Holy Spirit is a most holy province; and it is protected by awful warnings. This is a subject for calm and careful, but for open, speaking. The province itself is indeed a more awful one for those who set foot in it without due authority, than it is for those who, after learning from God's own actions, say seriously to such people, "You ought not to trespass there."

To those who do so, the writer solemnly commends the foregoing considerations. He believes that many have exceeded due bounds, honestly believing that they were walking in the right path. Such as these he earnestly begs to return as quickly as possible to their places in the ranks of the Church Militant, committing themselves unreservedly to Him who is ever ready to receive back those who return to Him, being convinced of the error of their ways.

CHAPTER VIII.

EXPECTATION OF THE GREAT ADVENT.

AFTER an examination of the general characteristics of the so-called "Catholic Apostolic Church," and especially of the two most prominent features in the Tenets therein held, we find that there are absolutely no grounds left for secure footing. What seemed plausibly solid at first has melted away when the light of God's Holy Truth was turned upon it. Apostles are seen to be no Apostles, and Prophets so-called to have no claim to prophetical gifts. But these two are the keystones of the edifice. "We admit," says one speaking in a tone of authority' "that if God hath not spoken to us by His Prophets, nor hath restored to us Apostles, then however free from intentional schism, still in the flagrant commission of schism we are found."[1]

Besides which, their boasted Catholicity is contracted into the narrowness of a modern Sect, with leading Tenets newly invented, and with primitive Truths added

---

[1] *Discourse delivered in the Catholic Apostolic Church, Gordon Square, on the occasion of consecrating the Altar*, &c. London: T. Bosworth, 1853, p. 7.

as an afterthought. At the same time, this system has been shown to have grown out of the general tendencies of this century towards the entire Catholic Faith, involving a wider grasp and a deeper hold of Divine Truth; and there is reason to believe that most at least of the Members of the so-called Catholic Apostolic Church are honest seekers after Truth, who have been misled by the shadow, mistaking it for the real substance.

These conclusions have been reached from definite and evident premises. On the one hand, the arguments advanced in favour of this system when probed have revealed their unsoundness within; and on the other, an artillery of formidable objections has massed itself in position around.

The mode of argument changes in the present chapter. We enter upon a solemn and mysterious subject, which is full of the most interesting speculation for those who look onwards to the future, but has been guarded jealously by no one less than our Lord Himself.

On the one side, He tells us that "of that day and that hour knoweth no man, no, not the angels which are in Heaven, neither the Son, but the Father."[1] An extraordinarily strong saying, which excludes even the Son of God from the knowledge of the time of the Great Day. And on the other, we hear from St. John, that "Blessed is he that readeth, and they that hear the words of the prophecy" in the Revelation, "and keep those things that are written therein." Attention and caution are thus inculcated on us.

[1] St. Mark xiii. 32; St. Matt. xxiv. 36.

As Irvingism took its start from the prophetical studies which prevailed at the beginning of this century, so the prophetical teaching of these people is the most prominent in their evangelizing efforts, and the immediate expectation of the Great Advent is the most powerful motive in their lives. Believing, as they do, that the Lord will come at once, and that the faithful amongst them will in a few days "be caught up to meet the Lord in the air," they pass their time on the very tiptoe of expectation. Terrors are thus intensified to the utmost, and a sanctified ambition is roused to its height. Preaching is enforced by a very mine of awful reasons for shuddering, and on the other hand places in the Lord's own retinue are offered for merely ecclesiastical obedience. I have seen the syllabus of numerous courses of preaching by these Evangelists, and have never found one which has not commenced with the Lord's Coming, and ended with "Believe in the Restored Apostolate." At first sight doubtless, even taking into account the drawback, we are inclined to say, what an incalculable help to Christian faith it must be to be able to have such a belief! How happy these people are to possess such a motive! is it wise to disturb them? But in the second place, we ask, "But is this belief true? Is it healthy? Is it after all the great Christian motive?" We must therefore proceed with our examination.

And first, we should commence by acknowledging again the vast power here exerted for effecting a holy life, and the coincidence of this watching for the Coming of the Lord Jesus Christ with numerous commands given by our Lord and His Apostles. The fervency of expectation which characterized the earliest ages of the Church is not a little remarkable. The inevitable effect of the elapse of century after century is manifested in the prevalent lack of looking forward to that Great Day of the Lord, which has been declared to be full of so much horror, and especially of such inconceivable blessing. And any putting forward of sound reasons and genuine incentives for watching for the Great Advent, must be of incalculable advantage to individual Christians and to the Universal Church.

But then on the other hand, even this motive is not after all the great Christian motive. If it were, in what an abyss of disadvantage would all those Christians lie, whose lot was not cast near to the Great Advent! No: it is the love of God that should abound more and more, it is the love of Christ that should constrain us. It is the realization of our present nearness to God in Christ, it is the apprehension of the incipient, but priceless, privileges of faith, which should carry Christians of all ages,—not of the first and last only,—as far as motives will go, in zeal and faithfulness through the temptations which are spread in their way. True, that the love of the Lord Jesus may be strengthened by the expectation of meeting Him soon. But the chief stress in Holy Scripture laid by the nearness of His appearing lies upon His judgment, upon the measures which the Lord of the house will take when He finds His servants not watching. The true love of Christ is a plant which grows best in the open sunshine, away from the turmoil of the winds, sheltered in its own quiet nook. The comparative coldness in the Eucharistic Service of this Community when compared with the loving realization of the Lord's Presence in the Church of England, as described by many,[1] shows a tendency of the system which might have been anticipated from an observation of the excessive degree, in which the expectation of the Great Advent absorbs the religious life of these people.

Connected with this subject, the theory in vogue amongst "Catholic Apostolics" about Sealing presents grounds for grave criticism. Not now to insist upon the inconsistencies already pointed out,—that the arrangement of tribes is purely arbitrary, that each Apostle has not sealed his 12,000, and that there is no chance of each tribe affording the proportionate quota demanded of it,—what an extreme of ecclesiasticism is it to imagine that the titles to places in the retinue of the Lord are exclusively bestowed by means of one rite administered once for all by one set of men. In what part of the Church, and in what age, was a single rite ever supposed to convey supereminent honours in the next Life?

The moderate Catholic Doctrine about outward observances and about the Catholic Church is this:— "The way of life, as revealed by the Lord Jesus Christ, and through the Holy Spirit, is before you: Eternal Life is won by following it, and everlasting perdition is incurred by rejecting it: such is the covenant of God: we can tell you no more: He is the wise, unerring Judge, who will have mercy where He sees reason to have mercy,

[1] Above, Vol. I. pp. 333—335.

but we warn you to walk in the way which alone He has revealed." That is a broad, intelligible issue.

But in Irvingite "Sealing," one ceremony rises into colossal size. Verily, the patent of precedence is easy of procuring—easier than if it were purchasable, since it is thus within the reach of all. But again, "Sealing" with its tremendous advantages is made really to depend, not upon a true attachment to the Lord Jesus Christ, but on an acceptance of twelve men. What is this but in effect preaching Paul, and Apollos, and Cephas? When the courses of sermons addressed to outsiders always end with the Tenet of the Restored Apostolate, what is this but to make these Apostles more prominent even than the Lord Jesus Christ Himself? On his death-bed Irving strongly deprecated any such result. But false principles often lead round to the very point, which at the outset people are above all anxious to avoid.

Such is the tottering superstructure which has been reared upon the Doctrine of the Expectation of the Great Advent. In all our careful criticism we should be especially anxious not to underrate this attitude of reverent and anxious watching. The last message of our Lord, when He left the earth before the ardent gaze of His Disciples, was to the effect that He should come again. With affectionate reiteration He bid them and all His people to watch. He has warned us against the dangers of a spiritual slumber.

So it is, that many outside the Irvingite Body have in this century looked for the Lord's Advent, with quite as much earnest longing and anxious preparation as any of these people themselves. Instances have occurred of persons who never received these Apostles or accepted the Sealing, but have kept their affairs wound up in expectation of being caught up into the air. Irvingites indeed are but a small section of those who have specially studied prophecy in our days. A large number of the students who met at Albury never believed in the subsequent manifestations or appointments. And the entire company of Albury students constituted only a small part of those, who were interested in the prophetical researches of our time, and pursued them to definite results. Whoever wished to learn what has been maintained and taught in our days, would in fact not turn so much to the teaching of this Community, as to the Books written under the names of Elliott, Wordsworth, Williams, Waldegrave, Bickersteth, Tregelles, Cumming, and others. So that a strong expectation of our Lord's Coming, and a devotion to this Great Event, are by no means necessarily mixed up with any exclusive Irvingite Tenets.

The fact is, that considering the great importance and thrilling interest of the Apocalypse, and of other prophecies in Holy Scripture which regard the future, the study of prophecy is a subject of purely legitimate speculation in the Church. Of course this speculation, like all other speculations, must be kept within due limits. Not only there must be no interference with any authorized Doctrine, the analogy of the faith also must not be traversed or disturbed. Again, an extreme and loving reverence must always moderate and soften all such speculation. Under these conditions, prophetical researches are plainly lawful and right. And inasmuch as the subject is mainly speculative in its nature, there is the more room for differences of opinion and variations in investigation. Therefore in such a brief notice of the various schools of interpretation of the Revelation of St. John as I can now give, and in such comments as I am able to offer upon opinions received in some quarters, I shall speak with less confidence as putting forward my own opinions, than when it is my duty, standing upon the firm foundations of the Catholic Faith, to show how parts of it are contravened by the fond inventions of men.

There are then various Schools of Apocalyptic interpretation. These Schools differ in numerous points of general or minute interpretation, and it is difficult to classify them. But perhaps we may collect them into four main groups, each of which however will include several varying acceptations of the prophecies that are found, especially in the Apocalypse.

I. The first group has been termed that of the *Futurists*, that is, those who regard all the Revelation as looking to a future fulfilment, except perhaps the Introduction, and the Letters to the Seven Churches.

Amongst these Futurists, using the term in a comprehensive meaning, but by no sort of means as exhausting the group, come the Irvingites, though they differ from the holders of an extreme future construction. They suppose that we are now in the midst of the accomplishment of the details included in what may be considered the Second Part of the Apocalypse, which relates to the

Sealed Book. The present time they consider to be the period of the Sealing of the Servants of God upon their forehead : the four angels meanwhile, at the four corners of the earth, "holding the four winds of the earth, that the wind should not blow on the earth, nor on the sea, nor on any tree."[1] Into close criticism upon the exact Tenets of the Members of the Catholic Apostolic Church, we are not now entering. The Apocalypse is a mysterious book, hard indeed to fathom. It is quite within the bounds of legitimate speculation to regard the chief part of it as destined in the future, be it immediately, or be it later, to meet with a literal fulfilment.

Here of course many Futurists part company with Members of the Catholic Apostolic Church, when the latter assert that we are now without doubt upon the very brink of that seething period, when the Apocalypse will be verified by a succession of events corresponding to the striking descriptions contained in that Book. But even here, again, many other people join with them. And with respect to the hidden preparations of the future, who can say that they are not even now at our very doors, in the every-day meaning of that remarkable expression? Provided that there be no dogmatizing upon these speculative matters, and no interference with the analogy of orthodox belief or with Catholic Doctrines themselves, such opinions are perfectly allowable, and may be made the topics of reverent discussion within the boundaries of the Church.

[1] Rev. vii. 1.

II. The next group consists of those who have been termed *Præterists*, that is, people who believe that nearly all of the Apocalypse, except the final portion about the New Creation, has been fulfilled already. This group consists chiefly of German Interpreters, though it includes also several Patristic and some Roman Catholic Authors.

According to this mode of explanation, a great part of the Book is taken up with references to the great Catastrophies, viz., that of Judaism as effected in the Conquest of Judæa and the destruction of Jerusalem, and the fall of Pagan Rome as accomplished by the advance of Christianity and the inroads of barbarians. The passage from the sixth to the eleventh chapters inclusive, is supposed to be devoted to the former of these subjects; and the twelfth and thirteenth chapters are applied to the fall of Pagan Rome.

These opinions have been widely held, and have been maintained with much show of reason. There are several features of resemblance which are very striking. The two great events alluded to were of extreme importance, and concerned the whole Church in early and critical periods of her existence. They were near to the time of St. John,—indeed one of them, and the date of the composition of this Book, hang in great measure mutually upon one another, and would well be included within the range of his vision or prophecy. Not to enter into any criticism, such interpretation again is legitimately within the circle of such Christian speculation upon mysterious subjects, which belongs to the liberty of the Catholic Churchman, always provided that he do not actually or by implication violate the lawful scope of any Christian Doctrine.

III. The next group, if it may be called a group, is represented with great ingenuity and completeness in Elliott's *Horæ Apocalypticæ*. In the words of this Author, it may be called the "Protestant continuous Historic Scheme of Interpretation."

As the readers of that work are aware, Mr. Elliott has with great learning tried to adapt to the course of the Apocalypse the history of the Church from the beginning, supposing that various people who have figured prominently in ecclesiastical events are set forth in some description or expression of St. John. The arrangement is unfortunately to some extent disfigured and distorted, as is too often the case in these speculations, by a narrow-mindedness, which limits the view taken to the survey presented to one, who has taken his stand upon a point not very high in one corner of the Catholic Church. Still, considered generally and as a whole, such a speculation seems perfectly allowable, even if it be not persuasive. And the fact that there are several people who accept the laborious conclusions of Mr. Elliott, renders it quite possible that there may be really more in such a system of interpretation than some minds, perhaps differently constituted from others, may discover. There are certainly several curious coincidences, though many of the presumed adaptations seem fanciful and far-fetched. Very possibly a considerable amount of truth may after all lie at the bottom, even when the superficial adjustments appear awkward and incongruous.

IV. It will have been observed that there is a resemblance between the first and last of these groups. Both have grown out of the prophetical studies of the present century. And both agree in assigning to the Revelation a literal and matter-of-fact interpretation. The persons therein mentioned are taken to be definite persons, sustaining a separate personal part in the drama of the Church. Mr. Elliott introduces Wycliffe, Huss, Wesley, and numerous others. It is taken for granted by the Irvingite Evangelist,[1] that Antichrist is to be a monarch, the personal head of a kingdom.

That this mode of exposition must be both a difficulty and a snare is only to be expected. A difficulty, because to select personages and special events out of the vast roll of ecclesiastical and other history, as governing the issues of periods, involves a delicate and hazardous exercise of historical philosophy. And that it is a snare, is shewn by recent interpretations of prophecy, which have variously ascribed to the Duke of Reichstadt, to the Emperor Louis Napoleon, to changes of Ministry in England, and to Revolutions in France, an importance which is now seen to be wholly disproportionate. A hill seems to one who is at the foot of it to tower into the clouds, which when viewed from a distant height is almost lost amidst the surrounding mountains. The facts of history rise and fall in relative consequence before the reader, according to the tastes and opinions of separate historians. To ascribe to them their true value in such momentous questions, is surely beyond the misty sight

[1] *Sermon in Gordon Square.*

Individual Applications unsatisfactory. 271

of this present world. And indeed so generally equal do the more prominent events and persons of various ages and countries appear, when we extend to each an impartial and conscientious consideration, that we come to the conclusion, that it is not true to the real conditions of the cases severally to chose out any special ones, and to ascribe to them the extreme prominence, which would have led to their being singled out from the rest, for representation in the Vision of St. John, as pivots in the history of the Church.

But then, the question may be asked, whether this is not to reduce the grand Revelations of the Apocalypse to practical nonentity. The answer to this question is found in a description of the fourth and last group of interpretations.

Observers then of the processes which have been briefly described, find that they can discover no firm standing-ground in them. The upholders of such literal interpretations appear to be wanderers upon a sea of speculation, without trustworthy chart or compass. They cannot agree amongst themselves about the true course: and where they do agree in the main, as for example, about a pre-millennial reign of our Lord, their conclusion is open to grave objection. Is it not then possible, and even probable, that they are in error about their fundamental principles?

Now the Apocalypse seems to be pre-eminently a spiritual Book. It contains things which are unearthly and strange. We hear of the Throne in Heaven,—the four beasts,—" the Lamb as it had been slain,"—" souls under the altar,"—"angels holding the four winds,"—stars,—the bottomless pit,—"a woman clothed with the sun, and the moon under her feet, and upon her head a crown of twelve stars,"—Satan and another beast,—an anachronistic Babylon,—and the war in Heaven,—not to carry the list further. And all through the History of Redemption we find the veil, which screens the visible from the spiritual world, occasionally lifted up. The angelic song at the Nativity, the Temptation in the Wilderness, the mysterious dealings with diabolic agency during our Lord's Ministry, and the Agony in the Garden, afford signal instances of this, which are continued through the visions of St. Paul, on to the grand Revelation of St. John.

That Apostle was therefore translated behind the scenes, and saw the machinery at work. He appears to have been shown seven distinct pictures,[1] including the sight in the vestibule. He had first an interview with the Great High-Priest, Who sent His messages to the Seven Churches of Asia. Then in the Sealed Book he learns the Prophetic History of the Church. Thirdly, in the Book that he eats, he views the Mysteries of the Church. Then in the Vials he is taught the Judgments of God. In the Vision of Babylon he is shown Unfaithfulness in the Church. Sixthly, the scenes in Heaven reveal Christ with His Elect. And finally in the New Jerusalem he looks onward to the Church in her triumphant condition and existence in Heaven hereafter. These successive scenes are taken not to be

[1] See *Williams on the Apocalypse.*

necessarily in chronological order, but in some instances to overlap and to intertwine one another.

The Apocalypse is thus supposed to be a disclosure of what happens all through the existence of the Church. It speaks of principles, and generally of spiritual Beings in the mass, with only occasional reference to individuals. Human and earthly literalness is alien to its tone and tenor. "A thousand years is as one day, and one day as a thousand years." Human agents are no doubt often the outcome upon earth of these spiritual agencies: but they are not the primary verifications and applications of the descriptions in this Book. The grand importance of these descriptions is not weakened, or their wide influence narrowed, by an exclusive reference to any single man of whatever age of the Church. The Apostle tells us of vast spiritual movements which, so to speak, underlie the Church's history, not of the superficial life which attracts the notice, and absorbs the interest, of weak-minded men, whose intellects are occupied with the visible occurrences of this world, and are unable to pierce through them to the mighty operations of the supernatural world.

Interpreted then by the rule of this central and governing idea, the Revelation, and the other prophecies which are to be taken in connection with it, are not supposed to be full of personal applications. Antichrist is not a single individual,—head of a monarchy or otherwise. He is the manifestation of the spirit of opposition to Christ, whensoever or wheresoever found. If there is to be a special and more violent outbreak before the final consummation, there is no proof that it will burst forth under single guidance, though it is quite possible that one man may in power and influence and excess far out-top the rest.

Again, as the late Bishop Waldegrave argued with much force and gentle persuasiveness in his *Bampton Lectures*,[1] the notion of a Millennium, in the light of this idea, will fly away. The entire Reign of the Lord in His Church occupies the place of this superstructure, which seems really to rest upon a slender foundation. And Christians, instead of merely looking forward to expected blessings, will come to realize and value those which they have already got. The Presence of the Lord now vouchsafed, opening out benefits and delights to all

---

[1] "My principal endeavours have been directed to showing, that the Doctrine of a personal reign is unsupported by Scripture, when rightly understood.

"That Doctrine perplexes the minds of many of our brethren, who cannot see their way clearly open either for its adoption or for its rejection. It also impairs the usefulness of others who have overcome this hesitation. It may not perhaps in every case occupy a place in their private studies and public ministrations, which belongs of right to more humbling, and withal more edifying, truths of God. But it does most certainly introduce into the whole system of their Scriptural exposition a dislocating principle, which men, not imbued, as they are themselves, with the spirit of genuine godliness, may easily apply to the overthrow of the whole fabric of the Christian Faith. Nor is the mischief confined to such extreme and exceptional cases. For certainly, under the semblance of providing for the future, they close against the spiritually-minded some of their richest storehouses of present consolation, and open to the carnally-minded a long vista of speculations, in which they find a welcome refuge from present self-examination.

"It was a deep and painful conviction, that these serious evils are inherent in popular Millenarianism, which led me to undertake the task which I have so inadequately discharged."—*Bampton Lectures.* London: Hamilton and Adams, 1855.

who truly seek Him, both as He is generally present in His Church, and as He especially condescends to come in His Holy Sacrament, will thus afford a loving fulfilment of prophecies to those, who by habitual faith enter into it more and more, and learn to live ever nearer and nearer to Him.

But perhaps an objection is made to this method of interpretation, that the meaning of the Apocalypse is thus volatilized and dispersed, a well-known rule in the diagesis of Holy Scripture being, that when the literal is possible, the further we stray from the literal the worse the interpretation. Indeed, we cannot doubt that this is an excellent rule, and that rival modes of interpretation of Holy Scripture may be well tested by their violation of it or conformity with it.

But the method of interpreting the Apocalypse which is now being described does not really violate the rule in question. There is an ambiguity in the word spiritual which must be noticed. Sometimes this word is taken to connote vague and misty principles, the product of the intellect, mere abstractions, entities if they may be so called without any real separate existence, capable of alteration or modification according to the opinion and choice of various people. No such meaning is intended here. If the descriptions of the Apocalypse are to be accepted in a spiritual sense, they must yet be supposed to relate to beings or things which have a real existence. If there is a spiritual machinery regulating the Church,— and it is difficult to see how this can be denied without erasing whole passages from the Bible,—then this must be quite as real as any human agents, and vastly more powerful and influential. So that the various parts of the Apocalypse may have the most literal application.

Much more literal indeed than under any other system, because in other cases it requires the utmost ingenuity to bring together two things which are dissimilar, and when they are brought together and placed side by side the incompatibility is only too apparent. Instead of Constantine, Augustulus, Pope Hildebrand, Luther, Huss, Charles the Fifth, the Napoleons, and the French Revolutions, all magnified into undue proportions according as we stand nearer to them and fix more intensely our gaze upon them, we shall have existences of the next world, which must surely agree with St. John's descriptions. True that we cannot see or say how. But then it is often our greatest wisdom to measure the strength of our faculties, and to recollect that many difficulties will be done away when we "see face to face," which we feel when we only "see through a glass darkly."

Again, be it remembered and reiterated, that within the Church there is room for all such speculation, provided that it is pursued with reverence and soberness, and in cases of difference of opinion with brotherly love. Taking my stand thus, I find reasons of considerable weight which lead me to urge that such a way of viewing the prophecies of the future in the Apocalypse and other parts of the Bible as has been last described is the truest to calm and sound judgment, to firm and powerful faith, and also to earnest piety.

Let any one who doubts this think of the constant

changes which in the last half-century have been forced upon those who have dogmatically taught the nearness of the Great Advent. Which of those men who were assembled at Albury, or followed Irving to Newman Street, would have dreamed of the history of those events being written in the year 1877, without any such momentous revelation having occurred in the world as they anticipated? Since those times, crisis after crisis, as they were deemed, has passed by, and the Lord has not come. Especially the year 1866—an epoch fixed upon by nearly all in this nineteenth-century school of prophecy as pregnant with vast changes of a sacred nature—elapsed without any sensible effect. Of course this unexpected postponement is explained as plausibly as ingenuity can manage; but is the explanation satisfactory? Is not the history of the world gradually proving in its steady and majestic roll, though occasionally the surface is somewhat turbid, that such prognostications are without foundation?

Indeed, this is by no means the first period in the career of the Church, when expectations have been rife that the present dispensation was drawing to a close. What could be more natural than that people should imagine that the Church's existence would not be prolonged beyond 1,000 years? Accordingly, when the first millenary was coming to an end, the opinion was widely spread that the Lord's Advent was at hand.

" So deplorable was the aspect of the times, that it seemed to offer a spontaneous solution of the prophecy of the Apocalypse which represents Satan bound 1,000 years, and afterwards loosed a little season. A thousand years had elapsed since the birth of our Blessed Lord: and those who looked upon the state of religion, and morals, and society generally throughout the world, saw much to convince them that the 'falling away' foretold by the Apostle had actually commenced. Accordingly we find that it was beginning to be a general opinion, especially throughout France, that the time of Antichrist had arrived. 'Most of the good and just, candid and simple,' says Aventinus, 'have testified in their writings that the reign of Antichrist commenced in those days, because they saw events accomplished in them which Christ our Saviour had predicted so many years before. The whole world unhinged, as it were, by the storms of war: the whole human race encircled by the whirlwind of arms: Easterns and Westerns hurrying to the fight one with another: all men assailing and wounding each other. Normans, Gauls, Germans, Saxons, Hungarians, Italians, Britons, Christians, mutually worn out with domestic quarrels and intestine feuds: Greeks and Armenians, Turks and Arabians, Spaniards and Saracens, Asiatics and Africans, in battle-array against each other: Jerusalem twice taken, twice stormed!' . . . . A long list of prodigies and extraordinary calamities follows, which Zonaras, Sigebert, and others describe more minutely."[1]

This description shows, not only how at that period people imagined that the great revolutions mentioned in the Apocalypse were being inaugurated, but that there then existed grounds for this imagination at least as

[1] *Manual of Ecclesiastical History*, chap. xi., by Rev. E. S. Foulkes. Oxford: J. H. Parker, 1851, p. 323.

strong as any in our own era. It was a critical and anxious time. And many therefore were disposed to magnify events of which they were the witnesses to a degree which we now see to have been full of exaggeration.

Or pass on to the period of the Reformation, and the same phenomenon is conspicuous. Indeed this was exactly the time when from the changes that were going on, and the excitement that prevailed, we should expect strong expectations to be cherished, that the Lord was then coming, and that events were paving the way for His approach. We have already seen how in the seventeenth century the supposed approach of the Millennium was the cause of the appearance of several persons claiming to be Prophets. And one of the principal Tenets of the Anabaptists of Münster, was the near coming of the end of the world, and included speculations about the manner of the Lord's Advent. In our own country the Fifth-Monarchy men of Cromwell's time present an exemplification of the same tendency.

The next period which was agitated by these expectations has been the nineteenth century, which indeed has possessed all the essential conditions for the wide spread of these opinions. First the world was shaken and dazzled by the horrors of the first French Revolution, the collapse of the entire framework of society in that country, and the extraordinary career of the first Napoleon. These stirring events have been followed by a general popularization of forms of government, by brilliant inventions, a vast increase in the wealth of the world, and a general examination of accredited opinions, followed by a considerable modification of the principles upon which they have been held, and in some cases by an entire alteration of sentiment. All this time, on the other side of the Atlantic, a colossal nation has been rapidly growing, and vast cities have risen up before their names were even known generally in Europe. What wonder then, if people have been led to exaggerate what they witnessed, and to suppose that the final crisis of the entire world's history was upon them? Abounding blessings have brought also abounding evil. At this therefore, at least as much as at any previous period, there has been reason to imagine that the consummation was drawing nigh.

But then the careful and wise student of history will hesitate to follow, and will see upon what a slender foundation this vast fabric of dogmatic teaching has been reared. He will recollect that his Lord Himself said that God the Father has kept in His exclusive power "the times and the seasons." Not that he will not watch. On the contrary, he will remember that "that day cometh as a thief in the night." His attitude will therefore ever be as of the servant who is waiting for his Lord. For indeed, if we read Holy Scripture thoughtfully and cautiously, we cannot but see that the Lord may appear at any time. It may be ten years hence, or twenty years, or fifty years, or a hundred years, or more,—or again, next year, or this year, or this month, or to-morrow, or to-day, that we shall hear the sounds of His approach. The chief features about the Great Advent are the intellectual uncertainty of the time of its occurrence, and by consequence the practical nearness of it to us all. The boy who may be questioned at any moment by his master must be always ready. And the motives of the Great Advent are clenched in each of us by the fact that death at all events moves us a stage onwards, and because no man knows when his own call may be given.

Doubtless the motive would be stronger, if we knew that the Lord were at our gates. But this is not the way in which Almighty God deals with His people generally, and why should we be singled out for an easier path of duty? The truly Scriptural attitude of reverent watching is really much higher and better than rash dogmatism and feverish expectation. There is more room for the natural growth under Divine influence of holy graces, and for the training of the Christian in the sincere love of Christ. If it be said that such an attitude is apt to settle down into one of total indifference, the answer is that the latter is impossible for the true Christian, who thoroughly realizes his condition, and knowing "how short his time is," and the imperfection of his present state, has learnt after St. Paul to look eagerly onwards to the time when he shall "depart and be with Christ."

Such has been the hope of millions of Christians who have been and are quite as faithful and earnest as any of those who are absorbed in the immediate expectation of the Lord's Advent. Free from rash dogmatizing, living in constant waiting, their hopes and hearts are centred in Heaven, and their lives are "hid with Christ in God."

CHAPTER IX.

THE DOCTRINE OF THE INCARNATION.

THERE are two grand principles which, as has been already explained, underlie and pervade the whole of the system of teaching under consideration. These are the expectation of the immediate Coming of our Lord and pe tli respecting His Incarnation. In the increase of both former, Irving and his friends were amongst the pioneers of this century. And as is usually the fate of the leaders in exploration, they fell into errors which a maturer experience would have guided them to avoid.

They were in front of a re-action which asserted itself in two directions against teaching which was more or less prevalent in the eighteenth century. Not only amongst Presbyterians of Scotland, but in many quarters in England also, the idea was entertained which cannot be described as less than horrible, that the Blessings of Redemption are meant to embrace only a chosen few who have been predestinated to bliss. The entire freedom of the mercy shown in the Incarnation, and the all-embracing love of God, limited only by the sin of men, postulating and proved by the liberty of will, which is one of the glories of the human race, were successfully vindicated by Mr. Campbell of Row, and by Irving himself. The general acceptance of these Doctrines, at least amongst the best-informed Theologians, owes not a little to the early movement in which Irving was conspicuous as a prominent figure.

But both he and the Body which has derived its popular name from him, had more to do with the dissemination of a better understanding of the principle of the Incarnation as distinct from Natural Religion. The pendulum had swung after the period of the Reformation much too far in the opposite direction. In doing so, it had given birth to the Sect which has borrowed one of the terms belonging to the Church, and has dubbed itself with the title Unitarianism.

This tone of thought left its impress upon the religious phraseology of the time. At the beginning of the present century, people used to hear constantly such terms as "Providence," "an Infinite Goodness," "the Deity," and so forth, which were preferred to more definite phrases that are now generally in vogue. Questionings about the existence of Almighty God had led minds away from the Truths of the Incarnation,—as there is great danger of similar discussions doing at the present day,—to a too exclusive consideration of the moral government of Almighty God. The Church Seasons were neglected. Religion was confined almost to Sunday. The knowledge of the "One Holy Catholic and Apostolic Church" founded by our Lord, and gifted by Him with the sources of order, permanence, grace, and spiritual rule, was to a great degree in abeyance. One School taught sedulously and earnestly, though all but exclusively, the Doctrine of the Atonement. The other Doctrines of the Creeds were held in England by a few faithful secluded treasurers of the old tradition, or else in a dull orthodoxy which had lost its living force in descent from holier times.

It was when the religious spirit of the age was roused, and was longing after more satisfying sustenance for the weary soul, that Irving settled upon the great Doctrine of the Incarnation. And where he led the way, his followers afterwards advanced. Avoiding in part his error, they have yet only a defective knowledge of that grand subject. Both with respect to the Doctrine at its source, and in the application of it further down the stream, they have as will be seen erred not a little.

It will be best to take the latter point first.

Irvingites are so much taken up with the idea of the Incarnation, that they are apt to insist exclusively upon the necessity of human agency for the salvation of people. This principle, besides being constantly asserted, is exemplified in the strong despotism which reigns amongst them ; in their exuberant hierarchy, in the exaggerated stress laid upon ordinances, and in the minute elaboration of their system. It is found in the unelastic stiffness of their operations, of which those complain who have not been administrators of it, and which probably constitutes one cause why their numbers are so small as they really are. Maintaining in opposition to Theistic tendencies, that the Lord has personally interposed, they attribute to all rites and agencies which are conducted by men an importance which similar rites and agencies do not possess anywhere in the Catholic Church.

Where then lies their error? Their error of principle, that is, for we have seen some of their errors of detail. For it may be urged, that if the Doctrine of the Incarnation is true, the results presented by them are involved in the acceptance of it.

The answer is found in the fact, that the Doctrine of the Incarnation is always, by Catholic Theologians and in Catholic practice, taken in combination with, and balanced by, the Parent Doctrine, so to speak, of the Deity. This it is which renders so utterly objectionable the assertion, that God the Holy Ghost is only in the Church as the Spirit of the Man Christ. True that He did come to the Church on the Day of Pentecost, there ever to dwell as sent by our Lord, and thus He continued and extended, if we may so say, the Incarnation. That again our Lord during His Life on earth established certain definite, outward, palpable agencies and ordinances for being the means of conveying grace to His people: and that He stamped the principle, involved in the Holy Ghost appearing in a bodily form, upon His Church, then founded and endued with the promise of continuous permanence. But nevertheless, any separation of the Holy Spirit from the Divinity, any limitation of His action or nature, except so far as He works specially in the Church in compliance with His mission, is both dangerous and wrong. Revealed Religion must be ever taken in connection with Natural Religion.

Thus the Incarnation does not supersede true Deism, but witnesses to it, and strengthens it. Grace does not override, but purifies, and invigorates nature. One who has suffered from the dry and dead humanity of their system well says:—" SOLUS CUM SOLO—communion of the spirit close with God. This is the secret of success. No breath of man, Angel, Pastor, Deacon—may come between the soul and God. If it does, sickliness and dissipation of grace will surely be the consequence."[1]

The incessant preaching of Apostles, as evidenced in numerous publications and by the testimony of those who have left the Body, must keep souls back from that personal communing with God through our Lord Jesus Christ, which is the true lesson of the Incarnation, and the inestimable boon of the Church in all her ministrations, and especially at the Holy Sacrament. Bishop, Priest, or Deacon stand reverently aside, in self-forgetfulness and self-obliteration, when they have brought the soul to Christ. And even He does not let people rest upon Himself, but presents the prayer or offering with pleading and intercession to Almighty God, He Himself with the Father and the Holy Spirit forming that Triune BEING.

It is when this truth of Natural Religion, which lies at the source of and above the Incarnation of the Son of God, is forgotten and obscured, that dulness and dryness and narrowness creep over sacred ordinances. That is to say, of course, always supposing that the Incarnation is received. Because the two Doctrines

[1] *Apostolic Lordship*, p. 33.

must go together: and denial or neglect of either is sure to lead to vast spiritual loss.

But the application of the Doctrine of the Incarnation by these people is also inconsistent and defective. Inconsistent, because, as has been already shown, the continuous tenor of the Catholic Church would be broken, if these Apostles were really appointed as they claim to have been appointed. They have had no outward sight of the Lord in the Flesh: they have been recognized by no existing Church authorities: they claim an appointment outside of the line of succession which our Lord initiated upon earth: they have taught Tenets alien to at least seventeen centuries of Church existence. And besides these incontrovertible facts, the balance of evidence from Holy Scripture is against their claims and their peculiar teaching. It is hard to conceive a more violent wrench of the continuous machinery of the Church following upon the lines of the Incarnation, than would be wrought if the Lord of the Church so secretly interposed for the benefit of all, in the midst of only a small class of His people in one corner of His domain.

But besides this, the means adopted by them for keeping up the Doctrine of the Incarnation are defective. We may allow them due credit for their teaching in the main upon Holy Baptism, and upon the sacrament of the Holy Eucharist. Also for recovering other practices, such as perhaps the Scriptural anointing of the sick with oil. But if we examine their calendar, what do we find? No notice of the Epiphany, of the

Annunciation, or of Trinity Sunday, or of any Saint's Day except All Saints' Day, or of Fridays, or Ember Days, or of Lent;—no Fast-days, except Good Friday.

No wonder, an English Churchman is inclined to say, who traces to the Sacramental part of the year so much of his own personal attachment to the Lord Jesus Christ, if more is not made of Him. No wonder, if at the Holy Communion and at other times that warmth of feeling towards Him, and that outward devotion which we ourselves witness, are not evident. No wonder if we are hearing from these people always about Apostles, and so little about the Lord Jesus Christ; if their Evangelists are busied in teaching about Apostles to those who have come to know Him, instead of about Him and about the riches of His Grace to people who are living in ignorance and sin. The closer realization, in these days as compared with the beginning of this century, first of the events in our Lord's Life and the consequences flowing from them, and secondly of His contemporaneous work in pleading for and aiding His people, in Presence as well as Grace, is very remarkable. And this is probably due in the main to the annually increasing observance of the Church's commemorations, and to the growing sense of the Doctrine of His Real Presence at the Holy Communion. That Irvingites have generally a defective appreciation of the latter as well as the former has been already shown.[1] The Jewish observances about shewbread have been allowed to lead them astray. Their

---

[1] Vol. I. pp. 333—335.

attitude is too much towards the ordinance, and too little towards the Lord Jesus Christ Himself.

But it is time that we mount up the stream, and examine the original error at the source, which vitiates the waters all down the channel.

Though Irving's language is usually condemned in the Body, and his teaching is said to be "not altogether to be defended," yet the opinion which is generally entertained is in effect much what he taught. He maintained, as will be remembered, that our Lord took our fallen nature, though He was without any spot of sin. His sinlessness was referred by Irving to the continued effect of His Divine Nature, the fallen nature in Him thus being preserved from sin. Such in the main was Irving's teaching. The opinion now advanced is as follows:—

They believe that the Saviour took man's flesh of the seed of the woman as the Blessed Virgin presented it to Him, and thus was in all points as we are, yet without sin: of which He was eminently void both in the flesh and in the Spirit. But then they assert that this voidance of sin was due, not at all to the flesh which He took: for, they say, unless we adopt the pious but untenable notion of her Immaculate Conception, St. Mary had nothing to offer but the flesh of Adam under all the conditions of the fall: His freedom from sin was due therefore exclusively to Him who took man's flesh.

The Examination into the truth and error contained, in this Tenet involves a very delicate point of Doctrine, and a discussion upon it must traverse one of the chief religious controversies of the present century. It is clear that both Irving, and his followers in the Catholic Apostolic Church, have found themselves travelling in a difficult country, without having previously ascertained the directions of the true Catholic Church. They have followed the track prompted by their own private judgment: and now they find it hard to get back into the great high-road.

In approaching this subject, which, as is well known, has been called the Hypostatic [1] Union, or the union of the Two Natures in the One Person of our Lord, we must first, and indeed always, bear in mind the immeasurable distance between the Divine and human nature, between God and man. The One so Infinitely vast; Infinite in size, Infinite in duration, Infinite in wisdom and knowledge, Infinite in power, Infinite in purity and holiness. The other a small worm of the earth, subject to sickness, infirmity, and death, vitiated by folly and ignorance, weak and contemptible as regards strength, and defiled by sin. That these two could ever come together under one Personality is one of the wonders of Revealed Religion. Yet the whole must stand or fall together. It is welded into one mass by bands which stretch all round. We cannot gainsay it without imputing imposture to the Chief Agent. The way of Faith passes through fewer obstacles than the road to unbelief.

The point of union was the Conception and Birth of the Lord. He was Conceived by the HOLY GHOST, Born of the Virgin Mary. Nay, if we could mark the

---

[1] From Ὑπόστασις, the Greek term for "Person."

particular point of time, accuracy compels us to fix it at the first of these two Events. At that time then — as on the Festival of the Annunciation — the two Natures came together, each in its trueness, each real and genuine.

Now is it conceivable, that HE who shrinks from sinfulness with a horror which we cannot imagine, could so come together with degraded nature, as that it should be united with the Divine under One Person, and that the Very SON of GOD? A little consideration must surely make this position plain. There must then be a natural revulsion, so to speak, between the two. The opposition between fire and water cannot be more intense than that between sinfulness and Almighty God. It is clear therefore that the union could only take place, if human nature were presented under its most favourable form. What was that? Its original, unfallen state.

This is not to assert, that the nature which our Lord took was not perfectly and completely human in all the conditions of His Being, sin only excepted. For this very exception noticed in these last words, which is declared in the Bible, and is admitted by the Members of this Body, really carries with it the whole question under dispute. Because our nature without sin is in fact our original, unfallen nature. A man of trained, theological mind would never have asserted such a contradiction in terms as Irving advanced. How could He be without sin, without being like Adam when first created? And how could He be a fallen creature, and yet be utterly pure from every stain of sin? And how could He be God, without being perfectly pure, both in His flesh and in His Spirit?

These simple questions carry with them the whôle decision. Yet we are met with the objection that we cannot hold this ground without accepting the Doctrine of the Immaculate Conception of the Blessed Virgin. Is this so, or is it not?

This much is clear. That inasmuch as we see that human nature must of necessity have been pure for Him to take it, it must have been purified before He actually took it. The words of the angelic salutation prove this: Χαῖρε, κεχαριτωμένη,[1] "Hail, thou that art highly favoured," or "thou that hast been endued with grace." Grace therefore must have been shed upon the Virgin before the angel came. And this is only reasonable. If we place ourselves in a position to estimate beforehand without prejudice the state of one who was to be "blessed among women" in this extraordinary manner, we must inevitably include in our estimate the following suppositions :—we should take it for granted that she must come from a very holy family; that at least according to analogous improvement in the human race, each successive generation must have risen in a generally ascending scale of excellence, till at last one was born, who surpassed all who went before her in the graces of her nature. Still even this pitch of excellence would fall short of what was required for such an astounding motherhood. It would fall short, because the traces and stains of the

---

[1] The same word is used of the grace bestowed upon all Christians: δι' οὗ ἐχαρίτωσεν ἡμᾶς ἐν τῷ ἠγαπημένῳ.

infirmity and sinfulness engendered by the fall of Adam would still remain; whilst on the other hand it is impossible that the Divine Nature could be associated under one Personality with a human nature from so vitiated a stock. "Can a clean thing come out of an unclean?" It follows therefore that some extraordinary sanctification must have been made, before the " HOLY GHOST came upon her, and the Power of the Highest overshadowed her."[1]

The time of this sanctification has not been revealed. Nothing is said about it in Holy Scripture. The Church Catholic in her entire amplitude has never pronounced one way or the other: all that she has done has been to assign to the Blessed Virgin the name Θεοτόκος—" Mother of God "[2]—at the Council of Ephesus, in order to protect the Doctrine of the Incarnation which had been impugned by Nestorius. And indeed the intention of this name was simply to say that He Who was born of the Blessed Virgin was really God, being an abbreviation of the passages in Isaiah: " A Virgin shall conceive and bear a Son, and shall call His name Immanuel. . . . His name shall be called Wonderful, Counsellor, the Mighty God." That is to say, the intention was, to secure the assertion of our Lord's Divinity from the very first moment of His existence upon earth, not primarily to do honour to the Virgin-Mother. For the name was directed against Nestorius, who taught that there were two Persons in Christ our Lord; and

---

[1] Compare August., *De Peccatorum Meritis*, ii. 24.
[2] See for example Pearson *On the Creed*, Art. III.

that Mary was the Mother of Christ, but not the Mother of God. Hence arose the name, which may perhaps be translated into our language with more exactness "the Parent of God," than "the Mother of God."[1]

The Catholic Church therefore has never yet pronounced upon this subject: for the Eastern and Anglican Branches have never joined in the act of the Roman Communion. The question is left open.

There appear to be four theories possible upon this subject. The traces of original sin must have been put away, at the very least, contemporaneously with,[2] or just before, the Angel Gabriel's visit. Or secondly, this might have been effected by a gradual process, extending over some period in the Virgin's youthful life. Thirdly, she may have been sanctified shortly before her birth. Lastly, she may have been conceived Immaculate.

The first of these seems at first sight to be suggested by the words of the angelic salutation. The Blessed Virgin appears to have been wholly unconscious of any special appropriateness in her for receiving the favour of God. The account in St. Luke suggests the notion of an intensely human creature, receiving upon humiliation

---

[1] The term is Θεοτόκος, not Θεομητήρ, to coin the word which might have been invented and used, but never was. It was a translation of the Latin "Deipara." In course of time, however, Θεοτόκος was translated "Dei Genetrix," which was again translated Θεοῦ Μητήρ. But some reason must have prompted the original coinage,—evidently fear of exalting St. Mary too much, and so of suggesting the glaringly untrue sense which another term might have suggested.

[2] So St. Gregory of Nazianzum, Orat. xxxviii. n. 13, p. 671, repeated in Orat. xlv. n. 9, pp. 851, 852, and St. John Damascene, *De fide Orthodox.*, iii. 2, quoted by Dr. Pusey in his *First Letter to the Very Rev. J. H. Newman*, D.D, &c., pp. 91, 148.

a wondrous favour from Heaven. By the operation of a course of "natural selection," so to speak, conducted under the auspices of the HOLY SPIRIT, we find a human creature as near perfection as human nature will allow. Starting then in this way, may she not have been successively purified, till at last the final Touch was given, if we may so say, when the Angel came with his message from Above?

In this manner we might to some extent combine the first and second, and indeed the third of these explanations, so as to account for the purity which was necessary for the maternity of the Blessed Virgin. For it is impossible to suppose that she waited till the visit of the Angel for special sanctifying Grace: that she was till then behind the other Saints of God. If Jeremiah and John the Baptist were sanctified before birth,[1] why may not the preparations for her wonderful future have begun then, supposing that they were part of a continuing process?[2] In this way, during all her existence Mary would have been under the special care and training of God, to make her fit to become the Mother according to the flesh of the Lord Jesus Christ.

The third explanation is one which has the sanction

---

[1] Jer. i. 5; Luke i. 41, 44.

[2] This is mainly Thomas Aquinas' view. "He thought that the cleansing might be twofold; one preparatory to the Conception of Christ, not from any impurity of fault or from the *fomes*, but rather collecting her mind into one; but that, secondly, the Holy Spirit worked a cleansing in her, by means of the Conception of Christ, which is the work of the Holy Spirit. And in this way it might be said, that He cleansed her wholly from the *fomes peccati*, or the law in our members."—*First Letter to the Very Rev. J. H. Newman, D.D.*, &c., by the Rev. E. B. Pusey, D.D., 1869, p. 149.

of many great names. Aquinas lays his chief stress upon it.[1] St. Bernard, and the Schoolmen spoken of as a body, accepted it. It has the merit of philosophical simplicity: but most English Churchmen would think that it raises the Blessed Virgin into too great proximity to our Lord. The strength of this supposition lies in its securing her purity from sin all through her life. The weakness of it lies in its apparent want of exact coincidence with the hints given in the Scriptural account. Yet combined with the second and first, as the commencement of a continuing process of sanctification completed at our Lord's Conception, it would seem to present no grounds for valid objection.

With respect to the last,—that St. Mary was conceived Immaculate,—while we remember that it is supported by so large a Branch of the Catholic Church, we can nevertheless not help seeing that it is open to most grave theological and practical objections.

In the first place, how it trenches upon the singular grandeur of our Lord's Birth! His would be no longer the One Immaculate Conception: and hers too would be no longer the One Immaculate Maternity.[2] He stands alone since the early days of Adam, as untouched from the very first by any stain of sin. Such is the Doctrine of Holy Scripture, which ascribes sin repeatedly to every human being,[3] and repeatedly too exempts Him from

---

[1] "Beata Virgo contraxit quidem originale peccatum, sed ab eo fuit mundata antequam ex utero nasceretur."—*Summa Theol.*, iii. Q. 27, A. 2.

[2] Mill's *Five Sermons on the Nature of Christianity*, p. 167.

[3] 1 Kings viii. 46; Ps. cxliii. 2; Prov. xx. 9; Rom. iii. 9, v. 12, vi. 12, vii. 7; Gal. iii. 22, v. 17; James iii. 2; 1 John i. 8.

it.¹ We hear nothing approaching to this about the Blessed Virgin. That merely human creature, great as is her human dignity, is lost in the brilliant light that centres in her Divine Son. He is her sole title to eminence. Indeed whenever she is mentioned after His earliest childhood, He alludes to her in terms which at least at first sight appear to be disparaging. Whether it was that she did not understand His early devotion to His Father, or was over anxious to bring Him forward, or sought Him out in the midst of His preaching, or was blessed by one of the matrons who hung entranced upon His words, His reply cannot be said to be such as would have naturally been made by Him to a Being answering to Roman conceptions.²

So that the assignment of an Immaculate Conception to St. Mary infringes upon the singular pre-eminence which naturally belongs to the Son of God, Who is Very God as well as very Man. If there is but One Immaculate Conception, the principle is intelligible, and by the very force of its nature admits of no increase. But if we extend this pre-eminent mode of origination to another, why not also to a third? If for nature to be pure the parent must be pure, why are not the mother, and the father too, of the Blessed Virgin to be included? A clear and philosophical limit in the nature of things is

---

[1] Luke i. 35 (that Holy Thing Which shall be born of thee); John i. 29, xiv. 30; Acts iii. 14; 2 Cor. v. 21; Heb. iv. 15, vii. 26—28, ix. 14; 1 Pet. ii. 22; 1 John iii. 5; 2 Pet. i. 19.

[2] The apparent harshness in the term "woman" in St. John ii. 4 is entirely due to the English translation. The word γυναὶ—better than "lady" or "my lady"—has no such meaning.

attached to the number one, which no other number possesses. And in the present instance, the unapproachable character of the Being of our Lord renders Him appropriately the solitary exception to the law of original sin which has prevailed since the Fall of man. "As by the disobedience of one many were made sinners, so by the obedience of One shall many be made righteous."

And in addition to these theological reasons which appear to have commanding weight, this new dogma is not only without any Scriptural[1] or Primitive authority, but besides being opposed to the general drift of Holy Scripture, as has been shown already, runs counter also to the expressed words of many writers of repute in the early Church.[2] For example, St. Augustine speaks as follows in a passage which is worthy of being well weighed with respect to the whole of this discussion :[3]— "Why do you endeavour with elaborate argument to rise to the height of impiety by showing, that 'the Flesh of Christ being born of Mary, whose virgin flesh like that of all other human creatures had sprung from Adam, differs in no wise from the flesh of sin, and that the Apostle should be taken as saying, without making any distinction, that He was sent in the likeness of sinful flesh?' Nay, rather you should urge 'that sinful flesh does not exist, so as to exempt Christ from it.' What

---

[1] Except in the Vulgate reading of Gen. iii. 15. "*Ipsa* conteret caput tuum," which, to say the least, is (1) very doubtful, (2) the premiss of an exaggerated inference. See Dr. Pusey's *First Letter to the Very Rev. J. H. Newman, D.D.*, pp. 382—388.

[2] See Dr. Pusey's learned *First Letter*, &c., throughout.

[3] *S. August. contra Julianum Pelagium*, V. 52, t. x. 654.

indeed is the meaning of the likeness of sinful flesh, if sinful flesh does not exist? But you said that I did not understand this expression of the Apostle, though you did not yourself so explain it as that I could learn from your own lips, how one thing could be like another which is non-existent. For if it is positively insane to say this, and without any doubt the Flesh of Christ is not sinful flesh, but only similar to sinful flesh, what prevents us from understanding, that with His sole exception all other human flesh is sinful? Hence it is evident, that that concupiscence which Christ rejected in His own conception, has produced the origination of evil throughout the human race. Although Mary herself sprung from this, nevertheless she did not transmit it to the Body which she conceived from another Source. But if any one denies that the Body of Christ can therefore be said to have been made in the likeness of sinful flesh, or compare the Flesh of Christ to that of other human creatures who are born in the usual way, so as to attribute an equal amount of purity to both, he is found to be a detestable heretic."

These opinions have been expressed by many others of the early Fathers. A large number speak of Christ Alone as being without sin, making no exception in the case of the Blessed Virgin. Many also maintain positively that she had a flesh of sin, or imply this by speaking of her as having been cleansed and sanctified.[1]

---

[1] *E. g.* (1) Irenæus, Tertullian, Origen, Cyprian, Jerome, Hilary, Ambrose, Basil, Chrysostom, Gregory of Nyssa, Gregory the Great ; (2) Fulgentius of Ruspe, Fulgentius Ferrandus, Bede, and others. See Dr. Pusey's exhaustive *First Letter*, &c. Dr. Newman's argument, that because

"Supposing," said the acute Thomas Aquinas in later times, "that the parents of the Blessed Virgin had been purified from original sin, nevertheless the Blessed Virgin contracted original sin, because she was conceived in the ordinary manner."[1]

So that the idea of the Immaculate Conception of the Blessed Virgin is not only against the drift of Holy Scripture, but is opposed to the opinion of those Fathers of the early Church who have spoken upon the subject. And while there is entire liberty in the Church for holding any opinion which does not exempt the Blessed Virgin herself from the consequences of the fall, nevertheless the teaching both of Holy Scripture and of the Church point to some purification being wrought in her, when the Power of the Highest was about to overshadow her. "The body of Mary," says St. Augustine, "though it came from the evil stock, nevertheless did not transmit it to the Body which she conceived from another source."[2] And amongst the writers of the English Church, Heylin remarks: "Some reasons there were why .... Christ

the antithesis between Mary's obedience and Eve's disobedience was a favourite topic with the early Fathers, so as to become almost a proverb, therefore they thought that Mary resembled Eve in her immaculate origin, *pace tanti viri*, rests plainly upon an inadequate foundation.—*Letter to the Rev. E. B. Pusey, D.D.*, by John Henry Newman, D.D., of the Oratory. Longmans, 1866.

[1] "Secundum carnis concupiscentiam ex commixtione maris et feminæ."—*Summa Theologiæ*, iii. Q. 27, A. 2. The ingenious distinction between *active* conception, effected by man, and *passive* conception, or the bestowal of the soul by Almighty God, and the confinement of the Immaculate Conception to the latter, minimizes the Doctrine, but if the two are coincident, does not get rid of the objection derived from the inimitable character of the Conception of our Lord.

[2] *August.*, t. x. 654.

our Saviour should be born of the purest Virgin, though those reasons do not make it to be less a miracle ; for nothing but a miracle and the Holy Ghost could have begotten such a child upon such a mother." [1]

It is clear then, that it is not at all necessary to adopt the opinion of the Immaculate Conception of the Blessed Virgin, simply because we believe, as we must believe, that our Lord took, not the fallen nature of man, but our nature purified back to the state in which Adam was created. Indeed the chief argument from which this dogma was adopted, viz., that it was demanded by the pious devotion of the Members of the Roman Communion, throw us back, not upon the usual firm, tangible, objective grounds of Doctrine, but upon what Mr. Matthew Arnold has well described as the beautiful and poetic gallantry which has made "our Lady" the object of Roman devotion. Religion in this struggling world is composed of sterner elements. Doctrines come to us from other sources than concentrated and intensified sentiment. The omen is not favourable, when feeling dominates over logical reasoning and ancient authority. Development, even if admitted under limits, becomes abnormal, when the earlier conditions of the faith,— rudimental it may be in conception, yet full of the genuine forces of fresh life,—are wrenched and warped. The old canon of Catholic authority, *Quod semper, quod ubique, quod ab omnibus,* loses its meaning, when eyes are shut to the past, and attention is fixed exclusively upon the present.

[1] *Heylin*, p. 193.

But on the other hand, all this powerful tendency in one direction adds to the strong light in which Irving's heresy,—for palliate and excuse it as we fairly may, it is really nothing less,—is exhibited before a candid consideration. Our Lord was born of the seed of Abraham, but it was a purified seed,—He was "That Holy Thing," — it is gross profanation to imagine anything else. There was the true and unbroken descent from Abraham, — the capacities of pain and general suffering were there in high perfection, even the infirmities of our nature were not wanting:—but in front of the Approach of the Holy Spirit the human stock must have been purified from sin.

"This original and total sanctification of the human nature," says Bishop Pearson, "was, first, necessary to fit it for personal union with the Word, who out of His infinite love humbled Himself to become our flesh, and at the same time out of His infinite purity could not defile Himself by becoming sinful flesh. Secondly, the same sanctification was as necessary in respect of the end for which he was made man, the redemption of mankind: that as the first Adam was the fountain of our impurity, so the second Adam should also be the pure fountain of our righteousness. 'God sending His own Son in the likeness of sinful flesh, condemned sin in the flesh;'[1] which He could not have condemned, had He been sent in sinful flesh."[2] "It was necessary," he says afterwards, "we should believe our Saviour to have

[1] Rom. viii. 3.
[2] Pearson *On the Creed*, Art. III., *Conceived by the Holy Ghost*.

been born of a most pure and immaculate Virgin."[1] Again: "The Saviour of the world was born of a woman under the law, without the least pretence of original corruption."[2]

There are therefore two grand truths respecting our nature as it was taken by our Blessed Lord. First, it was the true human nature, subject to all human infirmities, except sin only, and full of all human perfections. He must have had, as Man, the highest capacities, bodily, mentally, and spiritually. The very possession of these perfect capacities must have made Him more alive to impressions, and more susceptible of pain of all sorts. Everything that affects any human being must have affected Him, because His was not an individual nature with idiosyncrasies of any kind, but an exhaustive epitome of human nature generally. So that there is really no reason to go further than this, in order to prove His perfect sympathy with every single human creature.

In fact, if He had taken our fallen nature, His sympathy would have been limited to certain classes of mankind similar to Himself: because our nature is inevitably narrowed by falls and imperfections. So that, in fact, Irving was cutting the ground from beneath himself, when in order to prove our Lord's perfect sympathy, he attempted to bring Him nearer to us by imagining that He took a nature fallen like ours. Because in that case our Lord would have resembled a

[1] Pearson *On the Creed*, Art. III., *Born of the Virgin Mary*.
[2] Ibid.

limited few, not every single human being, however unlike the rest in character. The old Calvinistic leaven was really working in him, at the very time when in company with Mr. Campbell and others he was striving to cast it out.

Secondly, therefore, and as implied in the first of the two truths, the Nature of our Lord was of the perfect, and not of the fallen stock. An entirely new start was needed, and that was accomplished through the singular character of His Conception and Birth. Hence comes the principle of the new birth in the Members of Christ. Only in them their fallen nature remains till the great Regeneration, whilst in Him it was never found.

It is impossible to examine these errors upon the great Doctrine of the Incarnation, without seeing how dangerous it is for people to form their own notions about the important parts of Revealed Truth, without previously ascertaining their exact lineaments as hitherto accepted and explained in the Universal Church. The Faith was once for all[1] delivered to the Saints. Those who lived close to the days which our Lord spent upon earth, must have known more about the true Faith than people living now, in the nineteenth century, with only the Holy Scriptures and their own reason to guide them. Even in the fourth and fifth centuries, the tradition must have been strong and ascertainable, whilst the finest intellects in the world were exercised on it, and many of

[1] ἅπαξ, Jude 3.

them were rearing invaluable beacons for the guidance of future ages.

The Members of the Irvingite Body indeed profess to proceed upon principles different from those which are now meriting our condemnation. But inasmuch as theirs is in fact only a Pseudo-Catholicism, the winds which are actually wafting their vessel are really such as are blowing against the Universal Church of God.

CHAPTER X.

TYPES AND SYMBOLISM.

CLOSELY connected with the Doctrine of the Incarnation is the employment of illustrations derived from types and symbols. For a purely spiritual religion, such as that which was aimed at by the Members of the Society of Friends, dispenses as far as possible with outward ceremonies and external signs and tokens. It is when the region of the Spiritual is left, and a descent is made into the visible and palpable, that types and symbols are introduced and sanctioned. No representation can be made of GOD the Father, because no man hath seen Him, nor can see Him. But when the SON of GOD assumed our flesh, He moved into the sight of men. Those who were with Him could declare " that which they had heard, and seen with their eyes, and looked upon, and their hands had handled of the Word of Life."[1] The principle of legitimate Symbolism was sanctioned for ever by the Incarnation.

Accordingly, the shadows of Redemption were cast before in the types recorded in the Old Testament. The system of the Law was a foreshadowing of the great

[1] 1 John i. 1.

Work of Christ in all its features. The deliverance out of Egypt, feasts and sacrifices, the doings of the great Day of Atonement, the constant operations in the Tabernacle or Temple, were, as is well known, full of typical meaning. And on the other hand, the period of the neglect of the Doctrine of the Incarnation was also the time when symbols in Divine Worship were neglected, and indeed condemned, as derogatory to the honour due to Almighty God. By a strange misapplication of a small part of the Old Testament, a vast portion of the rest was emptied, at one fell stroke, of all permanent meaning. The second commandment was interpreted as in effect condemnatory of the Law itself. People held themselves up haughtily, as being a long way in advance of the principles of the Law, given though it was from Above, and as moving about in a lofty spiritual region without any need of assistance from outward helps to devotion, or from representations of either Doctrine or Worship.

No wonder, as we see now, that Doctrine faded into the mist, and Worship became infrequent and cold.

The natural revulsion from this state of things, heralded by the poetic light which was shed over the relics of olden times,—as shown for example in the Poetical and Prose Romances of Walter Scott,—led Irvingites too far. We can easily imagine how attractive was the building up of a new system suggested by, and coinciding with, the hints given in the Old Testament, and presumed to possess Divine Sanction for all its arrangements. And it is at once evident how minds of a certain cast which will readily occur to us would be enamoured with continual discoveries, whether for the first time, or upon an examination of the system, of subtle adaptations, or more open resemblances. This is in fact one of the most fruitful sources of proselytism by these people. For it is most interesting as a characteristic of the present times, to observe the extreme violence on the one hand with which symbolical observances are greeted by some people, and on the other the ardency with which others cling to such observances when they have once embraced them. It is probable that many in the latter class originally felt all the dislike manifested by the former, when symbols in worship to which they were not accustomed were first presented to their acceptance.

Part of the teaching and practice about symbols, which has been in vogue amongst the Members of this Body, is excellent. For example, with respect to the difference between types and symbols:—

"A type is that which foreshadows something absent and future; as for example, Adam was a type of Christ; the sacrifices under the Law were types of the sacrifice of Christ. A symbol, on the contrary, is something used to set forth and signify things really present, but unappreciable by the senses. It may also present a visible memorial of additional important truth. For instance, the light which is kept burning before the Altar when the Holy Sacrament is there, symbolizes to us the Lord's invisible Presence: but it is also from its very nature a memorial to us that He Who is our Life, is our

Light also; and not ours only, but 'the Light which lighteth every man that cometh into the world.'[1]

"Symbolism is not peculiar to the services of the Church; not a piece of *priestly* device, as some have imagined, but a principle of universal application. The calling of a soldier, for example, is symbolized by his uniform; the royal authority of the Queen by her crown and sceptre; the endless constancy of wedded love by the giving of a ring; innocence and happiness by garments of white; mourning and bereavement by a dress of black. All the forms and customs of society are more or less symbolic, that is, arranged so as to express some intention or feeling. In like manner, the passions of the mind—joy, anger, indignation, grief, &c.—are shown by expressions of face or bodily gestures, which are all symbolic."[2]

Again, as to the place and object of symbols:—
"Symbolism is, in fact, the science of exhibiting invisible truth by visible and appropriate signs, in order that our senses may be made the helps and handmaids of our spirits, and we may be the better able to worship God. If this end be not attained, symbols are useless."[3]

Again, with reference to the dress worn in holy ministrations: "According to every principle of truth .... the most solemn and holy services should be symbolized by greater beauty and costliness in the

---

[1] No opinion is here expressed as to the question of reservation of the Holy Sacrament—a matter of the extremest delicacy, and requiring the very greatest caution.
[2] *On Symbols used in Worship*, pp. 1, 2.
[3] *Id.* pp. 28, 29.

furniture of the place where they are performed, of the vessels or instruments used, and of the vestments worn by those who officiate. This truth was shown by God in the Tabernacle, where the material principally employed in the outer court was brass. Some small parts were of silver, but there was no gold. On the other hand, in the Holy Place and the Most Holy, all was of silver and gold, except the five sockets of the five pillars at the entrance of the Holy Place, which were of brass. The Mercy-seat and Cherubim in the Most Holy Place were entirely of gold. There was therefore a gradual increase of costliness from the court to the Holy Place, and from thence to the Most Holy.

"Doubtless these things typified different degrees of spiritual worship; but they also symbolized the truth that the more sacred the place and service the more costly should be the means employed. A palace is not furnished like a cottage; a drawing-room is not furnished like a kitchen. We do not appear before a king in mean raiment. Nature itself teaches us that a distinction according to circumstances is proper, fit, and true. And to attempt to act otherwise in the House of God is to begin with doing violence to a natural instinct, implanted in us by Him Who is all-wise, and must produce evil results. If no part of the building is accounted more holy than another, all will at length be reckoned common; till the thought of its being the House of God having died out, men will not hesitate to walk into it with their hats on, even to spit upon its floor, and lounge about or sleep—things which they would not dare to do in the presence of an earthly monarch, nay, nor even in the houses of their equals. This is a very serious matter; for such is the constitution of man, that truth or error is received as much by the sight of the eye as the hearing of the ear; and it is certain that a false external symbolism will imbue the mind with false doctrine.

"It is barely possible for purity of heart to co-exist with voluntary impurity, either of our dwellings or our persons. And in like manner, it will be very difficult for us to maintain a conscious sense of the awe and reverence which are due to the Presence of God, if while our own houses are adorned with costly furniture, we let His House lie waste." [1]

The justice in the main, and the appositeness of these passages, form the apology for quoting them. Religious symbolism is simply the application to Religious Doctrine or Worship of the great fact in the constitution of our nature that we consist of bodies as well as souls and spirits. The Incarnation was the formal sanctioning in Religion of this inalienable principle of our being; and was the extension of it into a more effective system of faith and worship than had before existed. Not of course that any one can possibly expel it from Religion. The yellow garment of the bareheaded Buddhist priest, the salaams of the Moslem, the traditional dress of the Quaker, are all symbolical. But when the Son of God manifested Himself under a human Form to men, He showed that outward helps to learning and devotion are perfectly

[1] *On Symbols*, p. 35.

legitimate, provided that they truthfully set forth what they are presumed to represent, and are kept in due subordination to the right spirit of teaching or worship.

> "Segnius irritant animum demissa per aures
> Quam quæ sunt oculis subjecta fidelibus."
>
> The things we see, with vivid flash
> Rush in and move the mind ;
> But those we hear, far less distinct,
> A slower channel find.

Besides bringing out this principle,—which indeed has not yet been thoroughly learnt by us,—the Irvingites also acted upon another, which previously to this century was too much cast into the shade in this land. In the broad contrast which Luther and his later followers drew between faith and works, they laid great stress upon the ceremonial law being suspended by the Gospel. According to their teaching one would suppose that every shred of Judaism was cast away except the strictest Sabbatarianism. For curiously enough, they seemed to tighten the bonds of the latter, in proportion as they loosened the observances or the principles which were found in the Law.

Yet inasmuch as the Law was given directly from Almighty God, we cannot but suppose that, although it had mainly a temporal purpose, it was nevertheless constructed upon eternal principles. And this is exactly what the Apostle who wrote most against a bare Judaism,—presuming him to be the Author of the Epistle to the Hebrews,—strongly asserts. He calls the arrangements of the tabernacle, alike of the fabric and worship, "the patterns of things in the Heavens," or "the figures of the true."[1] So that in order to understand the true nature of the work of Redemption, or the appropriate manner of symbolizing that work in Christian worship, we are compelled to recur to the ceremonies of the Jewish Law. To neglect them is simply to treat Almighty God as if He were a merely human lawgiver, and to regard as nothing the long argument and repeated expressions in the Epistle to the Hebrews. It is to suppose that He did not understand the most fitting way of setting forth the Redemptive work, and had upon false principles reared a building which was only to attract notice as an ancient relic of a barbarous age.

So far then Irving and his followers did right. But they missed in their earlier career another principle which would have saved them from error, and in fact did not discover it till too late. The main guide in the employment of a true symbolism is the practice of the Primitive Church. The question of the true relation between the Jewish and Christian Churches had been lately worked out, when the eye-witnesses of the Lord's actions, and the hearers of His sayings, were alive to quote many apposite words or deeds of His, which have not been recorded for the direct use of future ages. There can be no doubt that the practice of the Church, in her more literary period in the fourth and fifth centuries, was true to the traditions which were carefully handed down from the twelve Apostles and their associates, who were the authorized depositaries of the Lord's Teaching.

[1] Heb. viii. 5, ix. 9—11, 12—23, 24, x. 1, 2, 11—14.

But the attempt to ascertain the Catholic teaching of the Church in her early days was an after-thought with the Members of this Body. In the time of their first organization, when they became committed inextricably to Prophets and Apostles,[1] the Catholic Church was not at all their rule of decision, but "the Bible and the Bible only." The Twelve Apostles and Twelve Prophets met together at Albury with only the Bible in their hands. Consequently, in such a subordinate matter as symbolism they could not help going wrong. And yet more than this. Being without the necessary guidance of the complete Catholic system in interpreting the Bible, they groped about in the dark for hints in type or symbol, and thus built up their Doctrines, both time-honoured and novel, as they might chance to be, into a heterogeneous structure upon an insecure foundation.

Hence came their idea that the four beasts, the four streams of Paradise, the four ingredients of incense, and the four colours of the Tabernacle, typified four Ministries in the Christian Church. Hence too their notion, so elaborately worked out, that all the parts of the Tabernacle represented Ministers of some order or other, such as the "Pillar of the Apostles," the "Pillar of the Prophets," the "Pillar of the Evangelists," and the "Pillar of the Pastors." And from their servile deductions from the letter of types and symbols, as distinguished

---

[1] "If there is anything wrong with Taplin," said one of their leading Members now deceased, "everything is wrong." Taplin is generally said to have called Cardale, which call was the original source of the Apostleship. But others say that it was Drummond.

from the broader analogy of Catholic interpretation, have arisen their mistakes in the general interpretation of the Apocalypse.

We must look then upon Irvingite symbolism with critical eyes. As an expression of a principle, far too much forgotten and neglected in the period previous to their existence and that of the Catholic Revival in the Church of England, it claims our commendation and adherence. But the applications of the principle made by these people must be tried by the rule of true Catholic Doctrine and observance. And, what is well set forth in their teaching if not in their practice, symbolism must be kept entirely subordinate to the Doctrine or Rites which it embodies. Modest and retiring, it must not attract too much attention, for that would contravene the very law of its existence. Lastly, symbolism must follow upon Doctrines and modes of worship already established: it must never at all be made the groundwork of Doctrine, and very seldom of worship.

CHAPTER XI.

EFFECT OF THE EXAMINATION.

THE System of doctrine and discipline in the Catholic Apostolic Church has now been subjected to a careful and complete examination, and it is time to collect the results which are supplied in this and in the history of the Body as previously given in the first Volume of this work. If in any way the results presented appear to tell too strongly against the Community, it will not be through any want of earnest anxiety on the part of the author to do full justice to every characteristic that weighs in its favour. The best way of discovering the place which it properly holds in the economy of grace is to note, as far as circumstances admit, all that can be justly said for, and all that can be fairly advanced against, the System before us. We shall thus be enabled to strike the true balance.

We find then a Body of people who come to Christendom and demand for twelve men, who they say have been Divinely appointed to be Apostles, the spiritual allegiance of every baptized person. This claim has been solemnly made upon myself more than once, accompanied with solemn denunciations of my wickedness in refusing to receive this claim,—made in no unchristian spirit,— and of the danger which a persistence in such a refusal is presumed certainly to entail. Moreover this claim has been admitted by several of my clerical brethren, who have either openly or secretly placed themselves under the guidance of these so-called Apostles. When therefore those who ought to be leaders of the flock are induced to acknowledge these new teachers who make such imperative demands upon all baptized Christians, it seems necessary that some one should carefully examine the grounds for those demands, and present them as fairly as he can for the judgment of the Church at large.

There is much in the manner in which the claim is advanced which is in keeping with the high nature of the claim. Many at least of the Evangelists and the other Members of the Body are thoroughly in earnest. If on the one hand there is evidently a want of previous Theological training, and of an accurate or wide view of the Church's tenure of Divine Truth, there is on the other an unhesitating acceptance of the new authority, and a positive and unswerving dogmatism which is quite in accordance with the postulate of a great Revelation actually delivered from Heaven.

This dogmatism, as we have seen, is carried out in the mode of rule adopted by the Apostles. So far so, indeed, as to suggest more than suspicion, that the rule itself is simply of human origin. For a close examination reveals in many cases an absence of the wisdom which is from above and bears the stamp of Heaven. Still the skill with which the Body has been conducted, and opposing forces whether of doctrine or discipline have been reconciled and brought into harmonious operation, the moderation and modesty with which claims have been put forward, and the success with which their manner of worship—including their Liturgy—has been constituted and regulated, are decidedly in the favour of the so-called Catholic Apostolic Church.

Many exemplary features in the habits of the Members should also be noted. Their great regularity in attending public worship, their devotion to sacred purposes of at least a tithe of their incomes, and the good characters which they severally bear, must be taken as witnessing to the validity of the claim, even when we subtract the strong inducements which always act upon a small Sect, especially when maintaining that they have a special Revelation lifting them up above the rest of the world.

Again, we cannot help remarking, and are glad to remark, that these people have been led amongst others to recover and to cling closely to some old treasures of the Catholic Church, which had in many places been obscured and forgotten. They have placed in conspicuous light the Church's duty of watching for the Lord's Second Coming, the Doctrine of the Incarnation, the necessity and the advantage of a grand and ornate mode of Worship, the Doctrine of Eucharistic Sacrifice, and the need of Catholic Unity.

All these points are in favour of the so-called Catholic

Good Characteristics. 319

Apostolic Church. If they are not sufficient proof of the justice of the claims advanced, yet they demonstrate that there is here a large amount of good, if mingled with evil or error. The theory of such a system being invented in Hell is utterly exploded. At least it must take rank amongst the numerous mixed Systems which Christianity has witnessed.

We may now turn to the other side of the question. First of all, the verdict of the Catholic Church is wholly on the opposite side. For at least seventeen centuries no traces can be discovered of the peculiar Tenet of a Fourfold Ministry, and especially of the need of Apostles and Prophets :—yet it is inconceivable that the Church should have been unconscious of such a mutilation. How could she possibly have continued through all that roll of years, in all circumstances of unity or division, of quiet life or controversy, of growth or languor, without manifesting any signs that she was conscious of having lost an important limb, which should have united her to Heaven above, and to the Incarnate Lord? Again, at the present side of the seventeen centuries just mentioned, even amidst a remarkable outburst of earnest piety and longings for the action of a more perfect organization, no integral portion of the Church, no eminent persons in the Church whether for learning or piety, no large number of the rank and file of Churchmen, have accepted these people. They themselves admit that their preaching is not received. *Qui s'excuse, s'accuse.* And in the first century no proof is adduced, except a few doubtful passages in the Bible, to say the most. So that Catholic Testimony is unquestionably and unexceptionally condemnatory of their claims.

Then as to Holy Scripture. · We have seen that the foundation claimed for these Doctrines, which ought to have such vital importance, is slender indeed. Careful examination reduces it to still more slender proportions, and reveals a sandy bottom of a very treacherous nature When props arĕ constructed out of dark symbolic hints, and only one straightforward passage can be adduced, which is capable of another and a more natural interpretation, and violence must be done to the next passage in order to press it into the service, it is clear that proof is hard to find. While no one who accepts Catholic Doctrines could possibly interpret any passage of Holy Scripture in the teeth of continuous explanation in the opposite direction.

Again, these people make a great display of Catholicity of teaching. How can they have the assurance to do so, we cannot but ask, when they are maintaining these Tenets in open defiance of Catholic opinion? No doubt, especially in the compilation of their Liturgy and in the ordering of their worship, they have followed the example of the Early Church, and have given a Catholic colouring to their entire system. Still this, and even more than this, is not enough to prove Catholicity. As we have already seen, we must pierce to the centre in order to estimate the true nature of anything. Catholicity is shown, not by a certain amount of outward conformity, or by embracing various Doctrines held in the purer days of the Universal Church; but by a maintenance of the Catholic Rule of Faith, holding what the Catholic Church has always held, and especially by rejecting what the Catholic Church has always rejected; also by preserving the continuity and succession of life.

This truth is strongly exemplified in the question of rejecting or retaining what is alien to the Catholic Faith. The original adoption of such alien Tenets is thoroughly uncatholic: because Catholic-minded people always enquire whether the Church has given any sanction to a new idea. But when the absence of such a sanction is positively demonstrated, as in the case of these so-called Apostles and Prophets, the refusal to give them up implies not only insubordination to the Catholic Church, but that the maintainers of these Tenets place themselves in the position of judges and condemners of the Catholic Church. For they assert that it has been the want of faith, and necessarily ignorance too, which have stood in the way of Apostles and Prophets rising up. And they can bring forward no evidence to show that the Catholic Church of any age ever entertained their ideas, while they maintain the importance of these ideas to be so vast, that it is absolutely incredible that the Church should not have been well acquainted with them, if they had been part of the Christian Faith.

Further, Catholicity in their case is precluded by the break in religious life which occurred between them and the Church. For the Church is like a vast forest-tree, in which the sap runs continuously through the trunk, the limbs, the boughs, to the branchlets and the leaves. Continuity of succession is therefore simply essential to any Religious Body being a true Branch of the Church of Christ. Other trees may be planted, parasites may grow from the bark and even send their roots into the wood : but they are not parts of that one Tree, because Christ our Lord Alone planted that, and they have been planted or sown in some other way. For this continuity the Apostolical succession of Bishops, though it does not by any means exhaust it, is nevertheless absolutely necessary, because the Sacraments must be duly administered, and they can only be thus duly administered by those who have the title from our Lord, handed down through the men to whom He Himself gave it, and who thus possess His own authorization so to administer them. No others can act with His authority. This is a matter of common-sense order. But these people have no succession of the kind. Not a single Catholic Bishop has ever joined them. They are therefore plainly from an origin other than the Catholic Church. This is quite sufficient as proof: but we may also remark that no integral Branch of the Catholic Church has after the fact acknowledged them. All have rejected them. They stand by themselves.

Passing then on from these decisive considerations, we have examined the leading portions of the scheme of teaching presented to our consideration. We here put the question, "Are these true Apostles or not?" to a theological proof. Examining the nature of the credentials of the Twelve Apostles of our Lord, we have found that their credentials as Apostles were wrapped up in the indisputable fact, that they were designated and appointed by our Lord Himself. If He stood, they stood: if He were to fall, they must fall. Their appointment was outward, public, unquestionable, and never questioned. We have seen too that the instances of SS. Matthias, Paul, and Barnabas, were not outside the pale of this principle: because the first of these was chosen to fill up a vacancy out of those who had associated with our Lord from the very first, under circumstances of exceptional solemnity, and by the unanimous determination of those who derived their title directly from our Lord in Person: because St. Paul was acknowledged by these very Twelve as one who had actually seen the Lord after His ascension, and had been positively and definitely sent by Him: while St. Barnabas is one who has had the same title applied to him by the same authority and that of the Universal Church, probably under a wider acceptation of the term Apostle than it has acquired after eighteen centuries of prescriptive and venerable use.

None of these points touch these present men, who indeed are by no means alone in the history of the Church in laying claim to the title Apostle. Montanists, Mormons, and others, have arrogated it to themselves upon similar, if not identical, grounds.

But we have dived deeper into the mysteries of this question. We have discovered, chiefly from St. Paul's case, and from the words which he has used about his own claim to the Apostleship, that four credentials are necessary to establish such a claim. Any one must prove (1) Appointment by our Lord in Person; (2) An outward Act of Ordination; (3) Acceptance by the Church; and (4) Success sufficient to justify the appointment. Of these four credentials, these men only attempt to claim two. They do not pretend that the Lord Jesus Christ has with His own lips sent them forth; they only maintain a secret call like that which every one of Christ's ministers have had, though in varying degree. It is notorious that they have never been accepted by the Church Catholic. Two credentials alone therefore remain.

Have they had such a success as to justify their claim after the event? They acknowledge their own failure. They have been unable to convince other Christians possessed of at least as much learning, candour, earnestness, and love of the Lord Jesus Christ, as themselves, though they have tried over and over again. The signs and wonders, in the expectation of which this movement was commenced, have not followed: and one of their own number has left them in consequence. According to their early principles, all the acts of the so-called Apostolic College have been invalidated ever since 1840. They began a practice of "Sealing" which they believed would convey a title to places in our Lord's own Retinue to the amount of 12,000 places for each Tribe, which they asserted must be filled up before He came:—three Apostles refused to seal at all, some "Tribes" have none sealed in them, and now nearly all the "Apostles" have gone to their rest. After more than forty years' operations, the Body numbers some 10,500, or so, all told.

This is the success which these men, at the end as they represent of the Church's career, seek to parallel with the wonderful growth of the Church in her earliest days under the fostering care of the true Apostles. The compilation of a Liturgy with many merits and several blots, the exertion of tact and skill in keeping together and conducting the affairs of the Community, and the maintenance of exemplary outward life in the several Members,—qualities of a strictly human character which have been paralleled in the case of many leaders of Christian Sects,—are held sufficient to counterbalance all the points of admitted failure just enumerated, and to establish a claim to Apostleship.

But they say that these Twelve men were appointed by the Voice of the Church. How, and by what Church? That Branch of the Catholic Church in England which derives its descent, first from the Branch of the Church which occupied these Islands in the time of the domination of the Roman Empire, and afterwards from St. Augustine coming here with a special mission and founding the Saxon Church? The English Church has, so to speak, washed her hands of the whole matter. Or the Roman Communion, which, unfortunately to the subversion of Catholic order, has a Branch here in a country already tenanted by the Church? They themselves admit that scarce any Roman Catholics at all have received them. Or the Orthodox Greek Church? She declines to have any part or lot with them.

No: the so-called appointment was made by the Angels, who had been ordained or consecrated by the Apostles. What a movement in a circle! Apostles consecrate Angels, and then Angels consecrate Apostles. How could they have been driven, it may be asked, to such shifts? Plainly because they had no external authority to rest upon. The Rock of the Incarnation, on which the ordained Ministry of the Church stands in palpable and definite descent and growth upon the Lord Jesus Christ, utterly fails these people. Having only a foundation in sand, they wattle together Angels with Apostles, and Apostles with Angels, inside the building, in order to make up for the absence of that other Foundation, Which no man can lay where it has not been already laid.

So then no appointment can be claimed for these men analogous to the appointment of the Apostles of our Lord, or of St. Paul. To what then can they appeal? To a presumed nomination by the Voice of the Lord Himself speaking by His Prophets. So then first, they claim no more than Montanists and others have claimed before them: and secondly, instead of a direct appointment made Personally as in the case of the Twelve and St. Paul by the Lord Jesus Christ Himself, they were nominated by a Prophet or Prophets, speaking in the power of the Holy Ghost, Who was sent by the Lord Jesus Christ, so to speak. At the very best showing therefore we have a doubly indirect, instead of a direct Personal action: two links intervene between the Lord Jesus Christ and His presumed Apostles. This of course

materially alters and weakens the appointment as analo‑
gous to that of the Apostles of our Lord.

Still it might possibly be asked with some lingering doubt, as we have seen, whether the utterance of the so-called Prophets, though long-drawn, so to speak, and dissimilar to what occurred in the first ages of the Church, was nevertheless the Speech of God, or whether it was the invention of man: in other words, were these true Prophets, or were they not?

In order to decide this question, it was necessary to review the position of the real and false Prophets whom the history of the Church has witnessed. We find that many false Prophets have risen since our Lord ascended into Heaven. The Montanist Prophets, George Fox the Quaker, the Camisards in France, Swedenborg, Joanna Southcote, Shakers, Mormons, Plymouth Brethren, Agapemonites, Mrs. Girling, and others, present to us instances of a special arrogation of spiritual gifts, enabling them as asserted to speak directly the Will of Almighty God. In the presence of all these claims, we found it necessary to examine the cases of true Prophets in the Bible, in order to discover how we might know whether any Prophet claiming to speak in the Name of God is a true Prophet or not.

After an exhaustive survey, the canons arrived at were the following:—First, the prophecies delivered must agree with the Faith already revealed; secondly, in the case of a new line of Prophets springing up afresh after an interval—especially an unprecedentedly long interval—of the cessation of the spirit of Prophecy, miracles have invariably accompanied the outburst of the supernatural Gift; and thirdly, the predictions given must be soon verified by the event.

A careful examination of the so-called prophecies of these men, as illustrated by their history, showed us that they cannot answer to any one of these three canons. They have attempted to introduce violent alterations into the Constitution of the Church, which by the negative Voice of the Church are shown to be alien to her, and subversive of her arrangements. They not only have no miracles which are not referrible to natural causes; but inasmuch as they have frequently argued at length, that miracles are not essential as credentials of Apostles, it must be concluded that they surrender upon this point. And thirdly, many of their prophecies have been falsified by the event: and of course falsified prophecies afford quite as strong a proof in condemnation, as verified prophecies do in confirmation.

This conclusion that these Prophets have quite failed to satisfy the examination warranted, and indeed ordered[1] by the Bible, was strengthened by various other considerations.

First, the prophecies themselves do not show any superhuman character. On the contrary, many of them are vapid in the extreme, and appear to bear just the character which a purely human imitation of prophetical Gifts would exhibit.

Secondly, these people themselves, by their gradual reduction of their so-called Prophets into a lower

---

[1] "Try the prophets whether they are of God."—1 John iv. 1.

position, and by the strong restraint which they place over them, and their rejection of so many "prophecies" uttered under circumstances and with a character precisely similar to the circumstances or character of others which were allowed, show that they are unable to treat them with the deference, which men really actuated directly by the Holy Spirit of God, and their utterances, must of necessity have demanded.

Thirdly, the strange travesty of the events of the great Day of Pentecost, according to which mere gibberish was uttered, in imitation of the Gift of Tongues by which the Apostles spoke to every man in the language to the use of which he was born, strengthens our position in the eyes of all who have not allowed themselves to be blinded. The fact that a defence has led these people, and must lead them, into the really disingenuous attempt to show, in opposition to the plain words of St. Luke, that the Apostles merely used unintelligible sounds, is one of very pregnant meaning.

Again, we saw, that although the twelfth and fourteenth chapters of the First Epistle to the Corinthians, even if interpreted with Irvingite meaning, would not prove their position, the passage is generally misunderstood by the Members of the "Catholic Apostolic Church."

Lastly, it was shown, that the mere power of the human mind to produce results, when the entire soul and self of the agent has been, under circumstances the most favourable, projected upon the effort with all the force and energy of long-continued preparation and enthusiastic desire, is such as to be equal without extraordinary supernatural aid to work such effects as have been here recorded.

We have also examined the views current amongst the Members upon the subjects of Unfulfilled Prophecy, the Incarnation, and Symbolism, and not only have derived nothing in proof of the justice of their position, but have instead discovered various points in which rashness in drawing conclusions, want of appreciation of their subject, and deficient acquaintance with the Catholic Faith, have made them appear to be unsafe guides to follow, when they quit the old ways of Christianity.

Such then being the general nature of the very powerful argument which is ready to the hand of any one who may set himself carefully to examine both sides of this general question,—one side being so weak, and the side of rejection being so overwhelmingly strong, —we cannot but wonder what the Members of this Body can advance in reply. How will they satisfy themselves and make any plausible answer?

From various discussions with them and from their numerous books, I believe that, except so far as such an answer might reiterate pleas already refuted in these pages, it would take the following form :—

"The argument which has been just recited is the pleading of a man who is only half informed upon the subject on which he writes. None can judge in this matter but those who have seen and witnessed the events that have occurred. Any other judgment is founded only upon indirect evidence and is therefore useless. We have seen and known the real life. And for certain, without doubt or hesitation, we know that it is of God.

"Again, it is wholly wrong to pass judgment in this manner. The world has always condemned the things of Christ. Noah preached without effect. Our Lord Himself was disregarded though He spake as never man spake. He who takes upon himself to sit over these holy subjects, and to express opinions about them from above, instead of looking up to them from beneath in the spirit of a humble and docile learner, is sure to go wrong. Let him beware how he provokes the Holy Spirit of God, and entails judgment upon himself.

"Thirdly, what is the alternative if we give up the earnest faith and the solemn and primitive worship of our Body? You wish us to return to the Church of England. Consider the state of that Church at the present moment. In the first place, see how she is bound hand and foot by the State. She is more of a Parliament Church, than a Branch of the Catholic Church of Christ. See for example how many people within her borders deny the Sacraments. One does not believe in the Grace of Baptism. A very large number openly cavil at, or secretly disbelieve, the Doctrine of Eucharistic Sacrifice. Observe the unbelief, the neglect of Ordinances, the cases before the Courts, the general lawlessness. We have none of this: indeed the Religious Life amongst us exhibits the strongest contrast to this sad view. How can we come back to the Church of

England as a Branch of the Catholic Church, when its Catholicity is denied by many if not most of its Members, and when there is the certain prospect of her breaking up into several separate Sects, as soon as disestablishment removes from her the strong hand of the State."

I have merely stated in this part of the Irvingite objection what has been actually advanced again and again to myself and others. It is well that we should know and calmly examine the charges which other people, differing from us in opinion, bring against us.

It will be best to take first the second of the three arguments just advanced. This is very similar to a plea before discussed;[1] but as it is very frequently urged, and reiterated by the Evangelists and other advocates of their Tenets, we shall do well to consider it again in a garb slightly varied.

It may be taken in two aspects:—either that every one ought to accept these Apostles as undoubtedly sent from Heaven, without careful enquiry or scrutiny; or secondly, that it is exceedingly presumptuous and wicked in the author of this work to put himself forward to make a public examination of these claims which are brought out under such awful sanction.

In the first case, these people have evidently misunderstood the principle involved in the passages in the Bible upon which they depend. Honest, candid, earnest enquiry is nowhere forbidden. We are ordered to try the Spirits, whether they are of God. Our Lord bid the

---

[1] Above, Vol. II. pp. 96, &c.

Jews of His time to search the Scriptures to see whether they testified of Him. The history of St. Paul's journeys reveals his encouragement of a similar mode of enquiry amongst those to whom he preached.[1] Our Lord recognized the use of reason when He told His disciples to be "wise as serpents" as well as "harmless as doves." Members of the "Catholic Apostolic Church" themselves appeal to the same principle in the treatises which of course they address to the outside world, and in which they marshal carefully all the arguments that seem to them to establish their position. So long as we keep far from us all prejudice, and unfairness, and excess, and violence, and strive simply to weigh carefully and equitably the considerations upon both sides of the question, and are also simply anxious that whatever is right in the Sight of Almighty God should prevail, we cannot surely be wrong. If there are flaws in the arguments used, Members of the Body can point them out. If the arguments are valid, no amount of invective against a presumed want of docility and humility can set them right. And when a real candour and submission to what is shown to be right are demanded of one side, they must be also conceded by the other.

With respect to the other view of this plea, viz., that it is presumptuous and wrong in any private individual who is no more than a Parish Priest of the Church of England to put himself forward to examine these claims, my excuse is this. Mr. Cardale, as Apostle for England, claimed spiritual jurisdiction over every Baptized

[1] Acts xvii. 11.

person, and over myself too,—and this under an averred Divine Mission. I have known Clergymen younger than myself, whom I have regarded as men with a great promise of doing good in the Church of Christ, admit these demands. They have appeared to me therefore to require a careful examination at the hands of some one. And I have further thought, that if the materials for forming a right judgment were collected into a convenient compass and made public, that much good must of necessity ensue under the good Providence of Almighty God. Moreover, having myself made a careful examination by reading everything I could find anywhere, and by enquiry at head-quarters; and having become convinced that many good persons have been mistaken or deceived by a plausibility which some of the arguments put forward wear at first sight, I am anxious with the Divine Blessing to strip off this plausibility, and by exhibiting the System in its true light, to win back, if possible, many souls to the Catholic Church of Christ, who have inadvertently been led into a positive schism. Therefore I have attempted to speak with all the fairness, and candour, and openness that I can command; and to examine every single allegation that I can discover. Whether this be right or wrong, others will judge:— nay rather HE especially, whose Guidance and Blessing has been continually invoked throughout.

Part of the reply to the first head in the plea which we are considering is implied in what has been just said. Besides this, how can any proof still lie behind which is equal to making good the deficiencies which we have discovered in the proofs before the world? Evangelists, apologists, and writers generally, must have been strangely wanting to their duty, whether from lack of ordinary ability or otherwise, if they have neglected to bring forward grounds sufficient to set the Christian Church right upon such vital points. . The numerous treatises, sermons, and pamphlets, which form almost a complete literature, and evince great mental effort on the part of their several authors, must be marvellously defective, if they do not tell us what according to these people all Christians ought to know to their eternal interest. And when men stop the enquiries or the doubts of others simply by dogmatic assertion of the proposition under dispute, or disciples try to close discussion by a mere reference to the *ipse dixit* of their Master, people of mature experience, and possessed of a knowledge of the class of phenomena under dispute sufficient to enable them to form an opinion, know what conclusion to draw. Mere dogmatism is weakness, when an open argument is conducted before a competent tribunal.

The sole resource therefore now left is an attempt to remove the field of action into the heart of the adversary's country.' What then can be fairly said in defence of this attack upon the Church of England?

That any one who reads the Bible, and studies the state of belief and practice in the Early Church, would wish many things to be very different in the Catholic Church generally, and in that Branch of it which occupies England, is but too true. The want of unity is a grievous loss which must be felt in many ways. Has the so-called

"Catholic Apostolic Church" remedied this, or is there the slightest chance that such a diminutive Body, with the defects and failures recounted, could ever remedy it? The infidelity, again, that prevails in many places, and the misunderstanding of and disbelief in the Doctrine of the Sacraments in others, are doubtless grievous disadvantages.

But we ought also to observe what an extensive improvement in the latter province has been made in the last forty years. This remarkable growth to the appreciation and acceptance of Catholic Doctrine, which has shown itself directly in one of the large schools of thought in the Church, and has spread indirectly but even in a more remarkable manner amongst the other two schools, affords the greatest hope of future good. After a period of sad deterioration, when Christian Truth was being confined to a few Articles in the Creed, and belief was being narrowed and pared down to mere sectarian dimensions, we are growing generally towards a condition of Catholic apprehension of Divine Truth, which ought to leave no just reason for any people to fall off into other associations, because every genuine aspect of the Truth would be appreciated within the walls of the Church. Perhaps this may be a pitch of perfection not to be reached upon earth. Still the remarkable extent in which the breadth of the Broad Church has of late acted upon High Churchmen, fostered by the spirit of comprehensiveness necessarily inherent in Catholic Truth, adds to the advantages which have been reaped in the last forty years.

It is needless to recount the signs of outward improvement which have spread over our land, in every diocese, and almost in every town and village. Such tokens of an undeniable amelioration are notorious. But we cannot omit to draw one inference, well warranted, or rather, humanly speaking, necessitated by these facts. Such an advance must under God continue. A careful observer might calculate a minimum ratio of the improvement to be anticipated in the next ten years, under the fostering care of the Holy Spirit, by observing the accelerated progress in each of the last four decades. Such an advance, both retrospective and prospective, cannot but argue a strong force of life moving in the English Communion.

Meanwhile the Colonial Churches, which, under the continuing neglect of past generations, had scarce any existence, have grown up in a cluster round their Mother, strengthening her in return for life and blessings received, and working out as in virgin soil some of the difficult problems, which in England have become encrusted with the deposits of a debased spiritual life, guarded from removal by jealous and persistent prejudice.

There is no Conservatism so strong and blind as religious Conservatism. And justly so. Religion is a matter in great measure of habit and feeling. In Religion wisdom is rare, zeal is comparatively common. Reasoning without zeal is about as frequently found as zeal alone, and is unfortunately in times of improvement at least as likely to lead people astray. An inadequate estimate of these truths conducts to error of two kinds.

Either people imagine that the difficulties, which are sure to arise when improvement is going on, are much more formidable than they really are; or they set down to the score of revolutionary change those portions of improvement, which in fact result from the return to a realization of the true principles of the Church's existence. The former of these errors is involved in the charge brought by the Members of the so-called Catholic Apostolic Church against the Church in England. The latter is seen in those who from want of penetration into the real nature of things, or from yielding without due thought to the irritation which any enforced change of habit rouses in us, impede improvement, perhaps with sullenness, perhaps with determined opposition, and in some cases with violence.

Meanwhile there are several forces which promote the advance. One of the chief of these is curiously enough a common misconception of the nature and meaning of the separate improvements introduced. Doctrines are caricatured: and strangest of all, the caricaturists doggedly refuse to believe that the supporters of the Doctrines in question do not embrace the caricatures made by these opponents, in spite of all the denials and explanations of the introducers themselves. Consequently, they spend their strength in an opposition, which, though hindering at first, turns out eventually, as far as real argument and permanent effects are concerned, to be a mere beating of the air.

Such has eminently been the case with reference to the use of crosses in churches. Some people have urged violently, that the introducers of such crosses wanted to pay them some extravagant veneration. The sober sense and the moderate habits of English Churchmen have utterly dispelled this illusion, in their experience of the employment of those symbols of the Faith.

Just so, people at the present time impute to the maintainers of the Doctrine of Eucharistic Sacrifice a glaring caricature of that Doctrine, which they get by taking the language used in the Roman Communion and giving it the stiffest matter-of-fact interpretation. Whereas what is really maintained is the teaching of Mede,—a strong opponent of Rome,—that what we plead in words when we say " through Jesus Christ our Lord," that we plead outwardly at the Holy Eucharist. Thus this Doctrine, into which there is not time and space to enter here,[1] assumes a thoroughly moderate character, and only explanation is needed to prove that it is really not open to the charges brought against it. It is most truly Evangelical, for it forms the main defence, application, and realization of the One Sacrifice, offered once for all by the One Great High-Priest in behalf of all His people.

Indeed, the great need at the present time is moderation both on the extreme left and on the extreme right, and more calm wisdom too in the centre of the position. And the great source of hope lies in the knowledge that in course of time such calm wisdom and such moderation,

---

[1] Amongst other writers, the Rev. M. F. Sadler, Rector of Honiton, has excellently shown the Scriptural nature of this Doctrine in *The One Offering*. George Bell and Sons : London, 1875.

as history has shown, always win their way amongst the English people. It is the veriest chimera to imagine that England will ever become Roman Catholic. Romanism is a long way from the hearts of the English nation, and is alien to their manner of thought and habit. The sanguine Head of the Roman hierarchy in our country once allowed ten years for the accomplishment of their conversion. The ten years ended some seven years ago, and to all appearance the conversion of England to the Papacy is as far off as ever. No: what English Churchmen will do is this :—They will take the Doctrines and observances which have the true stamp of the Catholic Church upon them, whether they are found in Romanism or whether they are not, and then they will interpret them in their own sober way, and hold or use them with their own sober moderation. The history of the last forty years has shown this, and it also has shown that we must expect delay and discouragement in the accomplishment. For on the one hand an exaggerated stress is laid upon everything that bears the trace of novelty both by adherents and opponents, especially if they are possessed of the fresh enthusiasm of youth; and on the other, there is a lamentable want of penetration often evinced, where we should expect a juster estimate of the nature of the contest, and of the principles really at stake.

A few more words are necessary to make this position clear.

One of the great grounds of contention at present is the true position of the Church of England as a Branch of the Catholic Church. The more stress must now be laid upon this, because if once the Members of the Religious Body under consideration were convinced of it, they would see that a return to her full communion would present the least difficulty of any course open to them. It is not necessary to demonstrate here the connection of the English Church with the Catholic Church, because they will admit that that is proved by the continuous life of the Church in England, including the unbroken succession of the Bishops and Clergy, and by the unintermitted maintenance of the Creeds and Sacraments. The only question is, whether the English Church will pull herself up to a more Catholic standard and to a closer union with the Catholic Church of all ages, or whether she will pursue a downward course. Late experience furnishes an answer in great measure to this dilemma: but I think it will receive most important illustration from the following truths.

As long as the Church after our Lord's time was confined to a small fraction of the then civilized population, she rejected all half-sympathizers, and continued to preserve in unity of mind and Doctrine the pure features of the true Faith once delivered to the saints. When the world "awoke and found herself Christian," and the Church became conterminous with civilization, the one unbroken tradition was able, through the prestige attaching to the one School which handed down the Faith, to keep itself pure and unspotted from the world. How severe the struggle was, is shown by the history of the Councils in the fourth, fifth, sixth, and seventh centuries.

Still under God's good Providence, Catholic orthodoxy and purity were victorious.

But now, at length and by degrees, we have come to this. Nations within the Catholic Church apply their own several acceptations to the One Faith, and stoutly maintain in each case that the acceptation as formed and interpreted by themselves is the only one admissible.

Thus the Greek Church will allow only its own realization of what is orthodox and must be observed. And under the Greek Church is included the vast area of nations whose civilization is built upon the influence of the ancient Greeks, or who in religious matters at least have been brought within that influence.

Again, the Roman Communion embraces the old Latin races, and the Celtic races too, who, as in France especially, showed a marvellous power of assimilating Roman customs and language, probably owing to some near relationship between the nations. The acceptation of the One Faith in the Roman Communion has been strongly affected by the forcible, imaginative, impressible, and impetuous natures of the Latin and Celtic peoples. Their religion is eminently unfitted for the phlegmatic, dreamy, homely, matter-of-fact Teuton. Romanism cannot successfully cope with the Teutonic mind. Accordingly, when German thought awoke at the Reformation, the attempt was made under Luther to form a German acceptation of the Common Faith. Most unfortunately this was a failure, owing to the omission of integral and essential portions. Especially the Episcopal succession was not transmitted. We are witnessing another attempt now under the Alt-Katholiks, which we must hope may not fail, though their organization, and especially their Episcopacy, are allowed to remain dangerously weak.

Between the Teutonic and Celtic Races,—not here to notice the Dutch, Danish, and Swedish Churches,—come ethnologically the English. For not only in the mixed Norman blood, but in the remains of Celtic life amongst the Anglo-Saxons, which, if Mr. Freeman will allow it, were much larger than is generally supposed, we find Celtic material. And the Saxon element is also modified by a Scandinavian admixture, and the addition of foreigners of numerous nations has helped to make us many-sided. Accordingly, through our origin as well as through our wide influence in the world, we are fitted to become the mediators, uniters, and consolidators of the several divisions in the Church of Christ. But none the less have we too, through our strong insular prejudice and narrow-mindedness, coloured and limited our acceptation of Catholic Doctrine and discipline, as it is needless now to prove.

These truths, which are surely in the main self-evident upon the stating of them, account for the present disunion in the Church of Christ. Hordes of ignorant barbarians swept over the civilized world, before the Church was strong enough to hold her ground without loss. The thorough Christianization of these fresh-lived nations has never yet been satisfactorily and perfectly accomplished. A strong attempt was made at the period of the Reformation; but though it effected a great deal, it cannot be called successful. But it was full of lessons for after-times. And our business now is to gather these lessons from the results of the work thus effected, and to apply them to our own age.

What we have to do then is clearly this. We must recur to the fount of pure water which welled forth from Heaven in the days of the early Church. We must throw aside the peculiarities introduced by each nation, and endeavour to discover and to keep the central Catholic Faith to which the Church witnessed in her undivided state. Not of course that each Branch of the Church may not adapt the Faith, as set forth in observances, to the special needs and habits of the people interested; provided only that the Faith itself and the essential Rites and Ceremonies are not violated. The inhabitants upon the sides of a river may decorate the banks after their own taste, if only they do not vitiate the stream, or in any degree dam up the passage. So far as portions of the Faith are omitted or slurred over, or important observances are allowed to fall into neglect, so far in proportion is the Church weakened, and room is left for error to spring up: for that is generally the perversion of some neglected truth. Accordingly, the English Church has been gradually working back more and more into a complete possession of the heritage of the Church: and it is the duty of all who are able to look beyond the scene immediately in front of them, to aid her in this improvement and advance.

Such then having been the gradual progress, people must not be too impatient, or too ready to find fault, or too prone to conclude that things are worse than they really are. On the one hand, if there is religious zeal, we must expect some religious sensationalism. When the excitement of novelty has worn off, soberness and moderation are sure to succeed. And on the other, when the opponents of Catholic Truths or Ceremonies come to see that extreme error is not involved, but that the Truths or Ceremonies in question are capable of a moderate interpretation, then the opposition will become faint, and after lapse of time will die away.

Still this description may be supposed not to embrace the entire nature of the present disputes in the English Church. The fact is then, that we are now coming into the thick of a struggle depending upon the working out of the problem concerning the due relations between the Church and the State. A few words are necessary to bring out the salient points in this struggle.

The secret of the present perplexity lies in the fact that through the developments and adjustments of the age, we have drifted away from the old English Constitution. When the Prayer-book was reduced to its present shape, the Clergy were represented in Convocation, and the Laity in Parliament and by the Sovereign. And in their order, both became consenting parties. But since that time, most important changes have been introduced both into Convocation as representing the Clergy, and especially into Parliament. The Clergy have as a Body grown considerably in late years, and now two influential classes are not represented in Convocation, viz., the Clergy engaged directly in education—a most important

Body,—and the numerous staff of Curates. So that Convocation does not possess the authority or the efficiency which is really within its reach if properly constituted.

But the changes in Parliament are, as regards the Church, much more sweeping. When the Prayer-book was last revised, the Parliament that agreed to it was the English Parliament alone. Now the representation of the Laity in Parliament was fatally spoilt in 1707, A.D., by the union with the Scotch Parliament. At the present we have therefore, besides the Laity of the English Church, first, the Scotch Peers and Commoners, including especially Scotch Presbyterians who are not in Communion with the English Church. Next, after 1800, A.D., we have Irish Members, including Roman Catholics and Presbyterians. And thirdly, English Nonconformists. It is perfectly plain therefore, that the idea of the English Parliament representing the Laity of the English Church is a pure figment. And the only extraordinary point is, that this is not notorious in the eyes of every well-informed man.[1]

But this anomalous condition of Church Government derives additional importance from another feature of the present day. The law-abiding instincts of Englishmen are demanding a strict enforcement of Church Law.

---

[1] The good people of Edinburgh or Dublin, whether individually or representatively, are not Laity of the Church of England, any more than the inhabitants of New York or Vienna. Parliament represents the Imperial, not the Lay, interest in the Church of England as Established. No argument is necessary to refute an opinion which is at variance with the elementary principles of representation.

Now from the nature of written law, it can only be strictly enforced by the judicial and executive powers, when there is at the same time a Legislative authority in action to redress the inequalities necessarily incident to a written code. But we have seen that the Legislative authority of the Church is at present only a rusty blade, which cannot be wielded without danger to the brandishers, and at best can only meet with a clumsy use.

But then it may be asked, how it is to be reformed. This is a delicate and difficult question, which must be worked out by the present generation. Besides the relations between Church and State, it involves also the mutual positions of Clergy and Laity: the former as the men ordained in direct succession from our Lord, and the only men of whose learning and character the Church possesses any guarantee; and the latter as responsible for the finances necessary for the maintenance of the Church, and as being very different from the uneducated Laity of former ages, including the period of the Primitive Church. It is clear that the Government of the Church must be regulated upon Ecclesiastical lines. And the ascending units of the Parish and the Diocese, and, in a fainter colour, of the Province and the National Church, should find their recognition according to their relative importance. The several Colonies of the English Empire where the same problem is being already worked out, though under conditions somewhat different, may supply hints, reference being always made to the Church of the first ages.

In the face then of this difficult problem, we may again take heart, because we find that several of the difficulties, of which some people make so much, and which are no doubt serious, are to be referred to the inequalities arising from ephemeral sources. Still even here we have not yet exhausted the trials of the present time. What shall we say for the infidelity which has of late become so rife?

No observer of the religious currents at the present time can make light of the strong unbelief of various shades which is prevalent, especially amongst laymen of acknowledged and indeed eminent ability, and of highly-cultivated minds. But we must remember, that if the existence of this widely-spread unbelief is brought as a charge against the English Church, it can only be so brought in a very limited degree. The large area which the Church covers, and the instinctive dislike of schism which actuates many, causes many people to be credited to her who are living practically outside her walls. No doubt much is due, and perhaps more than people think, to the confined and debased state of religion, especially in the last century. But those whose present religious system is built upon the acknowledgment of this neglect, cannot, except in a minor degree, charge it upon the English Church of the present day. Still taking this infidelity as it now actually exists, are there any considerations of encouragement to those who would wish to be true sons of the Church of Christ, holding the entire Catholic Faith?

In the first place then we should bear in mind, that

outbursts of unbelief of a most formidable nature have often occurred in the History of the Church. After the time of Constantine, just such an outburst happened under the able leadership of a master-mind, Julian the Apostate. The earnestness of the Reformation Period was followed by the infidelity of the eighteenth century. In fact, times of increased religious earnestness generally lead to times of falling away from the Faith. The usual sequel of scepticism has pursued the religious movements of the first and second quarters of this century more closely than usual. This is probably an advantage: for the waters are still at their height, and are more likely to return in increased volume than if the period of neap-tides had come round. There are various reasons, besides the failure of scepticism in bygone ages, for inferring that the present overflow of unbelief, formidable as it appears in several quarters, will in course of time subside.

It has developed no one antagonist system. Its forms are many. New teachers introduce fresh ideas which are, at least in a measure, destructive of the old. The question therefore arises, "Where will it all end?" Sowing doubt, erection or exaggeration of difficulties, destruction of idols, are easy enough. But to rear a new system, around which others than mere disciples will gather, and which will rival or out-top the Catholic Faith,—this is as far off as ever in the dim horizon. Meanwhile some of the leading minds amongst the new philosophers testify to the continuous homogeneity of the Catholic Faith. Strauss saw nothing admissible beyond a belief in the possible existence of good. In fact, descending the mountain, he found no place to rest permanently upon, between the summit and the plains or marshes underneath. The plateaux on the mountain-side would prove to be only resting-places for a limited number of people in their ascent or descent. So the forms of opposition accumulate. In philosophy, besides the old forms of Deism, Atheism, and Scepticism, we have Positivists, Agnostics, and others: in Religion, we find 153 Sects[1] in England, besides several others in America not found on this side of the Atlantic. And these numbers are on the increase. What can resist the indirect testimony thus borne to the one Catholic Apostolic Church of Christ by these multiplying forms of dissension and unbelief or half-belief?

Much too of the present scepticism can be traced to the fact that many people are now in positions of influence, whose progenitors, if I mistake not, have not been thorough Churchmen. John Stuart Mill succeeded to the general line of scepticism pursued by his father. Lessons and habits learnt in the mother's lap, or imbibed from the conversation of the father, are more deeply embedded in our characters than we are apt to think. And when to this we add the absence of a teaching, both dogmatic and large-minded, of Christian Doctrine from much of our Public School Education, and above all the absence of Theology till lately from the Honour-Examinations of our leading University, we find a

[1] *Whitaker's Almanack for* 1878, p. 158.

favourable atmosphere for scepticism, which might be dispelled with incalculable advantage to the Church.

But there has been also another cause of such scepticism, and that one which has worked secretly and most powerfully in the education of our ablest scholars.[1] The philosophy really taught is a heathen philosophy, kept forcibly, upon a presumed philosophic axiom, away from Revelation. It has been a principle of the traditional teaching in Oxford since before 1848, that in order not to impede the freedom of the mind in studying philosophic questions, and not to introduce extraneous modes of enquiry, Religion and Revelation must hardly be so much as named in the lecture-rooms of Moral Philosophy. As if, supposing Religion, or to use the scientific name, Theology, to be true, Theology and Moral or Mental Philosophy must not necessarily run into one another. As if Moral and Mental Philosophy, to be complete, must not take cognizance of Religious as well as other phenomena. As if, supposing Theology to be true, the existence of an Orthodox instead of a Heathen Philosophy is not necessitated. Who does not see, that in these studies, which at Oxford at least are the most potent in forming the future opinions of the most thoughtful men, the admission of this principle of the exclusion of Theology must perforce carry along with

[1] I am indebted for this suggestion, the importance of which cannot be overrated, to the late Rev. W. M. Hatch, M.A., Fellow of New College, and some time Warden of St. Paul's College, Stony Stratford, the results of whose labours in this province of learning, during his unfortunately short career, will be found in an Edition of *Aristotle's Ethics*, now being published by Mr. Murray. But perhaps I may say that in my own lectures I used consciously and determinedly to violate the principle here impugned.

it the exclusion of Theological principles from the opinions of educated laymen, as being fit only for clerical mystics in the cloister or the vicarage?

But at the present time, the course of events is pointing to the rising of a new School of Theologians. For several years, the teaching of the Broad Church School has worked insensibly in promoting a tone of larger comprehensiveness. Accordingly, there is room now for another School of Teachers, which shall gather up the good that has been taught in each of the three previous Schools, and include it all within the circle of its own teaching. From the Evangelical School it may learn strong spiritual religion, humble faith in the Atonement, and ardent attachment to the Person of our Lord Jesus Christ. From the High Church Movement, which has worked up into itself most of the best Evangelical teaching, it will imbibe also the realization of Catholic Doctrines, of Catholic Unity, of the importance of the Sacraments, and of external Religion, and the depth and vigour and general holiness ensured by these points of Faith and Life. And the Broad Church teaches us a large-minded spirit of comprehensiveness, and the importance of moral duties, and of Natural Religion. To combine these elements first in ourselves, and then to form a School for the combination of them all in normal Churchmen, is, I believe, the grand duty lying before us in the future.

Not of course that the best and most eminent men of any one party have not themselves included all that have been mentioned. The influence of any eminent man beyond his own party, supposing circumstances to have made him a party man, is generally caused by his maintenance of broad general principles, that bind others to him besides his immediate disciples or followers. Still it is time for Churchmen to join together, welcoming and embracing all that is good, instead of keeping up party names and party policy. Such a line of action may be accomplished by our younger Theologians, whose career is before them. No other line can possibly be grander.

In this should be included the great achievement of the formation of a Christian Philosophy,—work enough for earnest and thoughtful Christian Students.

But this discussion may be considered beyond my immediate purpose, which is, to place a truer view of the English Church, and of her difficulties, before those who regard the "Catholic Apostolic Church" with favour, and to enlist their hearty services in the work before us. Superficial observation should yield to a masculine grasp of the principles at work, and sentimental expectations of new ordinances should give way to a strong determination to vindicate, and minister, to the Catholic vigour of the Church in England. If there are difficulties now before us, yet from the testimony even of those who are not within our Communion, the English Church has never since the Restoration been so strong in the affections of the people, as she is at present. Even those who are just now least contented do not think of leaving her.

This century has seethed with discussion and controversy : we must not mistake the ephemeral for the permanent. In the Catholic Faith we have a firm foundation, for which as thinking men,—sympathizing even with those who are oppressed with doubt and perplexity, little as they may imagine it, and feeling occasionally their difficulties,—we cannot be too thankful. The strength of the Faith is such, that no opposition, no discouragement, no perplexities, no defections, can really shake it. By degrees, in God's own good time, it will we may be sure work its way, and shine brightly and ever more brightly unto the perfect day.

MAGNA EST VERITAS, ET PRÆVALEBIT.

CONCLUSION.

THE course of this history, and of the discussions suggested by the Tenets of the Body presented to our consideration, leads naturally to inferences concerning the Religious world generally, and the Members of this Body in particular.

We learn how,—not indeed through these people alone, though sometimes they have been in the forefront of pioneering operations,—Doctrines have been rescued during this century from previous neglect.

Thus we see how the Church of Christ may fall into a carelessness about the Second Coming of our Lord, and that it is the duty of all to look to it habitually with holy hope and desire.

Again, our eyes are turned to the Incarnation as implying general principles for the entire Christian Church. Amongst these are those involved in the Sacraments, in a true symbolism and external rites, and in the maintenance of a duly-appointed Ministry, coming down in unbroken succession from our Lord Himself.

We see too light shed upon the Unity of the Catholic Church, and upon the duty incumbent on all Christians of doing what they can to heal her wounds and close her breaches. For the course of argument has led us, when defending the English Church against assailants, to fall back upon the One Catholic Church, as the only source under our Lord of support for the existence or the authority of a National Church, or rather a National Branch of the Church.

We have also been shown how, according to the teaching of all the old Catholic Services without exception, the Sacrament of the Holy Eucharist holds the most prominent place in Christian Worship.

For we should never omit to bear in mind that controversy brings out features in the Truth which we are apt to disregard. When we are driven to cast about for ground upon which we can plant our feet firmly, we sometimes find that there is water beneath the green sward, and that the rock is not exactly where we expected to find it. So that when we gain the experience of past history, or of any more contracted field of dispute, we shall generally be able to draw lessons which will shed light upon our own grounds of belief.

But materials for such observation abound throughout the history of this Religious Body, and it is therefore not necessary to linger now upon what is evident and plain. The chief lesson concerns those people who, led as they have imagined themselves to be by special revelations from Heaven, have taken up a system of Faith and worship, the peculiar features of which are not adopted or sanctioned by any other Baptized Christians.

To these I would beg to be allowed to speak in all Christian earnestness and charity.

You have shown yourselves to be anxious to observe such arrangements in Christian Worship as you believe to be sanctioned by Catholic Antiquity. You are, as a Body, exemplary in attendance upon all the duties set forth in your own Liturgy. You try, as I believe, zealously to prepare for the Second Coming of our Lord and Saviour Jesus Christ. You are eager for the Unity of the Church, as is expressed by your own Tenets.

But if you examine the grounds of your peculiar belief, you cannot but see that it has no certain warranty, either in Holy Scripture, or still more in the Faith of the one Catholic Church. You must see that you are tacitly condemned by at least more than seventeen centuries of Churchmen. You must surely grant, after careful enquiry, that you have been deceived as to the nature of the Doctrine of the Incarnation, and the necessary credentials of both Apostles and Prophets. You must also admit that there is no sort of doubt but that the Bishops who succeeded the Apostles entered plenarily into their authority and position, except so far as the Apostles alone had the inestimable advantage of personal intercourse with our Lord. You must allow that just so much failure, and deadness in higher spiritual life, has followed you as we should anticipate, supposing that you had honestly taken up these ideas, and after all had no sound basis in accepting them.

Think then, I pray you, whether your present position be not this :—God has in this manner allowed you to be drawn to the appreciation of important parts of His Catholic Truth, because otherwise you might have missed in a measure the knowledge of it. You have thus been also the means of bringing on other people who would without you have missed it altogether.

Is not then your work so far finished? And is it not your duty now to give up these newly-invented notions and to return to that Branch of the Church which is close to you and is the mother of very many of you? Think what you would gain by so doing. Such a return would no doubt involve a great sacrifice. But what an example you would set by such manly and candid conduct. You are now distinguished amongst Christian Sects by the splendour and solemnity of your worship, by your observance of numerous Catholic ceremonies, and generally by the anxiety which you display to prove the Catholicity of the various details of your practice and belief. How can you prove your superiority and your Catholicity more conspicuously than by thus giving up all to follow Christ, in joining the Branch of His Catholic Church in this country?

Surely so many years with so little progress, and the deaths of nearly all your so-called Apostles before the arrival of the Lord, and your being brought by their deaths into the position of the Church after the demise of our Lord's Apostles, must show you that you have been led by a mere semblance of truth. You have cherished very high and exalted claims, such as could have been justified only by the conspicuous and striking success which the founders of your society sanguinely expected. Nothing approaching such success has ever attended your efforts. And you must surely see how futile it is to attempt to charge upon the wickedness of the world the failure, which is really due to the inadequacy of the means employed to produce vast results. Supposing that you had been labouring amongst those who knew not the Lord Jesus Christ, this argument might have had some power of persuasiveness. But when you reflect, that amongst the chief rejecters of your claims are good and earnest Churchmen, at least as anxious for true Catholicity as you can be, and as earnest in their attachment to the Lord Jesus Christ, you must see that you have been led to talk about the wickedness of the world, when you should have been induced to distrust your own system.

And if you should thus be induced to abandon your peculiar views, and in deference to the judgment of the Universal Church to surrender all at once your isolated position, you would be following the example of your prototypes in the early Church, the Montanists. You cannot object to your being compared to them, since they had the reputation of remarkable sanctity of life. Nevertheless they remained as a separate Body only for a comparatively short period,—and then returned to the bosom of the Catholic Church of Christ.

Supposing that you were thus to set a brilliant example of the return of a large number all at once, in manly candour and with an acknowledgment of error, to the Church of your Baptism,—for such the English Church is to most of you,—how would your act be commemorated and extolled in the future annals of the Church. And how warmly would you now be welcomed back by Churchmen. Acting in the spirit pourtrayed by the Good Shepherd in His parables, the English Church in all her grades would receive you with the liveliest joy and thankfulness.

We are all looking onwards to that blessed time when the Lord Himself shall appear in the Clouds of Heaven. Amongst other terrible reproofs, what will He say to those, who knowingly, after their error has been earnestly pointed out, and the grounds, upon which their error is irrefragably proved to be such, have been carefully unfolded, nevertheless continue to promote schism and to rend His sacred Robe? What will be His fearful rebuke to such as, straying from His pastures themselves, lead others away from the fold where alone His true Presence is to be found?

Nay, my Brethren in Christ,—for so may I call you?—do not so foolishly, and indeed so wickedly. You know,—for the course of your career has led you into these higher truths,—what is the heinousness of schism, and what are the blessings of Unity. You can enter into the deep meaning of that solemn and mysterious prayer of our Lord, offered up by Him upon the brink of His Passion. May you then, at whatever cost, come back into the Branch of the Church in this land, and accepting the whole Catholic Faith, dwell where for us, as far as the world will allow, there is "One Fold and One Shepherd."

APPENDIX II.

THE TWO SMALLER TESTIMONIES.

A. THE TESTIMONY ADDRESSED TO HIS MAJESTY KING WILLIAM IV., AND TO THE MEMBERS OF HIS MAJESTY'S PRIVY COUNCIL.

[Vol. I. pp. 177, 178—286.]

THIS *Testimony* is without a printed heading. But the copy from which I quote is headed in Mr. Perceval's handwriting,—

To the Right Honorable
The Members of His Majesty's Privy Council.

It opens thus :—

The handwriting of God is upon the wall: every eye has beheld it, but there has been no interpreter.

The constitution of the kingdom has been changed; in casting off its Christian character, its acknowledgment of allegiance to the Lord Jesus Christ, by the repeal of the Test and Corporation Act, and by the admission of Papists to Parliament and to Office; it has been changed by the Reform Bill, which has laid the foundation of the present order of things in wrong and robbery, through the violation of charters, the contempt of prescriptive rights, and the overruling the independence of the upper House of Parliament; for it is notorious that it was only carried through that House by the sworn servants of the crown counselling and constraining their royal master to consent to violate that independence, if the Lords would not pass the Bill presented from the Commons.

The attack upon the ancient provision for the poor, the cruel enactments of the new law, and the abominable doctrines put forth by some of its promoters; the whole spirit of interference with the Church, from the extinction of the Irish Bishoprics to the resolution of the House of Commons to desecrate the property of the Church to other uses, the hatred against tithes, and the many schemes for removing them as a nuisance, the Bill for rendering marriage a civil contract, the attempt to force open the Universities, the notices for expelling the Bishops from the Lords, the Bill for admitting Jews into Parliament, and the violation of charters by the Municipal Reform Bill,—. are among many evidences of the departure of the ancient spirit of the constitution, and of the danger of subversion, which besets every venerable institution of the realm.

Above all, the danger which at present theatens the House of Lords, if they assert their independence and perform their duty, brings forth into manifestation the entire change which has taken place in the feelings and principles of the nation, and is also a warning note to prepare the whole country for the struggle that is at hand.

And while things are thus, it is admitted on all hands, that at no period since the Revolution has there been so great a difficulty in forming or carrying on the Government as has been experienced since the passing of the Reform Bill. Whichever party is in power finds it equally impossible to bring forward such measures as it conceives to be most conducive to the wellbeing of the State, but is obliged to conciliate the prejudices of those whom it equally fears and hates; Government, in its strict sense, is at an end; the persons who hold office are the executive of a power unseen but not unfelt—"the pressure from without;" no plan can be undertaken with confidence;

no fixed principles acted upon; ephemeral and casual success of schemes, partly followed and partly defeated, is the utmost that is hoped to be attained. Every political journal, all writers of acknowledged political sagacity of every nation and party, have foreseen, and declared their conviction, that a crisis is at hand, the certain issue of which they cannot divine, but the consequences of which they all agree in dreading.

Such is the present state of Great Britain: and it is a heart-rending spectacle to look upon her as she is, or is about to be, in inevitable prospect, and to compare her with former recollections. Her institutions, which for ages have secured her from the oppression of a monarch, of nobles, or of the many, tottering to their base; some laid prostrate; the whole attacked on every side by ruthless men, and none to save her. Her readiest defenders caught into the eddy, and themselves from time to time the helpers forward of her destruction, the instruments in the hands of those whom they abhor; her king all but a captive in the hands of his own subjects; her proud nobility, who never feared to avow their rights, waning before the threats and violence of their enemies, and scarce venturing by subtlety to undermine, or to postpone, the measures which they dare not openly to resist; many of the flower of them basely courting the favour of the mob they hate, in the vain hope of concealing their elevated station, and thinking to hide themselves by merging in the common mass; her gentry, in like manner, pandering to the passions of the people; the people themselves preyed on by one another; the labourers oppressed, and in their turn rising on their oppressors, and by combinations effecting the ruin of their employers, and ultimately their own; and all, or nearly all, that are active in the land, madly bent upon destruction, to which there seems no limit while there is anything to destroy. Oh! England, thy judgment cometh upon thee like a whirlwind, and there is no escape.

* * * * *

For the cause of all these present and threatened evils, these manifested judgments, and tokens of coming judgment, is the same as in all similar cases of history—the sin of the land, manifest in the sin of the rulers. We have departed from God, and He is departing from us.

* * * * *

Of this entire desertion of the principles of former days, God has given the land a notable index, in that the name of one of the two great parties in the State has well-nigh completely vanished throughout the country, while that of their opponents remains, and is seated in the places of power. The watchword of the former was, the Divine Right of Kings, with its countersign, the Duty of Submission; the motto of the latter was, the People the Source of Power, with its answerable doctrine, the Right of Resistance. The war-cry of the one was, Church and King; the shout of the other, the Rights of the People. The name of the latter lives, because their principles are living and triumphant; not, indeed, as held by their forefathers, but expounded by the commentary of the devil, and enforced by every agency of hell: but the other name has vanished, because the principles it represented are gone; and the wreck and remnant of the Tories are gathered, with a motley herd, under the common name Conservative, which truly represents the only bond by which they are held together —the hope of preserving their rank, their privileges, their wealth, their lives, and the peace of the country, from the threatened mischief which they clearly see bearing down upon them, in all the doctrines and all the measures that are afloat.

* * * * *

He is the fountain of honour and dignity, and the protector of the poor and needy; and being despised and disowned by all, He has withdrawn honour from nobility, security from property, and protection from the poor. Distinctions of men have ceased to be venerable; rights of property have lost their sacredness, and have been despised—first in the weakest, the poor, then in the corporations, and the Church comes next; then the hereditary nobility, and, lastly, the hereditary monarchy will be the prey. For primogeniture and inheritance are of God and not of man, and need to be seen in the light of God in order to be regarded and maintained; and, because kings, and princes, and nobles have ceased to give honour to Him, His dearly-beloved Son, the first-born among many brethren, whom He hath appointed Heir of all things, therefore He is letting loose upon their hereditary rights the ignorant blindness of ungodly men, who can see no reason in the institution, and feel no blessing, but are only provoked to it by envy and covetousness.

* * * * *

In three great State measures, the repeal of the Test and Corporation Acts, the Roman Catholic Relief Bill, and the Act for reforming the Representation of the House of Commons, she has revealed and consummated the sin of departing from God, which has here been charged against this nation—has registered her adoption of the spirit of the age, and written Ichabod on the constitution of the kingdom. In the first, she avows that every infidel, Jew, and heretic, are as worthy to serve the State as Christian men, or, in other words, that her sons are no better than infidels; by the second, she receives into honour and trust the abomination of the Papacy, which God had exalted this land to withstand and protest against; and the third is at once the fruit and the recognition of the principle that the people are the true source of power. These three Acts are now the law of the land; and in them the mark of the Beast, the characters of Antichrist, are written on the forehead of the constitution, which of old was sealed with the seal of the living God, the impress of the Name of the Father, and of the Son, and of the Holy Ghost.

* * * * *

All authority in Church and State belongs to Jesus Christ,

the King and Priest of God, and is delegated by Him to whomsoever He will. * * * *

* * * * *

This is the first great principle upon which all government rests, that all who are entrusted with any authority are only vicegerents and stewards of the Lord Jesus Christ; and the second is, that men are put in the place of rule, not for their own sakes, but for the blessing and protection of His creatures, that they may nourish and defend all those whom God has placed under them. Now, to the end that kings, and rulers, and all people might know their duty, and not be left to conjecture what the Will of God might be, and take their own way, calling it His, but be instructed what His way is,—to this end did the Lord Jesus raise up and set His Church on earth, which should be His minister to kings and people, to declare His Mind and Will to them, and bring His Word and Laws, by which they would know how to do what was well-pleasing in His Sight, and thus His Blessings should descend upon them.

Now the Church, as the depository of all spiritual authority, is not, nor can be, at all subject to the State, but is bound to stand as the teacher and• instructor of kings and nations—the faithful witness of God whether they would hear or whether they would refuse; and the State is bound to uphold, by example of obedience, the authority of God in the Church, and to receive the law of God at the priest's mouth. But, on the other hand, God would not that the Church should usurp temporal authority in the State; but, though established in the State, and protected, and set in honour, and provided for by the State, there should have been no mingling. The rulers of the State should never have presumed to interfere in the internal arrangements of the Church, or even have been permitted by her to appoint the lowest deacon to office in her; and, on the other hand, the State ought never to suffer the Church to assume authority, or to meddle with the affairs of the Government.

The business of the State was to protect the Church of Christ, and to provide for that Church through the tithes of the country, which are the Lord's portion, and to look to the Church for faithfulness to her God and holiness of life, so that she might be their example and teacher in all things; and it was the business of the Church to take heed that she discharged that duty faithfully, thankful for protection afforded and sustenance provided, but steadfast and immovable in rebuking all evil, and testifying continually of all God's truth, regardless whether she pleased or displeased the rulers or the people.

* * * * *

[The *Testimony* goes on to show that all have been unfaithful in their several stations to these principles.]

In the French Revolution God has given to all the nations of Christendom the warning of what is coming upon them,— *the first shock of that earthquake* which will throw down every regal and ecclesiastical tower therein. That was the *first act of the great tragedy* which shall be consummated in every monarchy in Europe.

* * * * *

The people are openly claiming all power with us, as they did with them: and the rulers are bowing down before the people, and saying, Ye are our lords, and we are your servants; and God is rejected by both, and the honour of Jesus trampled in the dust.

The people are calling out for a reform in God's Church, and the rulers are bowing before the voice, and the Church witnesses not for the Head of the Church, but says, We are in your hands, have mercy upon us; and God is dishonoured, and Jesus, the High-Priest, is stripped of His office and authority in the Church.

The people are craving to have their love of money gratified, and cry for the abolition of tithes; and the people's servants, the rulers, say, God's due shall be yielded to you.

The people say, It is a burden too heavy for us to bear to pay tribute; and the rulers, the servants of the people, say, The burden shall be taken away; and yet they are God's ministers attending upon this very thing: and so of the rest. Religious tests, the tests of the acknowledgment of the Lord Jesus Christ, in those who are to rule in His name, are abolished, because the people said, Let it be done; the rights of bodies corporate are to be abolished because the people wish it; the Jew, who stigmatizes Jesus as the madman, the blasphemer, and the demoniac, is to be admitted to rule in His name, because all such distinctions between Jew and Christian are invidious in this enlightened age; and what other abomination of desolation can be named that is not now being set up? The marriage-contract, the witness for the union of the Church with Christ, is to be deprived of its true character, to please the men who cause and foment division in His Church. The rights of the noble and honourable are to be sacrificed to the spirit of anarchy that is maddening the people. Now all these things find their exact parallel in the legislative acts of the French Assembly in the three years preceding the murder of their king. * * * And then they rose up and murdered their king, and rejected God and His religion by law, and paid divine honours to a goddess of their own. * * *
Then He gave them a king of their own choosing: the child and champion of Jacobinism, the header up of anarchy in iron despotism, the scourge of France and of Europe—Napoleon the Destroyer.

Such an example we are following, and such is the judgment that awaits us. * * * *

[The signs of the last days are being exhibited; but He is preparing a place of refuge and building an ark.]

For the Church of God builded up in its spiritual ordinances, Apostles, Prophets, Evangelists, and Pastors must be prepared, as a chaste virgin, to meet the Lord. The body of the baptized, all who will receive the full blessing pledged to them in baptism, out of all the tribes of Christendom, gathered from all the sects and divisions wherein they are held captive into one spiritual body, shall escape the tyranny of the man of sin, and shall be taken up to meet the Lord in the air before He comes to judge. The baptized in their present standing, divided and opposed to one another, cannot bear witness to the truth as it is in Jesus. They do not bear witness; they will not, they cannot. But God would bring them out of their division, that they may bear witness, and that they may together be counted worthy to escape the things that are coming upon the earth.

* * * * *

In this land has God called His Apostles, and given Prophets, Evangelists, Pastors, and Teachers; and Prophets, Evangelists, Pastors, and Teachers will He have in all lands, through the ministry of His Apostles, who must be sent forth unto all the baptized, gathering everywhere, and building everywhere—teaching and ordaining ministers throughout the earth.

Already has the Lord prevailed in these kingdoms to gather His people in many places, and to build them into Churches, giving them His ordinances anew from heaven; calling His servants, by the voice of Prophecy, to serve Him in the ministries of His house, and setting over His flocks His Angels and Elders, and giving Evangelists, by the laying on of the hands of His Apostles. In London He has set His SEVEN CHURCHES, wherein He will show forth the pattern of the completeness of the Universal Church—one, holy, Apostolical. He has gathered His children out of every sect and division, from every name and denomination, showing Himself the common Father of all, with whom is no respect of persons. In Edinburgh, in Dublin, and in many other towns in England and Scotland does the Church appear, His people gathered by the cry, "The bridegroom cometh!" walking in the light of Prophecy, and in the strength and defence of the ordinances of God, received through

Apostolic ordination. And many are the places besides, where the people of the Lord, believing that which is here testified to you, are waiting and longing to be visited by the Lord in His servants, that they also may receive the blessing of His ordinances, by the laying on of their hands. In all these Churches are a people found walking in one faith and discipline, holding and rejoicing in one hope, waiting upon God, in the holy worship of His house, morning and evening; owning the authority of the Lord Jesus Christ, present in the midst of them by the rulers He has appointed; learning and practising obedience in the midst of a rebellious generation; laying aside their idols, and submitting to be taught, in this age of self-sufficiency and many teachers; and gladly bringing up the tenth of all their incomes, in this day when the fever against tithes is the epidemic of Christendom—the servant and the poor labourer willingly paying them, because they believe that it is the Lord's portion, which He has reserved unto Himself of all that He has given to His creatures, and which He has set apart for the support of His Priesthood, by a statute in Israel throughout all their generations.

And the Lord has laid it as a primary duty upon this His Church—still in weakness, just rising out of the spiritual death into which the whole of Christendom is fallen—to bear a testimony, in love and faithfulness, to the king and to his counsellors, to warn them of the condition of the nation, the very near approach of heavy calamities, and the speedy second coming of the Lord Jesus Christ.

* * * * *

[Such may be the deliverance of every man, but the warning is sent especially to rulers and counsellors. They are called upon loudly, from without, by the many-headed monster, to register the edicts of Antichrist; and the Lord calls upon them to rally round and uphold to the death His standard. This deliverance is given only to such as repent; otherwise the pestilence and the sword will go through cities and villages. The final conflict between Christ and Antichrist is at hand. But before that the Lord gives a sign, and sends a warning,— the handwriting upon the wall. Oh, that all would hear: but there is mercy and salvation for the faithful. The warning and invitation are sent: the Day is at hand.

The concluding words, embracing Mr. Perceval's signature, have been already given (Vol. I. p. 286).]

B.

TO

HIS GRACE

THE

ARCHBISHOP OF CANTERBURY,

PRIMATE OF ALL ENGLAND, AND METROPOLITAN;

AND THE OTHER THE ARCHBISHOPS AND BISHOPS OF THE UNITED CHURCH OF ENGLAND AND IRELAND.

THE Church of England, among all the divisions of the Catholic Church, is most to be commended for the measure of truth contained in her doctrinal standards, for the comparative purity and spirituality of her liturgies, unmixed with superstitious rites of Popery and relics of Paganism, and for her Church administration, wherein she rejects not, with the greater part of other reformed Churches, the Apostolic forms and ordinances of the primitive Church. To the care of Bishops, as heads under Christ, and pastors of that Church, are committed the souls of the baptized in their several dioceses; and in their respective places of chief rule they are the present depositaries and trustees of the priestly office, the ministry whereof has been preserved by God through the ages that have elapsed since the Day of Pentecost.

Thus recognizing your standing and authority, it might seem to require explanation that we should not merely seek, but, in the name of our Lord Jesus Christ, Head of His Church, and by His authority, *claim* your audience. Nevertheless, we pray you to bear with us while, in discharge of a duty, not undertaken at our own suggestion, but imposed on us by God, we address you in His name, and as His ministers; and whether our communication be received or rejected, its nature will sufficiently prove its own apology.

Is it any marvel that, in the state of all things around you, the heads of the Church should be *thus* addressed? Is it not time for God to work, when men make void His laws? As Bishops of Christ's Catholic Church, you are called upon to look at her condition in every land, and to sorrow over the misled, torn, and scattered sheep for whom He died. As Bishops of the National Church, you are not merely bound to look to the apprehended judgments and dangers that surround you, but to be grieved in contemplating the wickedness of His baptized people, who are the agents through whom the ruin is apprehended,—to mourn, not that you are smitten, but that your children are the smiters.

It cannot be that you shut your eyes to the state of things around you. We will not believe that they who should abide nearest in the secret of the Lord are involved in the delusion that all is well, and religion flourishing; and that while all abroad and at home is becoming more and more "like to a troubled sea which cannot rest," and all bonds of religious society and relationships of life are dissolving, and among none so rapidly as among the great professors of religion, you, the

Fathers and Guardians of the Church, should content yourselves with sounding words, that the influence of true religion increases, all her principles sapped, and daily sinking away.

It is notorious that through Europe priesthood is scorned under the name of priestcraft by the great mass of those who think for themselves—by almost all but those in whom reverence is sunk in superstition and idolatry; that the holiest truths of God are denied as irrational; the miraculous character of Christianity is assailed, and its most venerable mysteries are considered mere symbols for conveying a system of ethics, preferable, perhaps (but only because more comprehensive), to the lessons of classical philosophy; that the Continent is all but swallowed up by the mediocrity in all that instruct, all that can strengthen, and all that can minister the life of religion in the Greek Church; by the Pagan superstition, the perversions of truth, and the declining dotage of the Papal system in the Church of Rome; or, when vitality, or at least activity is most apparent, by the spiritual infidelity of Germany, and the fierce atheism of France.

There may be exceptions, holy and good men, Greek, Roman, and Protestant, if such can be considered properly exceptions. Until the very reign of Antichrist, when nothing else shall be allowed to peep or mutter, buy or sell, charges of universal apostasy will ever be exaggerations. But the general truth of this description is notorious; and our object in giving it is not to convict of sin, but to present in its true colours the condition of so large a portion of the baptized Church, the descendants of saints and martyrs—a condition which should draw from us, as from the prophet mourning over the vision of the desolations of Jerusalem, the exclamation of passionate grief, "Oh that my head were waters, and mine eyes a fountain of tears, that I might weep day and night for the slain of the daughter of my people!" (Jer. ix. 1.)

And as with priest and people, so by eternal disposition of

God with princes and people also. But into the civil condition of other nations than our own we enter not, save to observe that, as the Churches are ripe for judgment, and the priests and people for apostasy, so is it, for the most part, with the States. Their princes rule by force, and the people are either waiting for an opportunity to revolt, or are running a course of revolution and anarchy, to end again in iron tyranny.

But to come to our own country. The evil principles which affect the rest of Christendom are here to be found struggling with an energy and life unknown elsewhere, and with a force resistless, except God be pleased to come to our help, as in days of old. The priesthood universally despised, and the very nature and standing of the Church unknown and denied; the dignity of the one, and the legal establishment of the other, assailed; all forms of superstition and fanaticism practised, and all heresies and perversions of truth maintained. Nay, infidelity taught as a system by preachers and lecturers who make it their profession, and in public assemblies gathered for that avowed purpose.

Among the clergy, all shades of opinion, both on matters of doctrine and discipline: the Socinian in one class, and in the other the man who does not *object* to receive Episcopal ordination in order to qualify himself to preach his own levelling and disorganizing opinions in the Established Churches, and the Bishops without power, for all practical purposes, to enforce either the doctrine or the discipline of the Church on their beneficed clergy, even in cases where morality demands their interference.

Proceeding to the laity, alas! the disorganization, the divisions of the body of Christ! the sheep driven hither and thither, scattered among a thousand sects instead of one holy body! The thought that they owe any relative duty to the pastor of their parish, except just so far as they receive a benefit from that pastor,—gratitude, not duty,—or that they are bound to give honour to their spiritual pastor as to their natural parent —these considerations enter not into the mind of the most attached to the Church. In almost every parish one or more other temples, professing to be dedicated to God, vie with the parish church for the offerings of the people; and millions literally—nay, in the manufacturing cities, generation after generation—never enter their parish church, nor see that pastor who must answer for their souls; or, if ever, only when presented for baptism in order to be placed on the register. Again, we remark, we are not now dealing with the matter of the sin in all this—no doubt both pastor and people have their share in it, for which they must give account: we are addressing ourselves to the moral aspect of what you know, and we know, and the people of this land know to be the true state of things.

In the country parishes of England the clergy have more in their power. They are able to exercise a more perfect control over their parishioners. And yet here how many are the cottages whereinto they are forbidden to enter, or more civilly repulsed by the information that the inhabitants go to chapel. Even when the clergy seek conscientiously to fulfil their duty, how large a portion of their flock are withdrawn from their care, and now almost, and in many cases altogether, with their own allowance and consent, are handed over to Dissenting ministers; and all the while demoralization strides through the land, and the people are ready to rise against their rich neighbours, and the lawless, instead of being the exceptions, form the great body. It is useless here to trace to political causes the acknowledged demoralization of the agricultural population. Such is their condition; and most fearfully does it threaten the Established Institutions in Church and State. Nor does it mend the matter that, when the Bishops, in their places in Parliament, have protested, or their clergy have petitioned, against legislative enactments calculated to increase this evil state, the counsel of the one has been rejected, and the exertions of the others imputed to interested motives.

But in towns is the concentrated energy of evil. Here are the strongholds of Satan. Here all wicked passions and tendencies take root and grow. Here are contrived and practised crimes of every description, and licentiousness unrestrained: hatred of authority, envy of wealth, and of rank, and of goodness. Here are conceived the schemes of sedition, and rebellion, and infidelity, of destruction and robbery; and from town to town the people are banded together for the work of ruin.

And what power is there left in the Hierarchy to arrest the evil? You cannot reach the wicked doers with the voice of holy rebuke; and, if you could, they have thrown off your authority, and would refuse to turn at your word. Your means are insufficient; and whether you apply to the State, or to the laity as individuals, you must be sensible that additional endowments cannot be procured for ministers, nor additional places of worship; nay, this is the very point of time when they curtail your means, and you know not how soon you may be met with the maxim already proclaimed by royal authority in Scotland, but a maxim subversive of the very notion of a National Church, that, "wherever religious instruction and pastoral superintendence are, to a certain extent, afforded by any sect or denomination whatsoever, there the services of an Established Church are not required, and may be dispensed with." Better that the State should altogether withhold its protection, than impart it in a mode which saps the foundation of the Church.

And the consequences are inevitable, so far as human agency can operate. The altar and the throne are systematically assailed. The cessation of those mutual offices of parental blessing on the part of the Church, and of filial protection on the part of the State, is already decreed by the party really, if not by that ostensibly, in power. The infidels, and Dissenters, and Papists, in unholy union, are effecting this as a prelude to the destruction of both Church and Monarchy, amidst the applause of some and the apathy of others. And none know so well as those whom we address, that the most influential supporters of the Church, in and out of the legislature, are, in point of fact, abandoning the citadel while they defend the outworks; and in seeking to preserve, as they intend, the property of the Church, are yielding to their enemies the only standing and principle on which the Church can be entitled to that property to the exclusion of others.

Already has the property of the Church been torn by lawless violence from the lawful proprietors in Ireland; and in Parliament, both the political parties have in their turn proposed measures for sanctioning that spoliation. The Archbishops and ten Bishops, in that part of the kingdom which is filled with superstition and most needs the exertion of the clergy, have been decreed to be "nuisances, and abated accordingly." It has been attempted to extinguish the very performance of Protestant Worship in nearly one-third of the parishes there. And the zeal, combination, and energy which have effected so much, will with equal success, so far as human foresight can conclude, again put into action the instruments of assault which have already made such breaches. Oh! it is not the loss of power, of wealth, or of political influence involved,—but this, Fathers of the Church, is the overwhelming thought, that while you have been intrusted by God with His baptized people in this land, you are about to be deprived, by the hands of wicked men, of the standing, the means, and the opportunity through which you might draw back to yourselves the wandering sheep, whom the Great Shepherd, when He shall appear, will demand at your hands. Even now see you the wolves in sheep's clothing dissolving the ties which bind you to your flocks. Schismatics—heretics of every shade—fanatics and infidels filled with spiritual wickedness. The people, whom you *now* vainly seek to reach with your Ministry, exposed to every form of temptation, spiritual, moral, and political. In a word, behold the mass of wickedness involving the souls of thousands, who, by the Clergy of the Church, should have been taught and blessed in the ways of God in His house, and that mass rolling onward with accelerated rapidity into the gulf of revolution and atheism—your responsibility remaining, your means of fulfilling it fearfully diminished.

And is it possible that all this ruin at home and abroad—this laying waste of God's Church, planted by Him in the nations of Europe—can have been brought to pass without sin? These evils within and without—this feebleness, and dissolution, and decay—have they been God's work, His Church meanwhile having fulfilled *her* duties? It is not so; these are not a passing cloud, a mere trial of faith in adverse circumstances. The Lord Himself is the adversary; "He covers the daughter of Zion with a cloud in His anger, He casts down from heaven to earth the beauty of Israel, and remembers not His footstool in the day of His anger; He swallows up all the foundations of Jacob; He throws down in His wrath the strongholds of the daughters of Judah; He pollutes the kingdom and the princes thereof; He cuts off in His fierce anger all the horn of Israel; He bends His bow like an enemy; He stands with His right hand like an adversary; He despises in the indignation of His anger the king and the priest" (Lam. ii. 1—4, 6). And why should vain man seek to justify himself? rather let us confess the offences whereby God has been displeased. "The sins of our kings, our princes, and our fathers, and all the people of our land" (Dan. ix. 8). The sins of Christendom. For it is *not* the sin of one generation nor of two; and though now it has leavened the whole lump as it was never leavened before, nevertheless the leaven has been hid for generations past. But now, or it will be too late, must the sins be confessed and repented of; for though in all times they have more or less existed, it is not the less true that this generation fills up the measure of the iniquity of their fathers, and of this generation shall be required the accumulated guilt.

The time of judgment answers to the time of harvest, not of sowing. The causes which have produced the ripening for judgment must be traced to former generations.

Bear with us, then, while, in love to the Church of Christ and to you, and yet, as becomes the Ambassadors of Christ our King, we lay open the burden which He has endured in the iniquities of His people, whom He has redeemed and gathered into the fold of His Church—the sins of His baptized, in the generations past, which He hath long borne with and restrained, but which now are working their evil fruits in the spiritual desolation which surrounds us on every side. To this end it is needful that we should first call to mind the standing of the Church of God as He constituted her at the beginning.

[The main body of this *Testimony*, which extends to seventy-one quarto pages, as against forty-five of the *Testimony to King William*, is taken up with an exposition of Irvingite Doctrine which is found in an expanded form in the *Great Testimony*. It concludes thus :—]

We call not upon you to follow twelve men, but to have faith in the Living God, in His promises, and in His word. We remind you, as the priests of God, that ye have to render to Him His Bride.

*   *   *   *   *

We know the difficulties wherein you are now placed, and the full weight whereof you will undergo in receiving this our testimony. The calling of the followers of Christ is not to *honour* in this world, but to *reproach* for His Name's sake—to take up their cross and follow Him. Nevertheless, we call not upon you to take any step in your own strength, nor to seek to free yourselves from the obligations into which the sins of generations past have betrayed the Church, and which, finding the Church involved in them, you, as individuals, have voluntarily incurred. Your duty is to stand in your places where you are, acknowledging the Hand of God in His present work ; confessing the sins which, like a thick cloud, have hid the face of Heaven ; watching day and night for the salvation of Israel, more than they that watch for the morning; continuing instant in prayer, but joyful through hope because of the approaching deliverance of yourselves and your people, through the power of God in the Holy Ghost. Above all, praying for us, that, like as now we have been used of the Lord to bring the word of these good tidings to you, so also we may shortly be sent forth to you in the fulness of the blessing of the Gospel of Christ.

Fathers of the Church, our souls long over you in the bowels of Christ. Unfeignedly we implore all the blessings of goodness may be poured forth upon you, and into the bosom of your people. God forbid that we should cease to pray for you, that you may be lifted up into the hope of your calling, and draw up a spiritual people with you into the communion of the one fold. We feel the awful solemnity of the call which we make upon you—our own responsibility and yours ; and while we have sought to fulfil our part in faithfulness and truth, we have also sought to bear ourselves as those who "plead with their mother" (Hosea ii. 2).

May the God of all grace fill you with all wisdom and spiritual understanding in all things; preserve you from the pride which saith, "I am rich and increased with goods, and have need of nothing;" "I sit as a queen, and shall never know sorrow!" May He count you worthy of this calling, and fulfil all the good pleasure of His goodness, and the work of faith with power, that the Name of our Lord Jesus Christ may be glorified in you, according to the Grace of God and of our Lord Jesus Christ. Amen.

Glory be to the Father, &c.

APPENDIX III.

THE MYSTERY OF THE CANDLESTICK.

"THE Lord maketh known the mystery of the candlestick to the churches. JESUS, Thou art the light that lighteth every man that cometh into the world. Thou hast the seven Spirits, the seven lamps of fire that burn before the throne of God. Thou wilt again manifest Thyself in Thy Church. Thou art giving and wilt give Apostles, Prophets, Evangelists, Pastors. Thou wilt manifest Thyself in all gifts of the Spirit, in all holy fruits of the Spirit. The candlestick doth set forth the completeness of a Church; the centre lamp sets forth the Angel; the six lamps to the branches, the Elders. The three bowls are the three ministries supplying the lamp with oil. Oh! thou angel, take heed that the oil flow freely, and supply the light of thy lamp through thy ministries of rule, of prophetic utterance, of teaching and feeding the people. And all ye people, ye do support the lamps, ye are as the shaft and the branches; let the knops and the flowers be seen. Ah! let the gifts of the Spirit be manifested; the word of wisdom, with its branches; the word of knowledge, with its branches; faith, with its branches, healing and miracles; these are the knops. And let the beauty of the flowers be the rejoicing of the Church of God; love branching into joy and peace; long-suffering, into gentleness and goodness; faith, into meekness and temperance. Faith, hope, and charity,—let them be manifested, O ye Church of God, and God shall bless you; and Jesus your High Priest shall ever walk about with the tongs and snuffers; the tongs (raising the wick), the voice of apostolic exhortation and encouragement; the snuffers, the utterance of prophetic rebuke, to cause the light to shine more brightly. And O ye people, bring up the pure oil, the first love; not of constraint, but with a willing mind. Fill ye your deacons, the vessels for the oil, that these, the heads of the congregation, may bring it up unto the Lord, and the bowls continually be filled. The wise virgins must take heed that their vessels be kept filled. The Lord giveth the shaft with its branches first; then the lamps on the top. Understand ye, the Lord prepareth His way in causing the hearts of His people to desire the manifestation of His glory. Then He chooseth out His servants, to place them as lamps. Jesus alone doeth this. Peace be with you all. Amen."

APPENDIX IV.

LIST OF OFFICES IN THE LITURGY OR PRAYER-BOOK.

OFFICES FOR DAILY OR WEEKLY USE.

THE Celebration of the Holy Eucharist.
The Administration of the Communion on the Afternoon of the Lord's Day.
The Shorter Service for the Celebration of the Holy Eucharist.
The Creed of St. Athanasius.
The Office for Morning Prayer.
The Administration of the Communion after Morning Prayer.
The Office for Evening Prayer.
The Forenoon Service.
The Form for Removing the Holy Sacrament.
The Benediction of Holy Water.
The Litany.
The Afternoon Service.
The Shorter Morning Service.
The Shorter Evening Service.
Additional Prayers, &c.
Occasional Prayers, Thanksgivings, &c.

OFFICES FOR PROPER AND OCCASIONAL USE.

Proper Services for Holy Days and Seasons.
   In Advent.
   Christmas Eve.
   Christmas Day.
   Monday, Tuesday, and Wednesday before Easter.
   Thursday before Easter.
   Good Friday.
   Easter Eve.
   Easter Day.
   Ascension Day.
   The Eve of Pentecost.
   The Day of Pentecost.
   The Form of Consecrating Chrism.
   The Anniversary of the Separation of Apostles.
   All Angels.
   All Saints.
   The Prayers for the Three Seasons.
The Assembly of the Seven Churches :—
   General Forms to be used in Celebrating the Holy Eucharist.
   By an Apostle before a Solemn Council.
   By an Apostle for a Tribe.
   By an Apostle before a Visitation.
   For a Particular Church.
   For Unity.
   For Blessing on the Labours of Evangelists.
   For Increasing the Number of Evangelists.
   In Commemorating a Sick Person.
   In Commemorating a Deceased Person.
   For a Young Person.
   For a Woman after Childbirth.
A Form of Prayer to be used on Days of Humiliation.

Offices in the Liturgy or Prayer-Book. 385

Forms for Celebrating the Eucharist.
   In Times of Calamity.
   In Times of Sickness.
   In Times of Scarcity.
   In Times of War.
A Form of Thanksgiving on Days of Rejoicing.
Forms for Celebrating the Eucharist on the Restoration of Peace, &c.

SPECIAL OCCASIONAL SERVICES.

The Receiving a Catechumen.
The Dedication of Catechumens.
Holy Baptism.
The Order for Receiving any who have been privately Baptized.
The Churching of Women.
The Committing to Pastorship.
The Benediction of New Communicants.
The Renewal of Vows.
The Laying-on of Apostles' Hands.
The Solemnization of Marriage.
The Benediction of Newly-married Persons.
Benediction for Works of Charity.
Dedication for the Holy Ministry.
The Benediction of a Door-keeper.
The Benediction of Singers.
The Admission of Under-Deacons.
The Benediction of a Deaconess.
The Order for Admitting to the Office of Deacon.
The Office for Blessing Deacons.
The Receiving One of the Seven Deacons of a Church.
The Receiving a Deacon.
The Order for Ordaining Priests.
The Form for Confirming the Orders of Priests.

Receiving one of the Six Elders of a Church.
Receiving a Priest.
The Receiving a Priest for Temporary Service.
The Presentation for the Episcopate.
A Prayer on Behalf of a Called Angel.
The Office for the Consecration of an Angel.
The Order of Inducting an Angel.
The Order of Sending forth an Angel-Evangelist.
Forms of Benediction upon the Sending forth of Ministers.
The Laying the First Stone of a Church.
The Consecration of Churches.
The Consecration of the Altar, &c.
The Consecration of a Tablet-Altar.
The Forms for Benediction of Furniture, Vessels, and Vestments.

OFFICES FOR PRIVATE OCCASIONS.

The Benediction of a House.
The Benediction of a Chamber-lodging.
The Benediction of a Ship.
The Absolution of Penitents.
Prayer for a Woman after Childbirth, and Dedication of Infant.
Private Baptism.
The Administration of Holy Communion to the Sick.
The Benediction of Holy Oil.
The Order for Anointing the Sick.
A Litany in the Visitation of the Sick.
Commendation of a Departing Soul.
Prayers on Passing an Altar.

APPENDIX V.

SELECTION FROM THE CATECHISM.

PART III.

Q. You have said that you believe the "Holy Catholic Church:" What is the Church?

A. The Church is the Congregation of all who believe in the Lord Jesus Christ, and are baptized according to His commandment. It is the Household of God, the Body of Christ, the Temple of the Holy Ghost.

Q. How doth God make known His will in the Church?

A. Holy men of old were moved by the Holy Ghost to declare the will of God; and the words of God delivered by them, and contained in the Scriptures of the Old Testament, were committed to the Jews. These, together with the writings of the Evangelists and Apostles of the New Testament, have been preserved in the Christian Church, and handed down to us: and Christ hath set in His Church Ministers for the guidance of His people, in accordance with His written word. And to all men God bears witness by the Church, proclaiming His salvation, and blessing the works of His hands.

Q. What Ministries hath our Lord Jesus Christ given to His Church?

A. When He ascended up on high, He received gifts for

men: and He gave some men, Apostles; and some, Prophets; and some, Evangelists; and some, Pastors and Teachers.

Q. For what ends were these Ministries given?

A. They were given for the perfecting of the Saints, for the work of the Ministry, for the edifying of the Body of Christ; till we all come unto the unity of the faith and of the knowledge of the Son of God, unto a perfect man, unto the measure of the stature of the fulness of Christ.

Q. What is the meaning of the word *Apostle?*

A. Apostle is "one sent forth."

Q. How are Apostles distinguished from all other Ministers?

A. Apostles are neither of men, nor by man; but by Jesus Christ and God the Father, sent forth immediately and directly.

Q. How are all other Ministers set in the Church?

A. They are set in the Church by our Lord Jesus Christ, not immediately, but through ordination by Apostles, or by those whom they have delegated for that purpose.

Q. What do you mean by *Ordination?*

A. Ordination is the means appointed by God for admitting those who are to serve in the Ministry to some *order* or degree therein.

Q. How is Ordination conferred?

A. Ordination is conferred by the laying on of hands with prayer: and therein God bestows the gift of His Holy Spirit, for enabling him that is ordained to fulfil, in spirit and in truth, the work of the Ministry, in the order to which he is admitted.

Q. Which are the principal orders in the Ministry?

A. These three; namely, the order of Angel or Bishop, the order of Presbyter[1] or Priest, and the order of Deacon.

Q. You have now told me in what way men are ordained to, and set in, the priesthood and all the higher ministries of

---

[1] Or Elder.

the Church: doth not God previously call them to these holy ministries?

A. Yes; God calleth those whom He purposes to employ by the word of the Holy Ghost, through the prophet.

Q. How are Deacons chosen?

A. Deacons are chosen by the Congregation, or with their concurrence. The seven Deacons of each Church are elected by the Congregation among whom they are to minister; and they become their representatives, when confirmed in their places by the Apostles. Other Deacons are chosen to the work of the Ministry by the Apostles, or by some Angel having their authority, after due notice and inquiry.

Q. How are we to regard the Angel of the Church?

A. We should honour the Angel as the chief Minister and Pastor, to whom God has committed the charge of the whole flock, including the Priests and the Deacons; and who is appointed to offer in the Congregation the Intercession of the Church.

Q. How are we to regard the Priests?

A. We should honour the Priests as those appointed, under the Angel, to minister the Word of God and the Sacraments; to watch over our souls as good shepherds of the sheep; and to offer in the Congregation the prayers of the Church.

Q. How are we to regard Deacons?

A. We should honour the Deacons as the ministers of God appointed to guide us, both by word and example, in the paths of righteousness; to assist the Priests in the ministry of the Church; to help those who seek to them, in the management of their secular affairs; and to relieve the poor and afflicted.

Q. What is the rite of the laying on of Apostles' hands on the members of the Church?

A. It is a Sacrament or rite in which is bestowed the Gift of the Holy Ghost, the Comforter, upon those who have been baptized and are come to full age.

Q. What benefits are conferred upon them in this rite?

A. They are established and confirmed, sealed and anointed: and therein the Holy Ghost divides His gifts to each one severally, as He will.

Q. What is meant by speaking of the Gift of the Holy Ghost as sevenfold?

A. The prophet Isaiah foretold that the Spirit which was to rest upon Christ should be the spirit of wisdom and understanding, the spirit of counsel and might, the spirit of knowledge and of the fear of the Lord, and should make him to be of quick understanding in the fear of the Lord.

Q. What is the manifestation of the Spirit which is given to each, for the profit of all?

A. The Holy Ghost, in coming down upon them that are sealed, gives to one the word of wisdom, to another the word of knowledge, to another faith, to another the gifts of healing, to another the working of miracles, to another prophecy, to another discerning of spirits, to another divers kinds of tongues, to another the interpretation of tongues. All these worketh that one and the self-same Spirit, dividing to every man severally as He will.

APPENDIX VI.

PASSAGES FROM MANUAL.

THE Priesthood, Episcopate or Oversight, and Pastorship of the Christian Church are *One* in the Lord Jesus Christ, who is the "High Priest of our Profession," and the "Shepherd and Bishop of our souls." He fulfilleth these functions by exercising a fourfold Ministry or manner of operation, adapted to the several parts of the moral and intellectual constitution of man. All other men engaged in the Christian Church, in ministering before God and towards their fellow-men in spiritual things, are instruments in the hands of the Lord Jesus, used by Him through the operation of the Holy Ghost. They have no independent virtue, power, or office, as priests or ministers; and they are to be received, sought to, reverenced, and obeyed, simply because they are thus employed by Him.

* * * * *

Those, therefore, who were thus ordained to be presbyters, were admitted to the one priesthood of the Christian Church, the duties whereof they were enabled to fulfil as effectually as Apostles, or any others. And as the end of their ordination was to "take heed unto the flesh," who should all receive that direct fourfold ministration whereby the saints are to be perfected, therefore there must be contained in this order the four classes of Ministers corresponding to, or rather continuous of, those existing in the higher order. There must be among those having the immediate cure of souls, not only the ruling Elders, but also prophetic Priests, Evangelists (or preachers), and Pastors (or confessors); through whom, receiving grace and instruction from those in the higher order, the fourfold Ministry of the Lord would find its direct and immediate application to individuals.

But of the four, the Pastor . . . . . . has the especial supervision and care of the children of God; he is the immediate and intimate guardian of their souls. And as this is the characteristic of the pastoral Ministry in its direct and personal application, so in the operation of the fourfold Ministry through those in the episcopate (whose Ministry is directed to Churches, and who take oversight over both priests and people), the Pastors are, from the nature of their office, the immediate guardians, and in the natural course of their ministry have the especial supervision and care of the Churches. So that, being Pastors of Priests as well as people, chief Pastors they became under the Apostles, heads of the Churches over which they were placed in charge; and thus "the hierarchy of the church' becomes "complete in every several community," comprising the representative of the higher order of the Christian Ministry (who becomes the connecting link and the channel of communication between the rulers over the Catholic Church, to whom he is strictly subordinate, and the particular Church committed to his care), and also comprising the presbyters, admitted to the priesthood, but subordinated to the Bishop, together with those acting in the office of deaconship.

* * * * *

The distinction, therefore, of order is not a distinction in the priesthood considered abstractedly. The Priest, equally with the Bishop or the Apostle, possesses power to present and to convey, and if duly authorized and legitimately placed in jurisdiction, does effectually present and convey the gifts, the vows, the prayers of the people to God, and the words of absolution, of blessing, or of instruction from God.

The distinction of order is not a distinction as to the nature of the fourfold Ministry or manner of action in the priesthood. These offices, in their application to the heart and spirit of a man, are as effectually administered by a ruling Elder as by an Apostle; by a Pastor, who is only Priest, as by an Angel or Bishop. The distinction consists in the extent and nature of the jurisdiction (whether as relates to discipline or doctrine), and consequently in the proper subjects of the respective ministrations; it consists in the possession by the one of the power or capacity, not possessed by the other, to oversee, to direct in their duties, to instruct, to bless, and minister supplies of grace, not only to the people, but to the Priests, for fulfilling their duties, with which is connected .... the capacity for being used to impart the gifts of the Holy Ghost in ordination and otherwise.

For the fulfilling of these larger duties there is required a distinct standing and place from that requisite for fulfilling those common to the priesthood,—there is required the impression of a new and distinct character, and the possession of a further gift of the Holy Ghost, which must be conveyed and conferred by solemn ordination. And as by the constitution of the Christian Church, as interpreted by tradition, Priests are incapable, and by the law of the Church are not permitted, to admit others to the priesthood, so it would follow by just analogy, and so by the original constitution and law of the Church it surely was provided, that none can be admitted to this higher order except they be called immediately of God, and by Him, without the intervention of man, be constituted to be His Apostles; or except they be received into the episcopate by ordination, through the imposition of the hands of Apostles or their delegates. It is probably from this cause (and not for the reason usually alleged) that while the act of one Bishop is sufficient to ordain to the priesthood, "two or three" are required to the consecration of a Bishop; an analogy which has been closely followed in presbyterian ordinations, as might be anticipated.

In concluding these observations, we point out the following relative positions in which Apostles and other ministers may be regarded : 1. As called and set in the one priesthood, wherein all are equally Priests, Bishops, and Pastors, though they are not all equal Priests, &c. 2. In respect of order, the jurisdiction and episcopate of the Priest extends properly only to the laity, that is to say, to the souls of *individual men* (if of ordained men, that is merely accidental); while that of the Bishop is to Priests, as Priests, as well as to all the people. 3. In respect of ministry or class comprised respectively in each order of the priesthood; and herein there is co-ordination, in this sense, namely, that all are ministers of the Lord Jesus Christ, each with his proper gift; but still there is also precedency; for it is written first Apostles, secondarily Prophets, thirdly Teachers. 4, and lastly: and besides all these, Apostles are distinct from all others, and over them in the Lord, and none can be absolutely co-ordinate with them. They are called and set in their office immediately by God, and others are ordained by them or through them; they become antecedently the depositaries of God's promises to the Church, and of the great promise, the ministration of the Holy Ghost; and that which was thus exhibited at the first, both before the Ascension and at the day of Pentecost, is, or ought to be, the continuous operation of their ministry, viz., that they should be the instruments in the hands of the Lord for supplying with continual grace those whom they ordain, and through them the whole flock and Church of God.

APPENDIX VII.

ACCOUNT OF THE CATHOLIC APOSTOLIC CHURCH IN THE CENSUS OF 1851.

THE following sketch, supplied by a Member of the Body, will perhaps convey, with certain qualifications, a correct idea of its sentiments and position :—

"The Body to which this name is applied (*i. e.* The Catholic Apostolic Church) makes no exclusive claim to it: they simply object to be called by any other. They acknowledge it to be the common title of the one Church baptized into Christ, which has existed in all ages, and of which they claim to be Members. They have always protested against the application to them of the term 'Irvingites;' which appellation they consider to be untrue and offensive, though derived from one whom when living they held in high regard as a devoted minister of Christ.

"They do not profess to be, and refuse to acknowledge that they are, separatists from the Church established or dominant in the land of their habitation, or from the general body of Christians therein. They recognize the continuance of the Church from the days of the first Apostles, and of the three orders of Bishops, Priests, and Deacons, by succession from the Apostles. They justify their meeting in separate congregations from the charge of schism, on the ground of the same being permitted and authorized by an ordinance of paramount authority, which they believe God has restored for the benefit of the whole Church. And so far from professing to be another sect in addition to the numerous sects already dividing the Church, or to be 'the One Church' to the exclusion of all other Bodies, they believe that their special mission is to reunite the scattered Members of the one Body of Christ.

"The only standards of faith which they recognize are the three creeds of the Catholic Church—the Apostles' Creed, the Nicene or Constantinopolitan Creed, and that called the Creed of St. Athanasius. The speciality of their religious belief, whereby they are distinguished from all other Christian communities, stands in this: that they hold Apostles, Prophets, Evangelists, and Pastors to be abiding ministries in the Church, and that their ministries, together with the power and gifts of the Holy Ghost, dispensed and distributed among her Members, are necessary for preparing and perfecting the Church for the second Advent of the Lord; and that supreme rule in the Church ought to be exercised, as at the first, by twelve Apostles, not elected or ordained by men, but called and sent forth immediately by God.

"The congregations which have been authorized as above stated are placed under the pastoral rule of Angels or Bishops, with whom are associated in the work of the ministry, Priests and Deacons. The Deacons are a distinct and separate order of ministers taken from the midst of, and chosen by, the respective congregations in which they are to serve, and are ordained either by Apostles, or by Angels receiving commission thereunto. The Priests are first called to their office by the Word through the Prophets ("no man taketh this honour to himself,") and then ordained by Apostles; and from among the Priests, by a like call and ordination, are the Angels set in their places.

"With respect to times of worship, the Holy Eucharist is celebrated and the Communion administered every Lord's Day, and more or less frequently during the week, according to the number of Priests in each particular congregation; and where the congregations are large, the first and last hours of every day, reckoning from 6 A.M. to 6 P.M., are appointed for Divine Worship; and if there be a sufficient number of ministers, there are in addition prayers daily at 9 A.M. and 3 P.M., with other Services for the more special objects of teaching and preaching.

"In the forms of Worship observed, the prayers and other devotions to be found in the principal liturgies of the Christian Church are introduced by preference, wherever appropriate; and in all their Services the bishops and clergy of the Catholic Church, and all Christian kings, princes, and governors, are remembered before God. It may also be observed, that in their ritual, observances, and offices of worship, external and material things have their place. They contend that, as through the washing of water men are admitted into the Christian covenant, and as bread and wine duly consecrated are ordained to be used not merely for spiritual food, but for purposes of sacramental and symbolic agency, so also that the use of other material things, such as oil, lights, incense, &c., as symbols and exponents of spiritual realities, belong to the dispensation of the Gospel.

"Besides free-will offerings, the tenth of their increase, including income of every description, is brought up to the Lord (it being regarded as a sacred duty that tithe should be dedicated to His service alone), and is apportioned among those who are separated to the ministry.

"In England there are about thirty congregations, comprising nearly 6000 communicants; the number is gradually on the increase. There are also congregations in Scotland and Ireland, a considerable number in Germany, and several in France, Switzerland, and America."[1]

[1] *Census of Great Britain*, 1851: "Religious Worship." London: 1853, pp. cii. ciii.

APPENDIX VIII.

THE TABERNACLE.

[READINGS FROM THE LITURGY AND OTHER DIVINE OFFICES OF THE CHURCH, VOI. I. PART II. PP. 255—261.]

THE Most Holy Place, the type of the spiritual and heavenly, comprises in its symbolical significancy the immediate commission of priesthood and authority, given in trust to those who are sent forth "not of men, neither by man, but by Jesus Christ and God the Father," and which is continually derived to the Church through the apostles thus sent forth. And as at the entrance to the Most Holy Place stood the four pillars concealed by the Veil, so through the gifts of apostleship and of prophetic revelation, the fourfold Ministry becomes developed in the Ministers of the Universal Church, namely, the Apostles, and the Prophets, Evangelists, and Pastors immediately associated with them. And thus all of these, not being seen in active operation in any of the particular congregations, but being spiritually present in all the Churches, binding all together, and ministering grace and spiritual power from the Lord, are symbolically represented in the Most Holy Place.

The priesthood, to whose charge are committed the sheep of Christ's flock, gathered into their several congregations, is symbolized in the inferior division of the Tabernacle; the

Angel of the particular Church, prefigured by the High-Priest, being, as it were, the connecting link between the universal and the particular, and in some degree belonging to both; as the High-Priest had rites to fulfil both in the Most Holy and Holy Place.

In like manner the deaconship is represented in the outer Court, although not without the symbolical presence of the priest also; just as, under the Law, the priest fulfilled duties both in the Holy Place and in the Court; assisting the High-Priest in the former place, and being assisted by the Levites in the latter.

We have mentioned, that between the Most Holy and the Holy Place were four pillars of shittim-wood overlaid with gold, upon which was suspended the Veil of blue, and purple, and scarlet, and fine white linen, with Cherubim wrought in it. Moreover, in the Holy Place there were four horns to the Golden Altar, and the incense which was offered upon it was composed of four ingredients; there were also four bowls to the Shaft of the Golden Candlestick; and to the Table of Shewbread four rings were attached above the four feet thereof, and on it were four several kinds of vessels or instruments for the service of that Table. Between the Tabernacle and the Court were five pillars of shittim-wood overlaid with gold, upon which was suspended a veil, distinguished by the same four colours as those of the inner veil, and similar to it in other respects except that there were no Cherubim wrought upon it. In the Court without there was the Brazen Altar with its four horns; and upon the four pillars of entrance was hung a similar veil of blue, and purple, and scarlet, and fine white linen, but also without Cherubim. These series of pillars, giving access to the several parts of the Sanctuary, are obviously connected in their symbolical meaning; and for this reason we shall bring them together under review. They refer, as do also the forty-eight boards forming the framework of the Tabernacle, and the remaining fifty-six pillars round the Court, to the Ministers of the Church, as having authority to minister the word of teaching and preaching; and not as engaged in, or performing, liturgical rites. It will be, therefore, unnecessary to explain them at any length. But the number four, so continually recurring and brought into such prominence in all the above types, demands our attention; for, in its spiritual interpretation, it refers to most important elements in the constitution of man as created by God, and to the modes of His operations towards man through the ordinances of the Church.

The four pillars between the Most Holy Place (which symbolized the spiritual condition of the Church in the heavenlies) and the Holy Place (which symbolized the Church in its condition on this earth, one, and yet divided into separate congregations or Churches) are the types of those offices, the proper sphere for which is the Universal Church, namely, Apostleship (committed to men immediately called and sent forth of God), and the offices of Prophet, of Evangelist, and of Pastor, committed to men called and ordained of God, not immediately, but through the instrumentality of their fellow-men. As these Pillars were the means of access to and egress from the Most Holy Place, so the revelations and commandments which the Lord would give to the Church are derived to particular Churches through the Ministry of those set in the offices typified and prefigured by the pillars. The veil hung upon the pillars with its four colours, is that Ministry which, until the resurrection, is to be fulfilled by those standing in the four offices: and the figures of the Cherubim wrought upon this veil, and upon this veil only, signify, that the Ministry typified thereby is that fulfilled by apostles and those immediately associated with them, the highest spiritual Ministry of the Christian Church.

Every particular Church, so far as circumstances permit, is formed upon the model of the Universal Church. And as the

Lord, the Angel of the Covenant, ministers to His Church through four, so in like manner, the Angel of the particular Church ministers to, and on behalf of, the people committed to his charge, whether in the functions of the priestly office, or in those of the diaconal ministry, through four. This is typically represented by the arrangements, both of the Holy Place and of the Court.

The four horns of the Golden Altar in the Holy Place do not primarily typify the fourfold Ministry; but in a secondary sense, and inclusively, they do. The Golden Altar is the type of priesthood in respect of Mediation; which, though it be a function appertaining to the office of every priest, yet as a corporate act of the Church, as One Body, is fulfilled only by the Lord, and in the particular Church only by the Angel. It is thus that the Golden Altar becomes the type of priesthood under the headship of the Angel. In this, the primary and immediate sense, horns being the symbol of power, the four horns to the Golden Altar primarily set forth, that the Angel has power and authority, by the employment under him of four other Angels equal to him by ordination, but subordinate to him in jurisdiction, to fulfil this office of intercession, in four distinct congregations forming part of his flock, but locally distinct from the Mother Church. But as the Altar typifies the priesthood, and as, wherever the Angel's office is exercised, the presence and assistance of the four Ministries in the priesthood under him, are essential to the completeness of his office, the four horns of the Golden Altar must consequently be applied in a secondary sense to the four Ministries in the priesthood. And with this agrees the symbolical meaning of the four ingredients in the incense offered upon the Golden Altar; for they signify four different kinds of prayers (using the word prayer in a generic sense); of which different kinds we shall hereafter have to give the distinctive characteristics, and to show their connection with the four classes of ministry existing in the priesthood. These four classes, the four Ministries in the priesthood, are, the ruling elders (elders, presbyters, or priests, ruling in word and doctrine, and also in discipline), prophets, evangelists, and pastors, the three last being respectively of the order of priest, presbyter, or elder, although not *ruling* elders.

As the Golden Candlestick is the symbol of the sevenfold Eldership, namely, the Angel and six ruling elders,—it is not to be expected that the idea of the fourfold Ministry should be brought into prominence in this type; yet is it not wholly excluded. In each of the branches supporting the six side lamps were three bowls, referring to the offices of oversight, teaching, and feeding or pastorship, exercised by every elder, in which he is assisted by the subordinate priest; namely, by his coadjutor or help, who should be competent in all respects to occupy the place of the elder in his absence, and by the evangelists and pastors of the Church. But in the Candlestick itself, that is, the centreshaft, were four bowls: and these refer to the four offices, corresponding to the four of the Universal Church, which are committed to the four classes of ministers in the priesthood under the Angel. For although that ministry of the Word, to which the type refers in its liturgical aspect, is committed to the sevenfold Eldership, yet the whole body of the priests and all the ministries of the House of God contribute to that perfect condition of the Church, wherein it shines forth as the Light of the world.

The Table of Prothesis, also (upon which were the twelve loaves, representing the Church in the entirety of the priesthood), was fitted with its "four rings in the four corners that were on the four feet thereof," and furnished with four kinds of vessels or instruments for the service of the Table. By these also the four Ministries are symbolized: for the priests of each of the four Ministries are alike essential to the completeness of the presbytery and to the perfection of the Church; and all in their ordination are alike invested with authority to offer the Sacrifice of the Church, and to present before God the memorial of Christ, in the Holy Eucharist.

In the Court without, the four horns to the Brazen Altar are capable of an interpretation precisely analogous to that of the horns of the Golden Altar. They refer to the performance of the liturgical rites symbolized by this Altar in four distinct localities under the general jurisdiction of the Angel. They are also symbolical of those Ministries, through the instrumentality of which those liturgical rites are celebrated and fulfilled. These are the same or analogous Ministries, whether in the priesthood or in the deaconship of the Church, manifested in each, in a manner consistent with their respective standing and duties.

Lastly, the five Pillars at the entrance to the Tabernacle, of equal height with the four Pillars leading to the Most Holy Place, and like them overlaid with gold, but based upon sockets of brass, and the sixty pillars encompassing the Court without, of which four formed the entrance or means of access to the Court, set forth respectively Ministries under the Apostles, and exercised in the Universal Church. The five Pillars typify a Ministry committed to men, whose duty it is to prepare the way, and to give access, to the several rites symbolized by those in the Holy Place. The four Pillars giving entrance to the Court typify an office committed to men, and ordained for the preparation for and giving access to the rites symbolized by those of the Brazen Altar and the Court.

Upon each of these—upon the five Pillars and upon the four—hung a veil of the same four colours as those of the Veil which separated the Most Holy from the Holy Place, manifesting that we can make no progress unto the perfection of the Christian man except through the operation of the fourfold Ministry exercised towards us in every stage of our approach.

APPENDIX IX.

THE REGULATIONS FOR DISTRIBUTION OF TITHE.

(1849.)

I. GENERAL RULES AS TO THE APPROPRIATION OF TITHES.

1. EVERY ordained priest, being a fixed and regular Minister in a Church, and giving up his whole time to his spiritual duties, receives some proportionate part of the Tithe of the Church. Such proportion (that is, the ratio, not the amount) to be the same in all Churches, and to be subject to arrangement by the rulers of the Church Universal in such manner as circumstances may from time to time require. Supernumerary priests do not receive any fixed proportion of tithe, but may receive support from tithe in the manner hereinafter appointed.

2. Every called priest, giving up his time to preparation for his spiritual duties, and to such subordinate offices as may be required of him, and every deacon giving up his time to his duties, may lawfully receive support from the tithe of the Church in which he is serving, after providing for the Angel and those already ordained to the priesthood.

3. In every Church the number of fixed and regular priests who, under Regulation 1, are to receive proportionate parts of tithe, is not to *exceed* the following: namely, one Angel, one Angel's Coadjutor, and such a number of priests as with the Angel and Angel's Coadjutor shall not exceed one to every fifty of the regular communicants. Nor in any Church is the number of fixed and regular priests to exceed the following: namely, Angel and the Angel's Coadjutor, six Elders, six Assistant Elders, and thirty-six other priests, of whom at least one-third should be Prophets and Evangelists. Any other priests employed in the service of the Church are to be considered supernumerary, and not entitled to fixed portions of tithe.

4. The precise number and class of fixed and regular priests who are to receive tithe in any Church, within the above-mentioned limits, will from time to time be decided by the Apostle in charge of the Church (*i. e.* of Tribe), whose sanction is also necessary to the appointment of all supernumerary priests.

5. From all tithe received in a particular Church, one-tenth is to be separated and paid to the Seven Deacons of the Universal Church, to be applied by them under the directions of the Apostles to the Ministers of the Universal Church.

6. After separating the one-tenth for the Universal Church, the Angel receives one-tenth portion of the remainder, being the Angel's tenth or portion. (But see Regulation 17 of December, 1858.)

7. After separating the one-tenth for the Universal Church and the subsequent tenth for the Angel's portion, the remainder is to be divided into two [equal] parts, one of which is to be the fund divisible among the fixed and regular priests, or "The Divisible Tithe;" and the other part is to be "The Reserve Fund."

II. APPROPRIATION OF THE "DIVISIBLE TITHE."

8. The Divisible Tithe is to be appropriated in the following proportions: namely, to each priest not being one of the six ruling Elders, one portion; to each ruling Elder, two portions; and to the Angel's Coadjutor, or, in the absence of the Angel, to the Horn or presiding Elder, three portions, if the number of communicants do not exceed 400; four portions, if above 400 and not exceeding 600; and five portions, if above 600. The five portions being (in a Church sufficiently large to allow of it) that part which the Angel shares with the Elders, Prophets, Evangelists, and Pastors of the Church severally, and by which he makes provision for his Coadjutor.

9. In case the amount of each portion of the Divisible Tithe shall be diminished at any time, in consequence of the increase of communicants and the consequent appointment of additional priests, the Angel and priests previously in charge shall be entitled to receive out of the Reserve Fund such an amount as shall make up to them, or equalize, their former proportionate share or shares. That is to say, so far as the reduction is occasioned simply by the increase of the congregation and the addition of one or more priests, it shall be made up or equalized to the Angel or former priests; but so far as the reduction is occasioned by a falling off in the tithe considered relatively to the increase in the number of communicants, so far it shall not be made up or equalized. Priests newly appointed and not formerly in charge shall not be entitled to any such equalization of their portions.

REGULATIONS.
(1858.)
I. Distribution of Tithe—by whom.

1. God having given the Tithe of our Increase to be the endowment of His altar, He has placed the particular application of the same under the direction of the Apostles.

2. The Apostles, in the light of prophecy, and on ample grounds of reason, have entrusted the Angel of each Church with the distribution of the tithe brought up therein, under the immediate superintendence of the Apostle in charge, and according to the rules laid down by the Apostles and by the Apostle in charge.

3. It is fitting that both the Apostles and the Angels should be relieved, as far as possible, from active intervention and personal administration of money affairs, reserving to themselves, in their respective spheres, the direction, oversight, and control of what is done, and receiving appeals from any who may consider themselves aggrieved, but leaving details to their respective Councils and Ministers.

4. The proper Council and Ministers for these affairs, in aid of the Apostles, are the Seven Deacons in the Universal Church. The proper Council and Ministers of the Apostle in charge are the Archdeacon and the other Councillors whom each Apostle is authorized to appoint. The proper Council and Ministers of the Angel of a Church are the Seven Deacons of the Church.

5. In any Church in which the number of Seven Deacons cannot properly, by reason of the small number of communicants, be completed, the Angel, with the sanction of the Apostle in charge, may, in the Council of his Church, select and appoint any other Deacons, not being of the Seven, but so that the number of those to be so appointed, together with the

existing Deacons of the Seven, shall not exceed seven in all. And the Deacons of the Seven, and such additional Deacons, shall form a consultative body, or council, for assisting the Angel with their counsel in the secular affairs of the Church. But those Deacons only who have been duly elected and admitted to the office of Seven Deacon, shall be accounted as of the number of the Seven Deacons of the Church, and they alone shall be put in charge or possession of the goods or property of the Church.

6. All cash belonging to the particular Church ought to be placed and kept in some secure place of deposit, in the joint names or under the joint control of the Angel and of, at least, two (or of one, if there be but one) of the Seven Deacons of the Church. Drafts or orders on bankers should be signed jointly; except that, if the names of two or more of the Seven Deacons be associated with the Angel, the Angel's signature shall not be necessary, unless under special circumstances he shall deem it advisable.

II. OBJECTS TO WHICH TITHE MAY BE APPLIED.

7. Tithe not required for the support of the Angel and priests may be applied towards the support of deacons and called priests, as set forth in the Regulations of December 1849.

8. Under existing regulations, the Tithe of a particular Church is not the proper ordinary fund for the support of Evangelists employed in the Universal Church. But where the Tithe of a Church will permit, Evangelists so employed, whether priests or deacons, may be attached as supernumerary Ministers to the particular Church, and supported from the tithe, giving their assistance in the services of worship or otherwise in the particular Church, so far as their duties under the Angel Evangelists will permit.

9. The oil and incense used for lights and burning in the

worship of the Church should be voluntary offerings, as are the Sacramental bread and wine. The expenses, therefore, should be defrayed by means of offerings, and not out of tithe.

III. DIVISION OF TITHE INTO "DIVISIBLE" AND "RESERVE."

10. The division of the Tithe into two portions—"the Divisible" and "the Reserve"—must be retained, in order that, according to the rule of the Apostles, some portion or proportion may be given to every fixed and regular priest of a Church, giving up his whole time to the duties of his ministry; and yet that provision may be made for those who are without private means of support. In order more effectually to secure a proper provision for those who need it, it is expedient, under present circumstances, that the proportion forming the Divisible Fund should be diminished, and that forming the Reserve should be increased. (See Regulation 15, *post*.)

11. The portion of Tithe which a priest receives from the Divisible Tithe ought to be at his own disposal, without question or control. His devoting of it, when not needed for his own livelihood, and either wholly or in part, must be "according to the purpose of his heart," and "not of necessity."

IV. APPLICATION OF TITHE.

12. The present regulations for distribution of Tithe in England are to remain in force until altered by the Apostles, or the Apostle in charge, except as the same are varied or altered below.

13. The alterations now made are not to affect existing benefices, so as to reduce them, unless such previously existing benefices shall, for three consecutive years (dating back from the end of the current or any future year), be of the same amount, or of a less amount, than such benefices would be under the alterations now made. Whenever the portions of

the Divisible Tithe fail to give the requisite amount, the deficiency is to be made up from the Reserve Fund.

14. After separating the Tithe of Tithe, one-tenth of the remainder shall form the Angel's portion.

15. After separating the Tithe of Tithe and the Angel's Tithe, one-third of the remainder shall form "the Divisible Tithe," and the remaining two-thirds shall form "the Reserve Fund."

16. The thirteenth Regulation of December 1849 is rescinded. The fixed proportion to be assigned to an Assistant Elder giving up his whole time shall no longer be augmented by the addition of a half-portion from the Reserve, but shall consist of one portion only from the Divisible Tithe.

17. If in any year the one-tenth portion assigned to the Angel shall exceed £800, or the portions or portion assigned from the Divisible Tithe to an Elder or other priest shall exceed £150, such excess shall not be received by the beneficiary before the same shall have been reported to the Apostle in charge; who will decide in each case whether the whole or any part of such excess shall be received by the beneficiary, or shall be carried over to the Reserve Fund.

V. The "Reserve Fund."

18. The benefice of an Angel, whose tenth portion is insufficient to provide what he needs for maintenance, may be augmented from the "Reserve Fund," so as not to exceed the rate of £300 in the year, on the order of the Apostle in charge. The benefice of any priest, whose portion from the Divisible Tithe is insufficient to provide what he needs for his maintenance, may be augmented from the Reserve Fund, so as not to exceed the rate of £200 in the year, on the order of the Angel taking counsel with his Deacons: on the like order, any supernumerary priest, whose private means are insufficient, may receive from the Reserve Fund a benefice not exceeding the

rate of £200 a-year; and any deacon or called priest may receive not exceeding the rate of £100 a-year: but with this reservation, that no priest, deacon, or called priest, whose whole time is not devoted to his ecclesiastical duties (or, in the case of a called priest, to preparation also for his vocation), shall receive from the Reserve Fund more than after the rate of £60 in the year.

19. Applications from Angels for a larger benefice than £300 must be made to the Apostle in charge, who will refer the same to his Archdeacon and Council for their report, and will give his order upon such report.

20. Application from priests or deacons for larger benefices than £200 or £100 respectively, must be made to the Angel, who, with the consent of the applicant, will refer the same to the Council of his Deacons. And if they report favourably, such report will be forwarded to the Apostle for his sanction, who, if he shall think fit, will refer the same to his Archdeacon and Council.

21. The Reserve Fund is first to be applied in equalizing or making up the deficiencies in the shares of the Angel and priests, as directed in Regulation 9 of December 1849, and in Regulation 13 above. It is not to be applied to called priests or deacons, until all payments to priests shall have been satisfied; nor to supernumerary priests, until all payments to fixed and regular priests, giving up their whole time to spiritual duties, shall have been satisfied; nor to any party, until all payments authorized to be made to the Angel shall have been satisfied.

VI. SURPLUS OF TITHE.

22. The surplus of the Tithe, if any, after providing for the wants of the particular Church according to the rules, and satisfying all payments directed or authorized to be made thereout, and also retaining a sufficient amount to meet immediate payments, or any probable diminution in the receipts of

the following year, shall be paid over to the Archdeacon with the Apostle in charge, to be applied under the sanction or direction and at the discretion of the Apostle for the advancement of the following objects: namely, the promotion of the Evangelist work in the neighbourhood of the particular Church from which the surplus Tithe arises; the support of poor priests in other Churches in the tribe, whose wants the Seven Deacons in the Universal Church are unable at the time to supply; the promotion of the Evangelist work in the tribe; lastly, the promotion of the Evangelist work or support of poor priests in other tribes. And with respect to the last-mentioned object, the sums which, in the judgment of the Apostle in charge, can be appropriated for the purposes of other tribes, will be paid over to the Seven Deacons and placed at the disposal of the Apostles.

VII. STATEMENTS OF ACCOUNTS.

23. On the first of January in each year, statements of all receipts and payments on account of Tithes and Offerings in the preceding year are to be transmitted to the Archdeacon.

24. At the close of each financial year the Council of Deacons in each Church shall lay before the Angel a scheme or estimate for the application of the Tithe in the ensuing year; and the same, being approved by the Angel, shall forthwith be transmitted to the Archdeacon for the sanction of the Apostle, and when sanctioned by him the same shall be the general plan for the disposition of the Reserve Fund during the current year, so far as circumstances will permit.

VIII. TITHE CANNOT BE CLAIMED, EITHER LEGALLY OR OTHERWISE, BY ANY MINISTER.

25. It is the Law of the Church, that the duties of the sacred ministry are to be fulfilled without fee or reward. No Minister possesses, or is entitled to, any right or personal claim

to the Tithe, or to any provision out of the Tithe, save only as the Apostles may at any time direct those entrusted with the distribution to bestow the same. All benefices to Ministers, in the absence of special directions to the contrary, are paid quarterly, and each quarterly payment is made in advance, and without guarantee or pledge for any future payment. The present Regulations, and all former Regulations concerning the distribution of Tithe, and all expressions therein referring to Ministers receiving or entitled to Tithe, are to be construed simply as temporary directions to those who distribute the Tithe. All existing Regulations are at any time liable to be revoked or suspended, and either in whole or in part, or in any particular instance, by the Apostles or by the Apostle in charge; and the Tithe itself, and all accumulations thereof, are at any moment applicable, under the direction of the Apostles, to any other object which the Apostles, in their regard to the interests of the Church, may deem more advisable.

INDEX.

ABSOLUTION. *See* Confession.
Advent, second, ii. 2—10, 259—281; also i. 11, 27, 38—40, 109, 319—321, ii. 355, 360.
Agapemonites, ii. 204, 205, 327.
Albury, i. 35, 36; first meeting at, 36 — 40; attendants, 40, 41; second, 41; third, 42; fourth, 43—45; last, 45; church at, 113, &c., 136; Apostles at, 167—184, 192, 206, 240; congregation lessened at, 234.
Alt-Catholiks, ii. 343.
Ambrose, St., ii. 167, 175.
America, effects in, i. 193.
American impostor, the, i. 105, 106.
Amos, ii. 212.
Anabaptists, ii. 193, 279.
Angel-Evangelists, ii. 49; the five first, i. 171, *note.*
Angels, ii. 51, &c., i. 151, ii. 60, 144; Drummond's consecration as, i. 114—119; Irving's, 121—127; insubordination of, 206, 207.
Antichrist, ii. 4—7, 270, 273, 278.
Apostles, i. 164, ii. 21, 32—38, 51 — 53, 119 — 153, 322 — 327; prayers for, i. 109, 207, *note;* first, 110, 111; second, 136; next two, 139; two more, 149; separation of, 155—161; three anointings of, 162; the Twelve, 166; twelvefold unity of, 169; directions to, 186; journeys, 188, &c.; lessons in Catholicity, 195; collision with Prophets, 207; firmness, 209; victorious, 213; lose one, 214; weakness, 229, 237; resume work abroad, 239; only ten meet, 241; difficulties, 243; relations to Prophets, 301—304; iron rule of, ii. 91, 317.
Apostolic Lordship, i. 309, ii. 13, 19, *note. See* Grant.
Aquinas, St. Thomas, ii. 295, 296, 300.
Armstrong, Rev. Nicholas, M.A., i. 80, 108, 149, 166, 181, 185, 208; paralyzed, 313.
Attention, concentrated, ii. 247—249.
Augustin, St., of Hippo, ii. 159, 174, 177, 244, 298, 300.

Baptism, Holy, ii. 18, 19, 72; of fire, i. 81, 140, 145, ii. 86.
Barnabas, St., ii. 142, 323.
Barton, Elizabeth, ii. 193.
Baxter, Mr. Robert, i. 70, 72, 75—82, 98, 155, 156, 276.
Bayford, Dr., i. 139.
Bayford, Dr. (Junior), i. 115, 137, 307.
Bennett, Rev. W. J. E., i. 273.
Bishops, the successors of the Apostles, ii. 154—187.
Bishopsgate, Church of, i. 134.
Böhm, Mr. C., i. 315.
Burial, no Office for, ii. 63, 64.

Caird, Mrs., a dressmaker, i. 51; intends to be a missionary, *ibid.;* speaks in a tongue, 52; cured, 56; a prophetess, 58, 72; marries, 58; visits London, 59, 66; settles at Albury, 59; condemned by Story, *ibid.;* death, 60.

Caird, W. R., i. 58—60, 116, 295.
Calvinism, i. 49, 50, 80, ii. 282, 304.
Camisards, ii. 194, 327.
Campbell, Mary. *See* Caird, Mrs.
Campbell, Rev. J. McLeod, of Row, i. 49, 51, 54, 103, ii. 304.
Candlestick, mystery of, i. 119; Appendix iii. vol. ii.
Canning, Right Hon. C., i. 23.
Cardale, John Bate, examines into the tongues, i. 61, 62; holds prayer-meetings, 65; defends Irving, 90; called as Apostle, 110; character, 111; chief author of Liturgy, 112; author of *Readings on the Liturgy, ibid.*; ordains Place, 114; Drummond, 115—119; dictates mystery of candlestick, 119; ordains Irving, 123—126; Miller, 135; as Apostle, 138; visits Scotland, 141; South and West, 149; solicitor, of Bedford Row, 165; prepares Testimony, 177; see also, 180, 181, 185, 202, 206, 211, 219, 220, 240, 242, ii. 333; vigour, i. 244; seals clergy and laity, 251; is practically the College, 261; Letter, 273—277; strong will, 288; visits the Churches, 304; death, 314; strange arguments, ii. 180.
Cardale, Miss, i. 72, 76, 80, 99, 111.
Cardale, Mrs., i. 62, 72, 111.
Caricature of Doctrines, ii. 338, 339.
Carlyle, Mr. Thomas (the Apostle), i. 14, 88, 157, 162, 166, 174, 180, 267; death and works, 271.
Carlyle, Mr. Thomas (the author), i. 15, 147.
Carthage, Council of, ii. 172.
Catalepsy, ii. 253.
Catholic Apostolic Church, name, i. 4—6.
Catholic Church, the, marvellous growth in, ii. 80, 81.
Catholicity, ii. 110—118; false, 305, 320—322.
Celtic and Latin Christianity, ii. 342.
Census of 1851, i. 260; Appendix vii.

Chalmers, Dr., i. 16; engages Irving, 18; opinion of his preaching, 20; visits him in London, 22, 73; contrast to Irving, 149.
Chrysostom, St., ii. 179,-242, 244, 299, *note.*
Church, Irvingite Doctrine of the, ii. 18—23, 121, &c.
Churches, the seven, i. 153, 243, 304, 345; the Colonial, ii. 337.
Church's Broken Unity, articles in, i. 81, *note,* 273—277.
Clement, St., of Rome, ii. 169.
Clergymen, Irvingite, in the Church, i. 277—281, 342—344.
Coadjutor Apostles, i. 315, 316.
Communicants, ii. 71, i. 345.
Concentrated Attention, ii. 247—249.
Conception, Immaculate, ii. 289—303.
Confession, i. 324, 327, ii. 73.
Confirmation, ii. 72.
Constructive Objectivity, ii. 249—253.
Converts, i. 341.
Convocation, ii. 345.
Corinthians, St. Paul's Ep. to, i. xii. xiv., ii. 41—44, 241—243.
Council of Zion, i. 172, 202, 211.
Cures, supposed miraculous, i. 55, 56, 62, 64, 139, ii. 228—236.
Cyprian, St., ii. 167, 172, 299, *note.*

Daily Worship, i. 173, 230.
Dalton, Rev. H., i. 145; deprivation, 154; 157, 166, 180, 191; retirement, 240; return, 291; death, 313.
Daniel, ii. 214.
Deaconesses, i. 325, 331, ii. 55.
Deacons, i. 129, 325, 331, ii. 51—54.
Dialogues on Prophecy, i. 43.
Discipline, i. 308—313, 326, 328—331, ii. 91, 146.
Dow, Rev. David, i. 97, 157.
Dow, Rev. W., 157, 166, 181; death, 271.
Drabicius, Nicholas, ii. 193.
Drummond, Henry, M.P., parentage and early life, i. 30, 31; description of, 32—34; Albury Park,

Index. 417

35; *Morning Watch*, 46, 85, 132; utterances, 94, 95; perhaps calls Cardale, ii. 314; hesitates to act, i. 113, 115; ordained, 115—119; Apostle, 136, 138, 141, 149, 166, 167, 179, 180, 185, 191, 219, 237; re-enters Parliament, 254—256; death and character, 287, 288; also ii. 33, 36, 126, 238.

Ecclesiasticism, ii. 263, 264.
Ecstasy, ii. 255.
Elders, i. 119, 123, 127, 128, ii. 58, Appendix vi.
Elias Ministry, i. 264, ii. 5—10.
Elijah, ii. 210, 212.
Elisha, ii. 210, 212.
Elliot's *Horæ Apocalypticæ*, ii. 265, 269, 276.
English theory of Catholicity, ii. 111—113.
Ephesians, St. Paul to, iv. 11, ii. 23, 121, &c.
Epilepsy, ii. 253.
Equals, when they may appoint equals, ii. 155, 156.
Erastianism, i. 338.
Eucharist, Holy, i. 116, 125; weekly, 169, 196, 223, &c.; reservation at, 241, 257, 301, 323, ii. 70, 71, 309, *note*. *See* Liturgy.
Eucharistic Sacrifice, Doctrine of, i. 196—199, 223—226, 257, ii. 68, 331, 339.
Evangelists, ii. 47—49; origin of, i. 109; sixty, 171; at work, 176, ii. 51—54; preaching, 261.

Fancourt, Elisabeth, i. 62—64, ii 232.
Feasts, ii. 61, 287.
Finance, ii. 74, 75, i. 150, 325, Appendix ix.
Firmilian, ii. 172.
Four Beasts, ii. 24.
Four Cherubim, ii. 24.
Fourfold Ministry, ii. 23—32, i. 176, 203, 232, 259, ii. 51. *See* Testimonies, and Appendix vi.
Frere, Mr. J. Hatley, i. 10, 27, 28, 41.
Futurists, ii. 266.

VOL. II.

Galilean Ministry, the, the acceptable year of the Lord, ii. 217, *note*.
General Rubrics, i. 322, ii. 60.
George, David, ii. 193.
Gifts, Ordinary and Extraordinary, ii. 244.
Girling, Mrs., ii. 206, 327.
Gordon Square, Church in, i. 268—270; service at, i. 234.
Grant, Mr. W. (*see* Apostolic Lordship), joins the Body, i. 308; difficulties, 309; position, 310; treatment, 311; appeals, 312; retires, 313; also 315, 333, 335, 336, ii. 13, 70.

Hall, Miss, i. 66, 68, 75, 98.
Hammond, Dr. W. H., ii. 247.
Heath, Christopher, i. 152, 268, 318.
Hebrews, Ep. of, written by St. Paul, ii. 134, *note*, 312.
Hegesippus, ii. 170.
Helps, ii. 54.
Hierarchy, ii. 50—57.
Holy Water, i. 241, 301.
Horn, a, i. 243, ii. 54.
Hypostatic Union, ii. 290.
Hysteria, ii. 253, 254.

Ignatius, St., ii. 170.
Imagination, ii. 251.
Immaculate Conception, ii. 289—303.
Incarnation, ii. 11—15, 282—305, i. 83, &c., 96, &c., 175, 223; misunderstood, ii. 129, 306, 355.
Incense, i. 241, 265.
Infection, religious, ii. 253.
Infidelity, contemporaneous, ii. 348—351.
Irenæus, St., ii. 41, *note*, 171, 299, *note*.
Irving, Rev. Edward, connection with Irvingism, i. 2—6; birth, 13; boyhood, 14; at Edinburgh, 15; at Haddington, 16; at Kirkcaldy, 16—18; studies at Edinburgh, 18; at Glasgow, 18—21; in London, 22; popularity, 23; description of, 24; prophetical

E E

studies, 27—29; account of meeting at Albury, 36—40; preaching, 48; scene in church, 69, 70; difficulties, 71; to be a mighty Prophet, 80; on the Incarnation, 83, &c., ii. 284, 289, 304; condemned by London Presbytery, i. 88; by General Assembly, *ibid.*; tried and ejected by London Presbytery, 89—91; Gray's Inn Road, 92; Newman St., 92; new position, 96, 130, 140; deprived at Annan, 96—98; reception in London, 120—123; re-ordained, 123 —126; not then slighted, 126; helps to ordain Elders, 128; virtual retirement, 133; in Scotland, 141; rebuked by Apostles, 142; last journey, 144—146; death, 147; character, 147—149.
Irvingism, name, i. 2—6, 133; in the Church, 277—281, 342—344, ii. 67, *note*.

Jeremiah, ii. 214.
Jerome, St., ii. 167, 174, 299, *note*.
John the Baptist, ii. 216.
Jonah, ii. 214.
Justin Martyr, ii. 41, *note*.

King, or King-Church, Mr., i. 139, 167, 181; death, 294.
Kotter, Christopher, ii. 193.

Latin and Celtic Christianity, ii. 342.
Lay-Assistants, ii. 56.
Lectionary, ii. 62.
Lee, Dr., examines the tongues, i. 60, 73, ii. 240.
Lights at Celebration, i. 241, 265.
Liturgy, i. 226—228, 234, 235, ii. 58—67.
Lord Jesus Christ, our, credentials of, ii. 216—218.
Luther, ii. 312.

Macdonalds (Margaret, James, and George), i. 54—58, 103.
Mackenzie, Mr., i. 90, 158, 167, 181; retires, 204, &c., 236, 240; death, 270.

Matthias, St., ii. 141, 323.
McNeile, Hugh, D.D., i. 37, 40, 45, *note*, 50, 72, 104, ii. 226.
Melbourne, Lord, i. 91.
Millenarianism, ii. 193, 274.
Ministry, a, ii. 60.
Miraculous cures, supposed, i. 55; (Margaret Macdonald), 56; (Mary Campbell), 62; (Elisabeth Fancourt), 139; (Miss Hughes), 64; (general), ii. 228—236.
Montanists, ii. 191—193, 323, 327, 359.
Moralism, ii. 283.
Moravians, ii. 193.
Mormonism, ii. 77, 199—202, 231, 323, 327.
Morning Watch, i. 46, 130.
Moses, ii. 206—209.
Mysticism, ii. 93—95.

Norton, Rev. Dr., i. 277.

Objectivity, constructive, ii. 249—253.
Oil, consecrated, i. 248.
Old Church Porch, i. 273—277.
Optatus, ii. 176.
Origen, ii. 41, *note*.
Owen, Rev. H. J., i. 139.
Oxford Church movement, i. 130, 179, 226.

Parliament represents Imperial, not Lay, interests, ii. 346.
Pastors, ii. 23—32, 49—53, i. 327, *note*.
Paul, St., credentials of, ii. 134—141, 323.
Pentecost, Day of, ii. 128, 239, 329.
Perceval, Spencer, M.P., i. 41, 98, 139, 178, 180, 191; death, 285, 286.
Philosophy, Christian and Heathen, ii. 351.
Physiology and Theology, ii. 256.
Place, Mr., 109, 114, 159.
Plymouth Brethren, ii. 203, 327.
Policy, change of, i. 299.
Poniatowski, Christina, ii. 193.
Præterists, ii. 268.
Prayer, reflex force of, ii. 252.

Prayer-book (Liturgy), i. 226—228, 234, 235, ii. 58—67.
Prentice, Mr., i. 307.
Prince, Henry James, ii. 204.
Prophecy, new study of, i. 9—12, 27—29; five meetings on, 36—46; supposed outbreak of, in Scotland, 52, 57—62; in London, 66—82, 90, 93—95, 98—102; in England, 114—119, 123—126, 139; character of, 142—144, 155, 177, 306, 307; theory of, 212, ii. 188.
Prophetesses, Ursuline, ii. 193.
Prophetical Gifts, claims to, ii. 188—221; examined, 222—258.
Prophets, ii. 38—47, 51—53, 188—258, 327—330; prayers for, i. 207, *note,* ii. 249, &c., 329; first, i. 52, 57, 66—82, 89, 99, 111; Taplin, first ordained Prophet, 129; the first seven, 172, *note;* afterwards twelve, *ibid.;* in rivalry with Apostles, 206—209, 211; relation to Apostles, 301—304, ii. 146, 238.
Prophets, Celestial, ii. 193.
Prophets, Schools of Jewish, ii. 209.
Protestantism, i. 9, ii. 111.
Pseudo-Catholicism, ii. 305.
Public Worship Regulation Act, i. 338.
Pusey, Rev. E. B., D.D., examines the tongues, i. 60, 73, ii. 240; first Letter to Dr. Newman, ii. 294—299.

Quakers, ii. 194, 327.

Real Presence, Doctrine of, ii. 68, 69.
Reason without zeal, ii. 337.
Reformation, i. 9.
Reservation of the Holy Sacrament, i. 241, 257, 301, 323, ii. 309, *note.*
Roman theory of Catholicity, ii. 111—113.
Romanism in England, ii. 339.
Rubrics, General, i. 248.

Samuel, ii. 209—212.
Satanic agency, supposed, i. 100—102, ii. 256.

Scepticism, contemporaneous, ii. 348—351.
Scott, Sir Walter, the harbinger of a warmer system, ii. 307.
Sealing, i. 248—254, 292, ii. 64—67, 72, 148, 264.
Services, ii. 57—67; attendance at, i. 321; character of, 322; times, 323; of obligation, 324.
Shakers, ii. 198, 327.
Sitwell, Frank, Esq., i. 157, 167, 180, 193; death, 294.
Southcote, Joanna, ii. 197, 327.
Spiritual Gifts, desire of, ii. 244, 251. *See* Prophetical Gifts.
Spiritual interpretation of the Apocalypse, ii. 270, &c.
Statistics, i. 260, 344—346.
Staunton, Sir G., i. 60, 73, ii. 240.
Sterling, Rev. Mr., i. 261.
Stewart, Rev. G. Haldane, i. 41.
Story, Rev. Robert, of Rosneath, i. 21; at Albury, 42, 49, 51, 52; condemns Mrs. Caird, 59, 60; refusal to join, 102, ii. 11.
Sub-deacons, i. 325, 331, ii. 55.
Supernatural agency, ordinary, ii. 255—257.
Swedenborg, Emmanuel, ii. 196, 327.
Swenckfield, Hacket, ii. 193.
Symbolism, ii. 15—18, 93—95, 306—315, i. 119, 120, 127, 144, 170—172, 176, 180—182, 232, 241, 246, 257—259, ii. 24—29, 122, 123, 161, 162.

Tabernacle, a, ii. 59; mystery of the, i. 170—175, Appendix viii.
Taplin, Mr., first public utterance, i. 67; character, 68; 70, 72, 76, 90, 93, 114—119, 123, 129, 141, 151, 159, 315, ii. 226, 243, 314, *note;* death, i. 294.
Tertullian, ii. 41, *note,* 171, 172, 299, *note.*
Testimony, the Great, i. 182, 189—192, Appendix i.; the State, i. 177, 178, 286, Appendix ii. A.; the clerical, i. 177, 178, Appendix ii. B.
Teutonic Christianity, ii. 343.
Theology, a new School of, ii. 352.

Theology and Physiology, ii. 256.
Thompson, Dr., i. 61, 158, 307.
Threefold Ministry, among the Jews, ii. 160; three better than four, 161; in our Lord's days, 162; after He ascended, 163.
Tithes, i. 150, 325, ii. 74, 75, Appendix ix.
Tongues, supposed, i. 52, 57, 58, 60, 67—75, 89, 99, 100, 143, ii. 239, 243.
Trinity, Doctrine of the, ii. 67, 285, 286.
Tudor, Mr. J., i. 41, 77, 130, 157, 181, 185; death and works, 293.
Types, ii. 306—315, i. 119, 120, 127, 144, 170—172, 176, ii. 5, 15—18, 24—29, 122, 123, 161, 162.

Unction, ii. 74.

Under-deacons, i. 325, 331, ii. 55.
Unitarians, i. 4—7.
Unity, ii. 318, 355, 360.

Vestments, i. 198, 232, 235.

Waldegrave's (Bp.) *Bampton Lectures*, ii. 265, 274.
Watson, Sir T., ii. 233, 255.
Way, Rev. Lewis, i. 11, 36, 41, *note*, 43.
Wesleyanism, i. 7, ii. 195, 231.
Will, weakness of, ii. 250.
Williams, Rev. Isaac, *On the Apocalypse*, ii. 265, 272.
Wilson, Daniel, D.D., Bishop of Calcutta, i. 40, 104.
Wolff, Joseph, D.D., i. 31, 37, 40.
Woodhouse, Mr., i. 149, 167, 180, 181, 191, 192, 260, 314.

THE END.

CLAY AND TAYLOR, PRINTERS, BUNGAY.

www.ingramcontent.com/pod-product-compliance
Lightning Source LLC
Chambersburg PA
CBHW022105290426
44112CB00008B/552